HOW TO BE PERFECT

HOW TO BE PERFECT

The Correct Answer to

Every Moral Question

MICHAEL SCHUR

With philosophical nitpicking by Professor Todd May

QUERCUS

First published in Great Britain in 2022 by

QUERCUS

Quercus Editions Ltd
Carmelite House
50 Victoria Embankment
London EC4Y 0DZ

An Hachette UK company

A CIP catalogue record for this book is available
from the British Library

HB ISBN 978 1 52942 132 3
TPB ISBN 978 1 52942 133 0
Ebook ISBN 978 1 52942 134 7

Every effort has been made to contact copyright holders.
However, the publishers will be glad to rectify in future
editions any inadvertent omissions brought to their attention.

Quercus Editions Ltd hereby exclude all liability to the extent
permitted by law for any errors or omissions in this book and for any loss,
damage or expense (whether direct or indirect) suffered by a
third party relying on any information contained in this book.

10 9 8 7 6 5 4 3

Printed and bound in Great Britain by Clays Ltd, Elcograf S.p.A.

Papers used by Quercus Editions Ltd. are from well-managed forests and other responsible sources.

This business is everybody's business.

—ALBERT CAMUS, *The Plague*

Do the best you can until you know better.
Then when you know better, do better.

—MAYA ANGELOU

Tens of thousands of years ago, after primitive humans had finished the basic work of evolving and inventing fire and fighting off tigers and stuff, some group of them began to talk about morality. They devoted part of their precious time and energy to thinking about why people do things, and tried to figure out ways for them to do those things better, more justly, and more fairly. Before those people died, the things they said were picked up and discussed by other people, and then by other people, and so on and so on all the way to this very moment—which means that for the last few dozen millennia, people the world over have been having one very long unbroken conversation about ethics.

Most of the people who've devoted their lives to that conversation didn't do it for money, or fame, or glory—academia (and more specifically, philosophy) is not the best route, if that's what you're after. They just did it because they believed that morality *matters*. That the basic questions of how we should behave on earth are worth talking about, in order to discover and describe a better path for all of us. This book is dedicated, with my extreme gratitude, to all those who have engaged in that remarkable and deeply human conversation.

It's also dedicated to J.J., William, and Ivy, who matter the most, to me.

CONTENTS

Introduction

Today, you've decided to be a good person.

You don't know *why*, really—you just woke up this morning full of vim and vigor and optimism, despite a world that often seems hell-bent on bumming you out, and you hopped out of bed determined to be a little bit better today than you were yesterday.

This shouldn't be that hard, right? You just need to make some small changes in the way you live. You walk outside, see a plastic cup on the street, pick it up, and throw it away. That feels good! Yesterday you might have ignored that garbage and kept on walking, but not today, baby. Today you're *better*. At the grocery store you spend a little extra to buy cage-free eggs and milk from humanely treated cows. It makes you smile to think of those cows munching happily on organic grass instead of being cooped up in some awful factory farm. Remembering an article you read about the impact of the beef industry on climate change, you even pass on the hamburger meat in favor of veggie patties. Now the cows are even happier! Because they're not dead!

You're doing great today. The New You is *crushing it*.

You take a quick jog around the neighborhood (for health!), help an old lady across the street (for kindness!), watch a documentary (for knowledge!), check the news (for citizenship!), and go to sleep. What a great day.

But then you lie in bed, staring at the ceiling. Something's nagging at you. How much "goodness" did you actually achieve? You *feel* like you did some good stuff, but then again you also felt like you could pull off wearing a zebra-print fedora to your office holiday party last year, and we all know how that turned out.

So now imagine that you can call on some kind of Universe Goodness Accountant to give you an omniscient, mathematical report on how well you did. After she crunches the numbers on your day of good deeds and the receipt unspools from her Definitive Goodness Calculator, she gives you some bad news.

That plastic cup you tossed? It's eventually going to flow into the ocean, joining the Texas-size trash island that's threatening marine life in the Pacific. (You read about that when you checked the news before bed, but you didn't think *you* had anything to do with it.) The veggie patties were shipped to your local store from someplace very far away, rendering their carbon footprint massive, and the cows you pictured *are* in fact penned up in a factory farm, because the legal definitions of "organic" and "grass-fed" are embarrassingly loose thanks to shady legislation written by agribusiness lobbyists. The cows aren't happy. They're sad. They're sad cows.

It gets worse: The sneakers you wore on your jog were made in a factory where workers are paid four cents an hour. The documentarian who made the film you watched is a weird creep who likes to sniff strangers' hair on the subway—nice work putting ten bucks in his pocket—and the streaming service you watched it on is part of a multinational conglomerate that also makes killer drones for the North Korean air force. Oh and by the way, that old lady you helped collects Nazi memorabilia. "But she seemed so sweet," you say. Nope! Secret Nazi. She was actually on her way to buy more Nazi stuff—that's what you helped her across the street to do.

Well, great. Now you're miserable. You tried to be good, in your own small way, and the world smacked you across the face. You're also *angry*. You had good intentions, and at least you put in the effort—shouldn't that count for something?! And you're *discouraged*. You can't afford to do much more than what you did, because you're not a billionaire who can start some giant charitable foundation, and given everything else we have to deal with in our everyday lives, who has the time and money and energy to think about ethics?

In short: being good is impossible, and it was pointless to even try, and we should all just eat hormone-filled cheeseburgers, toss the trash directly into the Pacific Ocean, and give up.

That was a fun experiment. What now?

Most people think of themselves as "good," and would like to be thought of as "good." Consequently, many (given the choice) would prefer to do a "good" thing instead of a "bad" thing. But it's not always easy to determine what is *good* or *bad* in this confusing, pretzel-twisty world, full of complicated choices and pitfalls and booby traps and bad advice from seemingly trustworthy friends like stupid Wendy, who said the fedora was "ugly-cute" and convinced you to buy it. And even if you *do* somehow navigate the minefield of modern life and succeed at being good, you're just one person! This planet contains *eight billion* people, and a lot of them don't seem to care *at all* about being good. There are corrupt politicians, and conniving CEOs, and people who don't pick up the dog poop when their dogs poop on the sidewalk, and evil dictators, and stupid Wendy (what is her deal? Does she *enjoy* making other people miserable?), so it's hard not to wonder if one person being "good" even matters. Or, to phrase it the way I did when I started reading moral philosophy and thinking about this enormous, knotted, tangled mess:

What the hell am I supposed to do?

This question—how can we live a more ethical life?—has plagued people for thousands of years,[1] but it's never been tougher to answer than it is now, thanks to challenges great and small that flood our day-to-day lives and threaten to overwhelm us with impossible decisions and complicated results that have unintended consequences. Plus, being anything close to an "ethical person" requires daily thought and introspection and hard work; we have to think about how we can be good

---

1 Well, let's be honest: it's plagued *some* people. For every conscientious citizen, there's a whole bunch of cheaters and liars and *Wolf of Wall Street* maniacs who see ethical rules as annoying obstacles to getting whatever they want.

not, you know, once a month, but *literally all the time*. To make it a little less overwhelming, this book hopes to boil down the whole confusing morass into four simple questions that we can ask ourselves whenever we encounter any ethical dilemma, great or small:

What are we doing?
Why are we doing it?
Is there something we could do that's better?
Why is it better?

That's moral philosophy and ethics[2] in a nutshell—the search for answers to those four questions. And while the Universe Goodness Accounting Department had mostly bad news to offer us, here's some good news: Philosophers have been thinking about those exact questions for a very long time. They have answers for us—or, at least, they have *ideas* that may help us formulate our own answers. And if we can get past the fact that a lot of those philosophers wrote infuriatingly dense prose that gives you an instant tension headache, we might arm ourselves with their theories, use them when we make decisions, and be a little better today than we were yesterday.

I became interested in moral philosophy when I began the work of creating a TV show called *The Good Place*. If you've seen it, you'll recognize many of the ideas in this book because we explored them on the show. If you haven't seen it, (a) how dare you insult me like that, (b) I'm just kidding, and (c) don't worry! Because the whole point of this project is to take you on the journey I went on, from a guy who knew almost nothing about this subject to someone who could write a book about it. (Or at least, convince Simon & Schuster that I could write a book about

---

2 I, like many people, use the terms "morals" and "ethics" somewhat interchangeably, over the objection of hard-core philosophers and linguistics nerds. If you enjoy semantic rabbit holes, you can poke around various dictionaries and tease out the differences . . . and then join me as we blithely ignore those differences, because life's too short.

it.) I fell in love with ethics for a simple reason: Nearly every single thing we do has some ethical component to it, whether we realize it or not. That means we owe it to ourselves to learn what the hell ethics is and how it works, so we don't screw everything up all the time. We share this planet with other people. Our actions affect those people. If we care at all about those people, we ought to figure out how to make the best decisions we can.

Another thing I love about ethics is: It's free!³ You don't need to apply for a license to be ethical, or pay an annual fee to make good decisions. Think of the world as a museum, and ethical rules as a volunteer museum worker, standing silently in a green sport coat, hands clasped behind her back. We're all walking around the museum looking at art (in this metaphor: morally confusing situations), some of which we understand and some of which we definitely don't, because it's all swirly and abstract and confusing. And when we see something we don't know how to interpret, we can just ask the nice lady in the green sport coat what we're looking at and what it means, and she'll tell us, for free! I mean, we could just nod thoughtfully and *pretend* we understand it—a time-honored tradition, in both art museums and life—but there's just gonna be more confusing stuff in the next room, so we might as well get some help making sense of whatever we're looking at now.

Before we get started, I have one more piece of good news. The very act of engaging with these ideas and asking these questions means we've already taken a crucial step: we've simply decided to *care* about whether what we do is good or bad. Which means: we've decided to *try* to be better.

That alone is a big deal. A quick glance around will reveal a ton of people who have clearly decided they *don't* care about being ethical, so

---

3 Minus, I suppose, the cost of this book, if you chose to buy it. Also, I should add that actually *acting* ethically often requires us to spend money or time. I only mean to suggest that the ideas, or concepts, are freely available.

they're not really trying. Part of me doesn't entirely blame them, because attempting to be a decent moral agent in the universe—a fancy way of saying "trying to do the right thing"—means we are bound to fail. Even making our best efforts to be good people, we're gonna screw up. Constantly. We'll make a decision we think is right and good, only to find out it was wrong and bad. We'll do something we don't think will affect anyone, only to find out it sure as hell did, and man are we in trouble. We will hurt our friends' feelings, harm the environment, support evil companies, accidentally help an elderly Nazi cross the street. We will fail, and then fail again, and again, and again. On this test, which we take daily whether we want to or not, failure is guaranteed—in fact, even getting like a C-plus often seems hopelessly out of reach. All of which can make caring about what we do—or in the modern parlance, "giving a crap"—seem pointless.

But that failure means more, and has more potential value, if we *do* care. Because if we care about doing the right thing, we will also want to figure out *why* we failed, which will give us a better chance to succeed in the future. Failure hurts, and it's embarrassing, but it's also how we learn stuff—it's called "trial and error," not "one perfect trial and we nail it and then we're done." Plus, come on—the alternative to caring about our ethical lives is really no alternative at all. We're supposed to just ignore all questions about our behavior? Phone it in, morally speaking? I can't believe that's the right move. If we care about *anything* in this life, we ought to care about whether what we're doing is good or bad. (Later we'll meet a group of very bleak French guys who believed there's no God and we're just tiny flecks of nothingness floating on a big dumb rock in space—and even *they* didn't want us to just throw in the ethical towel.) This book is an account of my own journey through moral philosophy, but it's also about learning to accept failure—or really, to *embrace* it—as a necessary and beneficial by-product of our efforts to try, learn, and improve.

So. We're going to ask questions about what to do in certain situations, and attempt to answer them using some ideas that are 2,400 years old and some that were proposed basically yesterday. We'll start off easy, to introduce those ideas—what they say, what they ask of us, how they claim to make us better people if we follow them. Then we'll ramp things up, applying what we've learned to more gnarly and tangled issues, introducing new ideas along the way. And by the time this book is done, we will know exactly how to act in every conceivable situation, so as to produce a verifiably maximal amount of moral good. We will be perfect. People will gaze upon us with awe and admiration. All our friends will be so jealous.

I'm just kidding—we're still gonna fail all the time. But again, that's okay! So, let's start failing. Or, in the words of Samuel Beckett:

Try again. Fail again. Fail better.

A Few Questions Readers Might Have,
Before We Get Started

Do I need to know anything about moral philosophy before I read this book?

No. My goal was to write a book anyone could understand, regardless of your familiarity with the subject. It's intended as an introduction to these ideas for relative laypeople—like I was when I began reading up.

So, you're not a philosopher? Or a professor? Or even a grad student?

No. I'm just, like, a guy. But that's the point! Everyone holding this book is "just a guy," or "a lady," or "someone who's concerned with how to behave," or "a person who was gifted this book on 'how to be a better person' by a friend and is only now realizing that maybe it was some kind of veiled hint."[1]

---

1 Other "not interested in ethics" types who might theoretically be holding this book right now: a guy who needs something heavy to squash a bug; a kid from the 1950s who's using it to hide his comic book during class; a woman who got it from her office Secret Santa and needs to flip through the first few pages to try to convince her coworker Terrence that he made a good choice and she *definitely* wouldn't rather have gotten booze like everyone else; a dog who got this book in his mouth somehow and now everyone around him is like, "Ha ha, check it out, Buster's trying to read!"

If I want to learn about moral philosophy, why would I read your book instead of a breakdown from some smarter, professor-type person?

First of all, that's rude. But more importantly: I spent a lot of time studying this stuff and discussing it with some very smart and funny people, trying to present it in a way that doesn't give everyone a tension headache. My goal here isn't to revolutionize the field of moral philosophy. It's simply to relay its nuts and bolts so we can all apply it to our real lives.

Okay, you're just some guy. Then who the hell are you to judge me?!

Yeah, I thought you might ask this question. So, listen: This book is in no way meant to make you feel bad about whatever dumb stuff you've done in your life. It's certainly not meant to suggest I *haven't* done a bunch of dumb stuff in my life, because I definitely have, and continue to. Nobody's perfect. (As we'll see in chapter 5, "moral perfection" is both impossible to attain and a bad idea to even attempt.) Again, the goal is to embrace our inevitable failures and find a way to get some use out of them—to learn ways to *benefit* when we make mistakes instead of just stewing in our own guilt, doomed to make those same mistakes all over again.

I am a smart professor-type person, and I'm furious. You only discuss the works of a few of the great philosophers! How could you possibly ignore the work of so many important thinkers?!

Moral philosophy has been around for thousands of years, and every new theory relates in some way to theories that came before it. Sometimes you'll be hacking your way through a dense philosophical tome, and you'll come upon a sixty-page digression where the author discusses some *other* dense philosophical tome, and if you haven't already fought your way through *that* tome you get hopelessly lost, your eyes glaze over, and you just put the book down and watch *The Bachelor*.[2] If I had tried to cover all of moral philosophy I would have done nothing but read books for sixty years and then died, and I have kids and a wife and I like to watch basketball and stuff. Not to mention that some philosophy I *did* try to read was just incomprehensible to me. At one point I got really excited about metaphysics, which dates back to the ancient Greeks and involves questions about the very nature of existence. Sounds fun! I opened a book called *Introduction to Metaphysics* by the German philosopher Martin Heidegger, and the very first sentence, with translator footnotes, looked something like this:

> Why[1] are[2] there[3] things[4]?

> 1. "Why" is perhaps not even the right question; better to ask "how" or "to what end."
> 2. We are obviously making a priori assumptions that there "are," indeed, "things."
> 3. Heidegger employs the German word *IchschätzedieMühediesnachzuschlagen*, which has no direct translation, so I have chosen the crude English word "there," which is a tragic and grievous misrepresentation of Heidegger's intent.
> 4. "Things" might better be thought of as "loci of existence," or perhaps the neologism "essents," meaning "things that have essence," or perhaps a new word I just made up called "blerf," which has no meaning at all, but is somehow in its nonsensical nonmeaning the most accurate word one can use to delineate the difference between nothingness and somethingness.

That's a slight exaggeration, but only slight. I gave up after maybe four more sentences. Later I found out that Heidegger was basically a fascist, so I feel like I made the right call.

---

2 Hypothetically. I mean, *I* never did this. But hypothetically that is something someone would do.

But there's another reason I included what I included and ignored what I ignored: The works discussed in this book are simply the ones I *liked* and connected with. They're the ones that made sense to me, in a cartoon-lightbulb-turning-on-above-my-head kind of a way. This simple sense of connection matters with something like philosophy, which is a massive and diverse rain forest of ideas. No one explorer can map the whole jungle, so you end up gravitating toward certain thinkers and away from others based on nothing more complicated than how much they resonate with you.

My understanding of ethics (and thus: the crux of this book) is organized broadly around a group of theories—virtue ethics, deontology, and utilitarianism—which are currently thought of as the "Big Three" in Western moral philosophy. That focus marginalizes some of the most famous thinkers in history, like Lao-tzu, David Hume, and John Locke, all of whose writings overlap with one of these Big Three theories but maybe aren't *integral* to them. Also, because I wanted *The Good Place* to be secular, I shied away from religious thinkers like Saint Thomas Aquinas and Søren Kierkegaard. Should the ideas in this book pique your interest, and you grab a compass and head into the jungle yourself, it's likely that some of the folks I mostly ignored will become your personal favorites. And then you can write your own book, and talk about why your people are better than my people!

I am a different very smart professor-type person, and I must say you have *completely* misinterpreted [something]. How could you have so blatantly misread [that thing]?

In 1746, a group of British booksellers asked Dr. Samuel Johnson to write a definitive dictionary of the English language. Over the next eight years, he did just that—he *wrote an entire dictionary*. Using only *his own brain.*[3] After he was done, a woman approached him, annoyed, and asked how he could have possibly defined a "pastern" as "the knee of a horse" when it is actually part of the foot. Johnson replied: "Ignorance, Madam. Pure ignorance!" So, if I got something wrong, that's the reason: pure ignorance!

Wouldn't it have been smart to have someone help you with this? An actual, you know, philosopher?

Ah, but I did—Professor Todd May, longtime professional academic and author of several excellent books on moral philosophy. We met when I asked him to help the writing staff of *The Good Place* figure out what the hell any philosopher was ever talking about, and he then agreed to collaborate with me on this book—to "spot me," as it were, and help me not screw up the scholarship so badly that I get sued by Jeremy Bentham's great-great-great-great-great-great-great-great-great-grandkids. So actually, now that I think about it, if there are any problems with the actual philosophy in this book, it's not because of my ignorance. It's Todd's fault. Blame him.[4]

---

3 And several assistants, who helped him collect and organize all the entries, but the point stands. Johnson got paid the equivalent of about $250,000 in today's money for eight years' work. I hate to be "Hollywood" about this, but that dude needed a better agent.

4 Note from Todd: Fair enough.

PART ONE

In Which We Learn Various Theories About How to Be Good People from the Three Main Schools of Western Moral Philosophy That Have Emerged over the Last 2,400 Years, Plus a Bunch of Other Cool Stuff, All in Like Eighty Pages

CHAPTER ONE

Should I Punch My Friend in the Face for No Reason?

No. You shouldn't. Was that your answer? Sweet. You're doing great so far.

If I surveyed a thousand people and asked them if they think it's okay to punch their friends in the face for no reason, I'd bet all thousand would say no.[1] This person is our friend. This person did nothing wrong. We should not, therefore, punch our friend in the face. But the weird thing about asking *why* we shouldn't do this, despite how obvious it seems, is that we may stumble trying to formulate an answer.

"Because, you know, it's . . . bad."

Even sputtering out that simplistic explanation is weirdly encouraging—it means we're aware that there's an ethical component to this action, and we've determined it's, you know . . . "bad." But to become better people, we need a sturdier answer for why we shouldn't do it than "because it's bad." Understanding an actual ethical theory that explains *why* it's bad can then help us make decisions about what to do in a situation that's less morally obvious than "Should I punch my friend in the face for no reason?" Which is just about every other situation.

An obvious place to start might be to say, well, a *good* person doesn't generally do things like that, and a *bad* person does, and we want to be good people. The next step would be to better define what a "good person" really is, and that's trickier than it might seem. The initial

---

1 Though if I put it up as an online poll, it would probably be like 70–30 *in favor* of punching our friend in the face for no reason. The internet is terrible.

idea behind *The Good Place* was that a "bad" woman, who had lived a selfish and somewhat callous life, is admitted to an afterlife paradise due to a clerical error and finds herself ticketed for an idyllic eternity alongside the very best people who ever lived—people who'd spent their time removing landmines and eradicating poverty, whereas she'd spent her life littering, lying to everyone, and remorselessly selling fake medicine to frightened seniors. Scared she's going to be discovered, she decides to try to *become* a "good" person in order to earn her spot. I thought that was a fun idea, but I also quickly realized I had no idea what it really meant to be "good" or "bad." I could describe *actions* as "good" or "bad"—

> sharing *good*
> murder *bad*
> helping friends *good*
> punching friends in the face for no reason *bad*

—but what was underlying those behaviors? What's an all-encompassing, unifying theory that explains "good" or "bad" people? I got lost trying to find it—which is what led me to moral philosophy, which then led me to producing the show, which eventually led me to writing a book where I spend twenty-two pages trying to explain why it's not cool to randomly coldcock your buddy.

Philosophers describe "good and bad" in a bunch of different ways, and we'll touch on many of them in this book. Some of them do in fact approach the concepts of good and bad through *actions*—they say that good actions obey certain principles that we can discover and then follow. Others say a good action is whatever creates the most pleasure and the least pain. One philosopher even suggests that goodness comes from being as selfish as we possibly can and caring only about ourselves. (Really. She says that.) But the first theory we're going to talk about— the oldest of the Big Three, called "virtue ethics"—tries to answer the question that initially stumped me: What makes a *person* good or bad?

Virtue ethicists define good people as those who have certain qualities, or "virtues," that they've cultivated and honed over time, so that they not only have these qualities but have them *in the exact right amount*. Seems gettable, right?

Although . . . immediately we're hit with a hundred other questions: Which qualities? How do we get them? How do we know when we've gotten them? This happens a lot in philosophy—the second you ask a question, you have to back up and ask fifty other questions just so you know that you're asking the *right* question and that you understand *why* you're even asking it, and then you have to ask questions within *those* questions, and you keep backing up and widening out and getting more and more foundational in your investigation until finally a German fascist is trying to figure out why there are even "things."

We also might wonder if there's a single way to define a "good" person; after all, as the author Philip Pullman once wrote, "People are too complicated to have simple labels." We are all highly individualized products of both nature and nurture—complex swirls of inherent personality traits, things learned from teachers and parents and friends, life lessons we picked up from Shakespeare[2] and/or the Fast & Furious movies.[3] Is it possible to describe a set of qualities we *all* have to have, in the exact right amount, that will make every one of us "good"? To answer that, we need to unlearn all the stuff we've learned—we need to reset, take ourselves apart, and then build ourselves back up with a sturdier understanding of what the hell we're doing and why the hell we're doing it. And to help us do *that*, we turn to Aristotle.

---

2 "Love all, trust a few, do wrong to none."

3 "It doesn't matter what's under the hood. The only thing that matters is who's behind the wheel." And also: "I'm gonna knock your teeth so far down your throat you're gonna stick a toothbrush right up your ass to brush 'em." That franchise contains multitudes.

"A Flowing River of Gold"

Aristotle lived from 384 to 322 BCE, and wrote the most important stuff about the most important stuff. If you want to feel bad about yourself and your measly accomplishments, poke around his Wikipedia page. It's estimated that less than *a third* of what he actually wrote has survived, but it covers the following subjects: ethics, politics, biology, physics, math, zoology, meteorology, the soul, memory, sleep and dreams, oratory, logic, metaphysics, politics, music, theater, psychology, cooking, economics, badminton, linguistics, politics, and aesthetics. That list is so long I snuck "politics" in there *three times* without you even noticing, and you didn't so much as blink when I claimed he wrote about "badminton," which definitely didn't exist in the fourth century BCE. (I also don't think he ever wrote about cooking, but if you told me Aristotle had once tossed off a four-thousand-word papyrus scroll about how to make the perfect chicken Parm, I wouldn't blink an eye.) His influence over the history of Western thought cannot be overstated. Cicero even described his prose as "a flowing river of gold," which is a *very* cool way for a famous statesman and orator to describe your writing. (Although, also: Take it down a notch, Cicero. Coming off a little thirsty.)

For the purposes of this book, though, we're only concerned with Aristotle's take on ethics. His most important work on the subject is called the *Nicomachean Ethics*, named either in honor of his father, Nicomachus, or his son, Nicomachus, or I suppose possibly a different guy named Nicomachus that he liked better than either his dad or his kid. Explaining what makes a *person* good, instead of focusing on what kinds of things such a person *does*, requires several steps. Aristotle needs to define (1) which qualities a good person ought to have, (2) in which amounts, (3) whether everyone has the capacity for those qualities, (4) how we acquire them, and (5) what it will look (or feel) like when we actually have them. This is a long to-do list, and walking through his argument takes a little patience and time. Some of the thinkers we'll meet later have theories that can be decently presented in a few sentences; Aristotle's ethics is more of a local train, making many stops. But it's an enjoyable ride!

When Do We Arrive at "Good Person" Station?

It might seem odd to begin with the final question noted in the last paragraph, but that's actually how Aristotle does it. He first defines our ultimate goal—the very purpose of being alive, the thing we're shooting for—the same way a young swimmer might identify "Olympic gold medal" as a target that would mean "maximum success." Aristotle says that thing is: happiness. That's the *telos*,[4] or goal, of being human. His argument for this is pretty solid, I think. There are things we do for some other reason—like, we work *in order to* earn money, or we exercise *in order to* get stronger. There are also good things we want, like health, honor, or friendships, *because* they make us happy. But happiness is the top dog on the list of "things we desire"—it has no aim other than itself. It's the thing we want to be, just . . . to *be it*.

Technically, in the original Greek, Aristotle actually uses the nebulous word "eudaimonia," which sometimes gets translated as "happiness" and sometimes as "flourishing."[5] I prefer "flourishing," because that feels like a bigger deal than "happiness." We're talking about the ultimate objective for humans here, and a *flourishing* person sounds like she's more fulfilled, complete, and impressive than a "happy" person. There are many

---

4 *Telos* is a very important concept in Greek philosophy. Its adjectival form is "teleological," which is a word that makes you sound *very* smart, and which I thus recommend using often. Anytime anyone says something you don't understand in a philosophy discussion, you can say, "But shouldn't we be thinking of this in teleological terms?" and the other person will nod sagely, like: "Mm, yes, good point."

5 I try not to use the word "eudaimonia" in conversation, mostly because I'm never confident I'm pronouncing it properly. Is it "yoo-day-MOH-nee-uh," or "yoo-die-MOH-nee-uh," or "yoo-deh-moh-NEE-uh"? I've never really known, and every time I say it out loud, like to Todd just now on a Zoom call, I kind of glide over it or pretend to cough so he doesn't catch on.

times when I'm happy, but I don't feel like I'm *flourishing*, really. Like, it's hard for me to imagine a greater *happiness* than watching a basketball game and eating a sleeve of Nutter Butters, but am I *flourishing* when I do that? Is that my *maximum possible* level of fulfillment? Is that the be-all and end-all of my personal potential? (My brain keeps trying to answer "Yes!" to these rhetorical questions, and if that's true it's kind of sad for me, so I'm just going to power through, here.) Aristotle actually anticipated this tension, and resolved it by explaining that happiness is different from *pleasure* (the kind associated with hedonism), because people have brains and the ability to reason. That means the kind of capital-*H* Happiness he's talking about has to involve rational thought and virtues of character, and not just, to give one example off the top of my head, the NBA Finals and a Costco bucket of peanut butter cookies.

If "flourishing" is still a bit slippery as a concept, think of it this way: You know how some people who are really into jogging talk about a "runner's high"? It is (they claim) a state of euphoria they achieve late in a long race, where they suddenly don't even feel like they're tired or laboring because they've "leveled up" and are now superhuman running gods, floating above the course, buoyed by the power of Pure Running Joy. Two things to say about this: First, those people are *dirty liars*, because there is no way to achieve higher-level enjoyment from running, because there's no way to achieve *any* enjoyment from running, because there is nothing enjoyable about running. Running is awful, and no one should ever do it unless they're being chased by a bear. And second, Aristotle's *flourishing*, to me, is a sort of "runner's high" for the totality of our existence—it's a sense of completeness that flows through us when we are nailing every aspect of being human.

So in Aristotle's view, the very purpose of living is to flourish—just like the purpose of a flute is to produce beautiful music, and the purpose of a knife is to cut things perfectly. And it sounds awesome, right? #LivingOurBestLives? Just totally acing it? Aristotle's a good salesman, and he gets us all excited with his pitch: we can all, in theory, achieve this super-person status. But then he drops the hammer: If we want to flourish, we need to attain virtues. Lots of them. In precise amounts and proportions.

What Are Virtues?

We can think of virtues as the aspects of a person's makeup that we admire or associate with goodness; basically, the qualities in people that make us want to be their friends—like bravery, temperance, generosity, honesty, magnanimity, and so on.[6] Aristotle defines virtues as the things that "cause [their] possessors to be in a good state and to perform their functions well." So, the virtues of a knife are those qualities that make it good at being a knife, and the virtues of a horse are the horse's inherent qualities that make it good at galloping and other horsey stuff. The human virtues he listed, then, are the things that make us good at being human. This seems kind of redundant, at first glance. If on day one of tennis lessons our instructor told us that "the virtues of a good tennis player are the things that make us good at tennis," we'd likely nod, pretend to get a phone call, and then cancel the rest of our session. But the analogies make perfect sense:

THE THING	ITS VIRTUES	ITS PURPOSE
Knife	Sharpness, blade strength, balance, etc.	Cutting things well
Tennis player	Agility, reflexes, court vision, etc.	Playing great all-around tennis
Human	Generosity, honesty, courage, etc.	Flourishing/happiness

---

6 Aristotle lists a dozen or so, but given that it's been about 2,400 years since he made his list, I feel it's fair and just to make our own additions when we discuss virtue ethics in the modern world. Seems kind of silly to take the text of an ancient document so literally, you know?

We now know what we need (virtues) and we know what they'll do for us (help us flourish). So . . . how do we get them? Do we already have them, somehow? Were we born with them? Sadly, there's no easy fix here. Acquiring virtues is a lifelong process, and it's *really* hard. (I know, it's a bummer. When Eleanor Shellstrop—Kristen Bell's character from *The Good Place*—asks her philosophy mentor Chidi Anagonye how she can become a good person, she wonders if there's a pill she can take, or something she can vape. No such luck.)

How Do We Get These Virtues?

Unfortunately, in Aristotle's view, no one's just born inherently and completely virtuous—there's no such thing as a baby who already possesses sophisticated and refined versions of all of these great qualities.[7] But we're all born with the *potential* to get them. All people have what he calls "natural states" of virtue: "Each of us seems to possess his type of character to some extent by nature; for in fact we are just, brave, prone to temperance, or have another feature, immediately from birth." I think of these as "virtue starter kits"—basic tools and crude maps that kick off our lifelong quest for *refined* virtues. Aristotle says these starter kits are the coarse character traits possessed by children and animals—which, if you've ever taken a bunch of ten-year-old boys to Dave & Buster's, you know are often indistinguishable.

We can all probably identify some starter kit we had as kids. From a very early age I was an extreme rule follower—or maybe let's say I was "inclined toward the virtue of dutifulness," so I don't sound like such a suck-up. It takes a tremendous amount of convincing for me to break *any* rule, no matter how minimal the potential punishment, because my personal virtue starter kit for dutifulness came extremely well equipped—*lots* of tools in there. One of them is this little voice in

---

7 What a cool baby that would be, though! Man. Would love to meet that awesome, flourishing baby.

my head—present as far back as I can remember—that starts chirping at me if *anyone* violates a rule, and it doesn't stop until the rule is followed.[8] When I was a freshman in college, our dorm had a rule that all loud music had to be off by one a.m. If I was at a party at one a.m., *even in someone else's room*, that little voice would instruct me to edge over to the stereo and nudge the music down a little. Because *that was the rule.* You can imagine how popular I was at parties.[9]

But again, these starter kits represent only our *potential* to become virtuous—there's a huge difference between that potential and the real thing. Think of it this way: We sometimes talk of certain people being "born" with certain qualities—she's a "born leader," or he's a "born bagpiper," or whatever. What we really mean is that the person seems to have a natural *aptitude* for leading or bagpiping, and we often say it in awe because that skill doesn't come naturally to us. We've never even *thought* about trying to play the bagpipes, so whenever our friend Rob drags that floppy Dr. Seuss–looking contraption out of his closet and fires it up, we ascribe his talent to some internal, inaccessible setting that he seems to have magically had from birth. Then, when Rob gets a full ride to Ohio State on a bagpipe scholarship, we think, "Rob has fulfilled his destiny by capitalizing on his innate skill." And we also think, "Ohio State has a scholarship for bagpipers?" And then we think, "What the hell is Rob going to do with that degree? How's he going to make rent money—just, like, playing at Scottish funerals?"

Rob didn't come into the world with "The Bonnie Banks of Loch Lomond" humming through his head in concert B-flat. He was simply *inclined* toward bagpiping, in that mysterious way that some people are inclined toward math or painting or baseball, which is super cool when it happens to you or your kids and super irritating when it happens to

---

8 Many people I've talked to have some version of this little voice, to varying degrees. One friend of mine refers to it as the moral equivalent of that "ding ding ding" sound your car makes when you haven't put on your seat belt.

9 Not very.

other people or their kids. And then he took his aptitude and developed it, with many years of practice, into a *skill*. He found something he liked and felt natural doing, and then practiced for a million hours[10] until he became an expert.

And the same way we develop any skill, Aristotle tells us, we become *virtuous* by *doing virtuous things*. This is the "lifelong process" part of the equation: "Virtue comes about," he writes, "not by a process of nature, but by habituation. . . . We become just by doing just actions, temperate by doing temperate actions, brave by doing brave actions." In other words: we have to *practice* generosity, temperance, courageousness, and all the other virtues, just like annoying Rob practiced his annoying bagpipes. Aristotle's plan requires constant study, maintenance, and vigilance. We may have been born with those starter kits, but if we don't develop them through habituation—if we just kick back and rely on them as adults—we're doomed. (That would be like someone saying, "When I was a kid I loved playing with matchbox cars, so I think I'll hop into this Formula 1 Ferrari and run the British Grand Prix.") Habituation isn't very different from the "practice makes perfect" ethos that was drilled into us by high school basketball coaches or music teachers: we get better at the thing by doing the thing, and if we stop doing it, we'll get worse.

This habituation, the practice of working at our virtues, is really the whole shebang here. And the great thing about Aristotle's sales pitch is that he says habituation can work for *any* virtue—even ones we seemingly *weren't* born with aptitudes for, ones where our starter kits are old, rusted toolboxes that are missing all their screwdrivers. This is important, because aptitudes are seemingly randomly assigned to us. We all have things that come easily to us, and things that we—to use a technical philosophical term—suck at. I, for example, have a terrible sense of di-

---

10 Ugh, can you imagine how awful that must have been for his parents? I know I just invented Rob for this book, but I feel really bad for his fictional parents.

rection. I do not know where I am at any given moment unless I am in a place I have been ten thousand times before, and even then it's dicey—I frequently got lost during the seven years I lived in Manhattan, which is laid out in a *numerical grid.*[11] It certainly feels to me that no amount of practice could turn me into a good navigator. Virtues seem to work the same way—I had an aptitude for dutifulness, but not (for example) courage. You might recall having an aptitude for generosity but not temperance, or industriousness but not mildness. In order to flourish we need to develop *all* of these virtues, and Aristotle promises us that we[12] can, regardless of whether we are seemingly inclined toward some of them more than others. With enough work, no one is doomed to be forever deprived of magnanimity or courage or any other desirable quality, the way I'm doomed to get lost every time I walk around a parking garage looking for my car.

Habituation may be the most important part of Aristotle's ethical system, but it's not the only one. Just like we need a coach to get better at tennis or a maestro to help us learn the flute, we also need a good teacher to give us some flourishing lessons. The ancient Greeks were kind of obsessed with how important teachers (or "wise men") are for everything—civics, ethics, science, and so on. Socrates taught Plato, and Plato taught Aristotle, and Aristotle taught Alexander the Great,[13] so there's a lot of focus on the role of brilliant instructors (and wise friends) in transforming people from unformed little goobers into the civic-minded, flourishing people they want us all to be. And since they

---

11 I gave the character Chidi from *The Good Place* this condition, and called it "directional insanity," which is how I think of it.

12 Aristotle, like most educated and famous people in ancient times, was an incredible snob, so for him there were very few people who were capable of achieving everything he said we should try to achieve with respect to virtue and excellence and so on. He also restricted the possible field of such people to "free males." So. You know. Not great.

13 Who maybe didn't totally internalize Aristotle's lessons, it seems, about being a good person, given that he spent his life trying to conquer and enslave the entire world.

themselves were often teachers who founded academies, every time they talk about the need for wise teachers it's hard not to imagine them pointing to themselves and clearing their throats.[14] (The *Ethics* sometimes reads like an infomercial for Aristotle's academy.)

To be clear, the wisdom of wise teachers doesn't *replace* habituation. That dingdong who liked toy cars and then tried to race Ferraris probably wouldn't fare any better if he just read a book[15] on torque or watched Dale Earnhardt Jr. give a TED Talk. "Nature, habit, and teaching," says Aristotle, "are all needed." Because flourishing, you see, doesn't just require us to identify and then acquire all of these virtues—it requires that we have every one in *the exact right amount*. We have to be generous but not *too* generous, courageous but not *too* courageous, and so on. The toughest part of virtue ethics is identifying these amounts, and then precisely nailing each one. Aristotle called each of those maddeningly specific targets: "the mean."

"When Have We Actually 'Achieved' These Virtues?"

The mean, or "golden mean," as it's commonly referred to (though never by Aristotle himself[16]), is the most important cog in Aristotle's ethical

---

14 I stole this joke from Woody Allen, who used it in a comedy piece he wrote about Socrates. And yes, I am 100 percent aware of what it means to reference Woody Allen in the year 2022, and am doing so very intentionally. Just wait until chapter 10.

15 In 2017, President Trump put his son-in-law Jared Kushner in charge of constructing a new Israel-Palestine peace plan. Kushner had no experience authoring international treaties of any kind, so the announcement was met with skepticism. When Kushner released his plan at the beginning of 2020, he proudly announced that he had "read twenty-five books" on the history of the Israeli-Palestinian conflict. To date, Israel and Palestine have not achieved peace.

16 The actual term "golden mean" was first used by the Latin poet Horace several centuries after Aristotle died, but everyone attributes it to Aristotle anyway. It's like how Humphrey Bogart never actually says, "Play it again, Sam," in *Casablanca*. Another of Aristotle's most famous lines, "We are what we repeatedly do. Excellence, then, is not an act but a habit," was also never written by him. Will Durant wrote that *about* Aristotle in his seminal 1926 work *The Story of Philosophy*. But try telling that to the thousands

machine. It's also, in my opinion, the most beautiful. And the most annoying. And the slipperiest, and the most elegant, and the most infuriating.

Think of any of these qualities we're seeking—generosity, temperance, whatever—as a perfectly balanced seesaw, parallel to the ground. If we sit right in the middle, everything will remain upright, even, and harmonious. That's the golden mean of this quality: that perfect middle spot, representing the exact amount of the quality in question that keeps the seesaw level. Shifting toward either end, however, will throw it out of whack; one side of the seesaw will plummet to the ground, and we'll hurt our butts. (In this metaphor, our butts = our personalities.) The two extreme ends represent (1) a *deficiency* of the quality, and, on the other side, (2) an *excess* of the quality—way too little, or way too much. Extreme deficiency or excess of any one quality then becomes a *vice*, which is obviously what we're trying to avoid. Philosophers sometimes think of this as the "Goldilocks rule." For every aspect of our character, Aristotle's basically telling us to be: not too hot, not too cold . . . just right.

As an example, let's take mildness, which Aristotle describes as "the mean concerned with anger." People with a *deficiency* of anger are those who

> are not angered by the right things, or in the right way, or at the right times, or towards the right people. . . . Such a person seems to be insensible and to feel no pain. Since he[17] is not angered, he does not seem to be the sort to defend himself; and such willingness to accept insults to oneself and to overlook insults to one's family and friends is slavish.

---

of Instagram accounts posting that "Aristotle" quote over pictures of people doing yoga on a beach at sunset.

17 All philosophers until like thirty years ago used, by default, masculine pronouns in their writing—the theoretical people they discuss are always "he/him." Even the female philosophers did this. It's kind of a bummer. This book will use gendered and nongendered pronouns at random.

In other words: without *any* anger, if we saw something cruel—like a bully picking on an innocent kid—we might just stand there, slack-jawed and drooling, rather than responding with an appropriate amount of indignation. But if we have *way too much* anger, we might grab the bully and dropkick him into a lake and then grab his whole family and dropkick *them* into the lake and then burn their house down. The golden mean of anger—which, again, Aristotle calls "mildness"—represents an *appropriate* amount of anger, reserved for the *right* situations, to be directed at people who *deserve it*. Like fascists, or corrupt politicians, or anyone associated with the New York Yankees.[18] So, "anger" is the quality, and "mildness" is the dead-solid-middle-point *virtue* we're seeking.[19]

We can see the beauty of this idea, right? It's all about harmony and balance and gracefulness. It's the "Simone Biles doing a perfect dismount off the balance beam" of ideas. But when we think about it for even a second, it gets slippery. For starters, how do we *know* what's excessive or deficient? How do we know when we're angry in the right amount, for the right reasons, at the right people? This is the most common criticism of virtue ethics: *So, we just need to work and study and strive and practice, and somehow magically obtain this theoretical "perfect" amount of every quality, which is impossible to define or measure? Cool plan.* Even Aristotle has a hard time precisely describing a mean sometimes. Regarding mildness, he writes, "It is hard to define how, against whom, about what, and how long we should be angry, and up to what point someone is acting correctly or in error." And then he shrugs: "This much is at least clear: the intermediate state is to be praised, and . . . the excesses and deficiencies are to be

---

18 Ethically speaking, Yankees players and fans deserve an excessive amount of anger. It's the only exception Aristotle allows for. Don't try to look it up in the *Ethics*; it's in a different book. I forget which one, but it's in one of them. He also says it's bad to root for the Dallas Cowboys.

19 We can break all of the virtues down this way—for example, "pleasure-seeking" is a quality, and "temperance" would be the mean of virtue we're seeking.

blamed." The entire system can seem a little like Justice Potter Stewart's famous comment on "hard-core" pornography—that although he couldn't actually *define* it, "I know it when I see it."

That may seem like a tenuous basis for an entire ethical system. And yet: We kind of *get it*, right? We can probably all remember a time we got furious at someone or something, and later thought: "Ehhhh, I probably got too angry there." Or maybe a time when we let something go, and then felt like we should've raised our voice a bit louder. If we take the time to mull over what we've done, if we really commit to examining both our own actions and the actions of those around us, we can eventually come to understand what's too little, what's too much, and what's "just right." We need to Know It When We See It, and we'll only Know It When We See It if we're always looking for it.

This search for virtue can help us in other ways too. Once we start thinking of people as collections of these qualities, we can understand better what we like and don't like about them. Sometimes we'll say, "Luis is the *nicest* guy," or "Diana is the *sweetest* person in the world." But we don't actually want our friends to be extreme. (The actual nicest person in the world would be *so boring*.) Think of people you once spent a lot of time with—ex-boyfriends or -girlfriends, maybe. The things you loved about them were probably the qualities that were so balanced that they approached virtues. ("Damon was always there for me, but he also knew when I needed some time to myself.") The things that drove you nuts about them—that probably turned them into exes—were the qualities in which they were wildly deficient or excessive, and which they never seemed to modify in order to get closer to the balance you desired. ("Damon never used deodorant, and clipped his toenails on the dining room table, and cleaned the Cheeto dust off his fingers by wiping them on my cat."[20]) We can find these golden means only by practicing the

---

20 Also, importantly, realize that those people are thinking the same things about you. Probably not hard to remember a time when someone hit a breaking point with you over

art of finding them—by trying and failing and trying and failing, and by evaluating our successes and failures.

Golden Means: They Make You Less Annoying!

So now, at long last, we can loop all the way back to our original question and provide a sturdier answer.

We might have instinctively known it's bad to punch our friend in the face for no reason, but now we understand *why* it's bad: instead of exhibiting the *mean* of a virtue (mildness), it demonstrates a wildly excessive amount of anger. That seesaw would be way out of balance. We now also understand how to behave going forward: we may have been inclined toward mildness, understanding intuitively (thanks to a "mildness starter kit") that mild is a good thing to be; but if we don't *practice* mildness, learn how to fine-tune it, and regularly check in with ourselves about whether what we are doing is appropriately mild, we might someday end up drooling while other kids get bullied or punching our friends in the face. Virtue ethics gives us the whole picture: how we're doing, how we can get better, and what we should avoid.

Let's revisit my own personal example, with the virtue of dutifulness (which, again, isn't among those listed by Aristotle). We might say the *deficiency* of dutifulness would be lawlessness—breaking all rules and social contracts. The *excess* of dutifulness would be mindless obedience—the kind exhibited by soldiers committing atrocities because they were "only following orders." My personal relationship to dutifulness has at times tipped toward excess. Just ask my wife, my friends, or anyone who has been at a party with me right after the noise curfew hit. I rinse

---

some deficiency or excess of a quality that *you* suffer from. That time you got dumped is suddenly making sense now, right?

my mouth with mouthwash for thirty full seconds, because *that's what it says to do on the label.* I drive with my hands at "ten and two" on the wheel, because *that's what my driving instructor told me to do.* I've always seen this behavior as virtuous and written off annoyed reactions to it as unfounded—but after I read Aristotle I understood how an excess of dutifulness can negatively impact the people around me: I am constantly killing everyone's buzz. (The look on my wife's face when she tries to talk to me and then realizes she has to wait thirty seconds for me to finish my mouthwash routine would melt steel.) I've tried hard in the last few years to demilitarize my overabundant dutifulness, but it ain't easy! I'm forty-six, and I've lived this way all my life. I haven't been looking for that golden mean, and thus: I can be kind of annoying.

But again, I'm not a lost cause. I was born with a good starter kit for the virtue of dutifulness, which relentlessly warned me against violating rules—I essentially did everything my parents and teachers told me to do, because they were In Charge. Now, however, if someone in a position of authority told me to do something iffy I wouldn't just blindly obey, even if that person were wearing a uniform with a name tag that said "Official Rule-Making Authority Guy."[21] I might not have practiced finding the golden mean as much as I should have, but at least I now have a greater understanding of the world, knowledge about social interactions, a sense of propriety, and wisdom shared with me by a bunch of wise men and women—all of which help me modulate my inclination to follow rules. If I'd relied solely on my starter kit for my whole life, things could've turned out very badly. Given my predilection to do what I'm told, I'm lucky that the circumstances of my upbringing pushed me to only a mild excess of dutifulness that made me kind of annoying, and not an extreme excess that made me, you know, a war criminal.

To me, this is the true value of Aristotle's virtue ethics—despite being

---

21 Even thinking about that guy makes me nervous.

written so long ago, it's really on point when it comes to this one aspect of the human condition. If we're not careful, our personalities and habits slowly and inevitably calcify over time. Until I was about thirty, I was an avid music listener, in multiple genres. Then I got married and had kids and disappeared from the culture for a while, and now all I listen to is the same late-nineties indie rock and hip-hop albums, over and over. They're familiar and comforting, and playing them in my car has become an automatic response. Our behaviors create deep grooves in our personalities, like a heavy chair forming impressions in a shaggy rug, and it becomes harder and harder to escape them. The best thing about Aristotle's "constant learning, constant trying, constant searching" is what results from it: a mature *yet still pliable* person, brimming with experiences both old and new, who doesn't rely solely on familiar routines or dated information about how the world works.

Aristotle scholar Julia Annas, a professor at the University of Arizona, wrote a book called *Intelligent Virtue* in which she talks about the difference between a *rote* response to some situation that tests our virtues, and a deeper, more "intelligent" one: "The result [of practicing something] is a speed and directness of response comparable to that of mere habit, but unlike it in that the lessons learned have informed it and rendered it flexible and innovative." What a wonderful idea—that when we practice a virtue over and over and over, we become *fluent* in the virtue, and our responses emerge from a deep reservoir of understanding about the virtue, so instead of remaining stuck in a rut defined by our previous behaviors, we have a fighting chance to make a good decision regardless of how weird the situation might be. Because again, most ethical questions aren't as easy to answer as "Should I punch my friend in the face for no reason?" They're far more nuanced and complex, so it stands to reason that the harder we've studied, the better we'll fare when some entirely new situation arises to test our moral reflexes.

This "flexibility" of response is actually a bit like comedic acting. There are plenty of skilled comedians in the world who are funny and sharp and have good timing. But others—often coming from improvisational comedy backgrounds—seem more *thoroughly* funny. They're effortlessly funny, in every direction, all the time. They never strain, or flail, or panic, even when they have no script to work from or rehearsal to prepare with. I suspect this is because improv requires intense and constant training; small groups of people perform together, day in and day out, inventing scenes out of thin air. It teaches them how to be attentive, loose, confident, unrushed—how to calmly focus on all of the quickly moving parts of a scene at once, to anticipate each other's actions, and to avoid repeating themselves. I remember thinking about Steve Carell and Amy Poehler[22] that they knew their characters so well the *Office* or *Parks and Recreation* writers could place them in any scenario, at any moment, and they would know instantly how to be funny—they were *fluent* in their characters. They had practiced the skill of comedy so much, so often, for so long, that their responses to any unfolding scenario were flexible and innovative.

This is the full sales pitch for virtue ethics: If we really work at finding the means of our virtues—learning their ins and outs, their vicissitudes and pitfalls, their pros and cons—we become flexible, inquisitive, adaptable, and *better* people. In fact, the search for golden means is cumulative— the closer we get to one, the more it can help us in our search for others. Approaching the mean for kindness helps us get closer to the mean for generosity, which helps us get closer to the mean for loyalty, which helps us approach the mean for temperance, and so on. Eventually we'll truly flourish, achieving a mastery over the exact balances of hundreds of different virtues. We'll understand and adapt to any new situation, able to see and decipher the very foundational code of human existence—like Neo at the end of *The Matrix*.

See? Being good isn't so hard. You just have to understand the world as completely as Neo does at the end of *The Matrix*.

---

22 I know, I know, I'm name-dropping here, but the analogy is worth it. I promise I'll keep the Hollywood celebrity references to a minimum. It's what my very good friend Ted Danson would want me to do.

Needless Cruelty: A Good Thing to Avoid

We now understand why punching our friend in the face for no reason is *bad*—the person who does that fails to reach (or straight-up ignores) the golden mean of several different virtues. But we also started with a deliberately easy question, so let's make a tiny modification: "Should we punch our friend in the face *if he does something we don't quite like?*" Maybe this friend made fun of our new khaki shorts, causing us some small pain, and now we have to determine whether we are allowed to punch him in the face. A virtue ethicist would say that a punch to the face after such a minor slight exhibits the same excess of anger that it would if we were doing it for no reason at all. But we can also look at this from another angle, thanks to Judith Shklar (1928–1992), a Latvian philosopher who wrote extensively about freedom and liberty—topics near and dear to her, given her Jewish family's history. The Shklars had to flee Latvia to escape Stalin, and then had to keep fleeing to escape Hitler, and after finally reaching America, Judith got a PhD from Harvard and became the first woman ever tenured in Harvard's Government Department. In her masterwork, *Ordinary Vices*, she makes a compelling argument that cruelty—not pride or envy or wrath or any of the other classic "deadly sins"—is actually the worst human vice, and should be placed atop the list of things to avoid. "To put cruelty first," she writes,

> is to disregard the idea of sin as it is understood by revealed religion. Sins are transgressions of a divine rule and offenses against God. . . . However, cruelty—the willful inflicting of physical pain on a weaker being in order to cause anguish and fear—is a wrong done entirely to *another creature.*

When we think only of religious "sins" as the ultimate bad stuff we want to avoid, we end up manufacturing justifications for horrible atrocities; her example is the European conquerors coming to the "New World," encountering its Indigenous peoples, and rationalizing genocide as the will of a Christian God. If we elevate cruelty—transgressions against other humans—to the top of the "worst crimes we can commit" list, we can no longer find and exploit any such loopholes.

But Shklar has another beef with cruelty, which helps us understand why we shouldn't punch our friend after he makes fun of our khaki shorts. Cruelty, she says, is often way out of proportion to the behavior that prompted it. A man commits a minor crime (like in the famous *Les Misérables* example, stealing a loaf of bread when you're starving) and is then sent to prison, where his conditions are *incredibly* cruel. It's asymmetric: the cruelty of the punishment vastly outweighs the crime he's committed. Pretty compelling argument, right? The modern-day criminal justice system has put countless people in prison for extremely minor offenses—including some, like marijuana possession, that are now widely legal. But it's not just criminal acts that reveal this problem. Basic, garden-variety human interactions are rife with unwarranted cruelty. If you don't believe me, make a YouTube video and say something innocuous, like "Cheese is delicious!" or "I love Michigan!" and then read the comments. ("Go back to East Lansing, you ugly curd-loving moron" is one example of what might happen.)

Since our goal here is to become better people in our day-to-day lives, putting cruelty first in our list of things to avoid seems like a really good idea. Unfortunately, there's a hefty price to pay: because there is so much cruelty all around us, thinking of it as humanity's worst vice takes a heavy toll on our psyches. "If cruelty horrifies us," Shklar writes, "we must, given the facts of daily life, always be in a state of outrage." And she's right! A quick glance at the news reveals endless cruelty: racism, sexism, voter suppression, laws constructed to keep people in abject poverty, mean YouTube comments—putting cruelty first threatens to turn us all into misanthropes, says Shklar, which might be why we're tempted not to focus on it. But there is a way to escape the scourge of cruelty: knowledge. (Specifically: knowledge of cultural practices other than our own.) Quoting the great Enlightenment philosopher Montes-

quieu, she tells us that "'knowledge makes men gentle,' just as ignorance hardens us." This is an idea Aristotle would like, I think. The more
we try to learn and understand the lives being led by other people—the
more we search for a golden mean of empathy—the less we will find it
permissible to treat them with cruelty.

We've covered a lot of ground already! We not only understand that
we shouldn't punch our friend in the face for no reason (or for a bad reason), we also have a deeper understanding of why that's true. We know
what we're aiming for (golden means of various qualities), and what it
provides us (a deep understanding of our actions, rendering us "flexible
and innovative" in their applications to other, more complicated situations). We also understand why a cruel action (the wanton infliction of
pain on another person) should be atop our list of things to avoid.

But again, come on—should we punch our friend in the face for no
reason? That was a layup. The world, as we've said, is complicated, and
most decisions are not nearly that simple. In fact, what if we're in a situation where our choices are not

(a) punch someone in the face
or
(b) don't

but rather:

(a) punch someone in the face
or
(b) punch someone else in the stomach?

. . . What the hell do we do then?

Should I Let This Runaway Trolley I'm Driving Kill Five People, or Should I Pull a Lever and Deliberately Kill One (Different) Person?

Weird question, right? We were just goofing around, talking about *Les Misérables* and YouTube comments, and suddenly we're in some dystopian vehicular psychodrama. Obviously, chances are you've never been in this exact situation, and you probably never will be. But trust me when I say that any understanding of modern ethical decision-making requires you to think very hard about what you would do if you *were* faced with this choice, and more importantly, why you would do it.

So. You're driving a trolley, and the brakes fail. On the track ahead of you are five construction workers who will be smooshed by the runaway trolley—but there's a lever you can pull that will switch the trolley onto another track, on which is *one* construction worker. The questions are obvious: Should you do nothing, allowing five people to be killed? Should you pull the lever, killing one person? Also, why are these people working on active trolley tracks in the middle of the day? Who approved this? Jerry, from scheduling? That guy is so incompetent. I heard he only got this job because his cousin owns the trolley company.

This thought experiment and its many variations (which we'll get to shortly) are collectively called "the Trolley Problem." The original question was posed in 1967 by a British woman named Philippa Foot.[1] Now, I know what you're thinking: "Philippa Foot" sounds like the name of a fairy-tale mouse who lives inside a purple mushroom in an enchanted forest. But she wasn't a fairy-tale mouse, she was an esteemed philosopher, and the Trolley Problem is arguably modern philosophy's most famous thought experiment. In fact, it's *so* famous and oft-discussed that many academics kind of hate it now—they roll their eyes and look annoyed when it comes up, because it's all anyone has talked about for fifty years. It's like the philosophy version of "Stairway to Heaven" or *The Godfather* or something—an admitted classic that has suffered from overexposure. But suck it up, academic philosophers; we're gonna talk about it, because working through its complexities does a bang-up job of explaining why "doing the right thing" is so difficult.

Most people agree that in the original conception laid out above, we should pull the lever. We give this answer reflexively—it just . . . seems like the right move. We don't know anything about the people—they're just anonymous construction workers who inexplicably don't find it important to pay attention to the seemingly vital question of whether there might be a trolley bearing down on them—so we ought to save as many as possible, right? We have the chance to do something simple that spares four human lives. Pull that lever, baby, and we'll be heroes!

But hidden in this problem, lurking under the surface, are a whole bunch of booby traps—the troubling places that our answer leads us to once the original scenario is even slightly modified. For example, what

---

1 Though it wasn't *named* "the Trolley Problem" until Foot's essay was discussed by a woman named Judith Jarvis Thomson, whom we'll meet later and who is largely responsible for many of the maddening variations we're about to investigate. In the annals of Trolley Problem history, Foot gets all the headlines, but Thomson deserves a lot of the attention. (Also, Foot was British, so she called it a "tram," and "the Tram Problem" just doesn't have the same ring to it.)

if we're not the *driver*, but just an innocent observer, standing next to the tracks where (in this version) the track-switching lever is located? Now we don't have the same decision-making responsibilities that we might have if we were employed by the trolley company. Would we still pull the lever then? Or what if the potential smooshees aren't anonymous? What if we look out through the front windshield and recognize our friend Susan standing over there on the other track, and because we don't want to kill our friend Susan, who's so nice and thoughtful and once gave us her Beyoncé tickets when she couldn't use them, we actively decide *not* to switch tracks. Is it morally permissible to let five people get killed in order to save our friend Susan's life? Or what if we see Susan standing there on the other track, but not only is she not our friend, we *hate* her? She's condescending and mean and she refused to give us her Beyoncé tickets that one time even though she couldn't use them, and actually we were literally just telling our sister yesterday that sometimes we wish she'd be flattened by a runaway trolley. If we pull the lever now, did we do it because we wanted to save five lives . . . or because annoying Beyoncé-ticket-hoarding Susan had it coming?

Here's the one that always gets people: What if we're standing on a bridge that spans the tracks, looking down at the runaway trolley, and next to us is a big thick-necked weight lifter[2] named Don, who's leaning waaaay out over the edge of the bridge. We—experts in physics, apparently—calculate that Don is just massive enough so that if the trolley hit him, it would slow down and come to a stop before the five guys got smooshed. Which means all we have to do is shove Don the *teensiest* bit so he falls onto the tracks and *he* gets smooshed, saving five other lives. Would we shove him? Most people draw a line in the sand here, and say no—they wouldn't shove poor Don to his certain death. At

---

2 This variation comes from Judith Thomson's seminal 1985 article on the Trolley Problem; in her version, it's an overweight man. "Thick-necked weight lifter" seems less judgy.

which point, whoever is administering the thought experiment rightly points out that the action and the result are essentially identical: in one scenario we pull a lever, in the other we tip Don off a bridge, but in each case we are knowingly causing the death of one innocent person to save five others. But it *feels* different, right? There's gotta be a difference between pulling a lever from inside a trolley and *physically pushing someone off a bridge*. Also: Be more careful, Don. Stop leaning so far out over the railings of bridges. (None of the people in the Trolley Problem have any awareness of the dangers all around them. It's infuriating.)

We're not nearly done, by the way, with thorny Trolley Problem–related quandaries. What if we're doctors in a hospital, and five people come into the ER needing five different organ transplants or they'll all die: one needs a heart, one a liver, one a lung, one a stomach, and one a . . . spleen, I guess? Do you need a spleen to live? It doesn't matter. The point is, they all need organs. We, the exhausted doctors on duty tonight, walk to the vending machine to get a soda and see a custodian happily cleaning the floors. Maybe he's singing a little song to himself about how healthy he is, and how it's so cool that all of his organs are functioning perfectly. This gives us a great idea: We'll kill that custodian, harvest his organs, and divvy 'em up. His heart goes to the heart-needing guy, his spleen to the spleen-needing lady, and so on. Everybody wins! (Except for the custodian.)

Again, this seems abhorrent, but in essence it's no different from our action and its results in the original experiment: because of a choice we make, one innocent dies and five innocents live. Almost none of us would agree to that version, however. It's one thing to pull a lever, we think—it's another thing entirely to sneak up behind a singing custodian and garrote him with a piano wire so we can rip out his spleen. This is why the Trolley Problem is so compelling: our answers to the simple question "Is it okay to do this?" vary widely with each different version, even though the basic act (choosing to kill one person) and its end result (five others live) is always the same.

So . . . what the hell?

Utilitarianism—A Results-Oriented Business!

We have now arrived at the second of our three main Western philosophical schools: utilitarianism, most famously developed by British philosophers Jeremy Bentham (1748–1832) and John Stuart Mill (1806–1873), two deeply weird dudes.

Bentham had many admirable qualities—he argued for gay rights, minority rights, women's rights, and animal rights, which were not things a lot of people argued for in eighteenth-century England. He was also . . . let's say, "eccentric"? and declared that when he died his body should be given to his friend Dr. Thomas Southwood Smith for use in medical research. Smith preserved Bentham's skeleton, dressed it in one of Bentham's suits (as he had apparently requested), and commissioned a wax replica head when the preservation of Bentham's actual head—and I quote—"did not produce acceptable results." Apparently, in fact, it "went disastrously wrong, robbing the head of most of its facial expression, and leaving it decidedly unattractive." (I have decided not to include any photos of this. You're welcome.) The Bentham skeleton-wax-head contraption is called his "auto-icon," which I suppose is a better name than "nightmare death puppet," and in 1850 Smith donated the auto-icon to University College London, of which Bentham was a sort of "spiritual founder" (though not an actual one) so they took it in. Hilariously, according to the UCL blog, "The College did not immediately display the auto-icon, much to Smith's disdain." Seems like a real "can you blame them?" type of deal. For decades UCL kept their human scarecrow in a wooden cabinet, but in February 2020 they put it in a freaking glass case in the freaking student center, which I imagine everyone at University College London really enjoys and it doesn't at all make them want to barf.[3]

---

3 Here are a couple more fun little tidbits about the auto-icon from the UCL Culture Blog regarding the rare occasion when they drag it out of its display case: "It takes 3 peo-

Bentham's disciple J. S. Mill was also an early women's rights supporter, authoring a groundbreaking work of feminist thought called
The Subjection of Women in 1869.[4] He learned Greek and Latin by the
age of eight, and by the time he was a teenager he had an impressive
command of Euclidean math, politics, philosophy, and basically everything else, thanks to an overbearing dad who had some truly intense
thoughts on childhood education. By the time he was twenty he was
horribly depressed—a predictable outcome if you have the kind of father
who made you learn Greek and Latin in kindergarten. Mill pulled out of
his funk partly by reading Romantic poetry, which is a very nineteenth-
century-British-genius way to pull out of a funk, and went on to become one of his generation's most influential philosophers despite never
teaching at a university or even attending one. To cap off his singular
life, Mill died in 1873 of St. Anthony's fire, a rare infection where your
skin essentially explodes into bright red inflammations. But before his
skin exploded, he furthered Bentham's work on the subject of utilitarianism, and brought it to the forefront of Western philosophical thought.

Utilitarianism is one branch of a school of ethical philosophy broadly
called "consequentialism," which cares only about the *results* or *consequences* of our actions. The best thing to do, says a consequentialist, is
simply the thing that results in the most good and the least bad. Spe-

---

ple to move and, as Bentham's skeleton is bolted to his chair, it has to be moved in one
go. This involves two people carrying the chair and body, while a third holds on to the
feet to try to keep them still. The skeleton is held together with copper wire and hinges at
the joints, which means in theory the auto-icon could move like a living person. In practice this means that his feet want to stay on the ground or, if held high enough, dangle off
the chair. An absolute nightmare when you are trying to move delicately. Another reason
why we try not to move it is the fear of pests getting on to Bentham's clothes, eating away
and causing huge damage. The undershirt had to be replaced in 1939 because of this,
and it has been treated twice for infestations since the 1980's." So. That's fun.

4 I read *The Subjection of Women* in college, and when I started working on *The Good
Place* I went back and dug out my old copy. I was amused and horrified to see that the
cover of the edition we used was . . . pink. You know, because it's about "girls."

cifically, Bentham's initial phrasing of utilitarianism was that the best action is whatever makes the most people *happy*.[5] He called this the "greatest happiness principle," and it's both invitingly simple and kind of silly.[6] "Who gets to decide what 'happiness' is?" would be one question we might ask, given that some people, like me, are normal and well-adjusted, and other people put pineapple on pizza and enjoy listening to the Red Hot Chili Peppers.

Still, consequentialism has undeniable appeal. When I first read about it in college, I thought: "Cool! I *get* this one!" It's an ethical theory that feels *attainable*, because all that matters for any action is the outcome: more overall happiness = better, more overall sadness = worse, so all we have to do is create more pleasure/happiness than we do pain/sadness and we win the ethics contest! Consequentialists give us the comfort of *knowing* that what we did was good or bad, because the answer lies in verifiable results; it's an attempt to take morality out of the abstract and make it more like math, or chemistry. Think of the scene at the end of *Schindler's List*, when Oskar Schindler (Liam Neeson) laments that he hadn't done enough—that his gold pin could've been traded or sold, and the money then used to save the lives of two more people. Schindler had found a way to rescue persecuted people using his fortune and influence, so every pfennig he spent equaled some percentage of a human life. His moral calculation was crystal clear. And that's why *Schindler's List* is famously such a pleasant and relaxing movie to watch.

---

5 The differences in consequentialist branches consist mainly in what the aim or objective is—what they're trying to maximize by making all their decisions. Utilitarianism chose happiness, while other branches may choose kindness or income equality or roasted beet consumption or anything else. I use "consequentialism" and "utilitarianism" interchangeably, which would probably get me yelled at in a philosophy PhD program, but again, life's too short.

6 Obviously, Aristotle was also interested in maximizing happiness, but his definition—*flourishing* by exhibiting virtues in precise amounts thanks to a ceaseless process of searching for those virtues—holds a lot more water, at first glance, than Bentham just saying, "Let's maximize happiness!"

Okay, so, only the results matter. But how do we actually judge the results? If you're Oskar Schindler, and you trade a gold Nazi pin you don't really care about for two human beings, it's pretty easy to figure out that you created more happiness/pleasure (two lives are saved) than pain/sadness (you don't have your cool pin anymore). But most decisions aren't nearly that cut-and-dried. If we're going to judge *all* of our actions on this basis, we need some kind of calculator that can help us determine how many "happiness points" or "sadness demerits" each act creates. So, Bentham invented one. He came up with seven scales we should use to measure the pleasure created by anything we do:

Intensity (how strong it is)

Duration (how long it lasts)

Certainty (how definite it is that it'll work)

Propinquity (how soon it can happen)

Fecundity (how "lasting" it is—how much other pleasure it can lead to)

Purity (how little pain it causes in relation to the pleasure it creates)

Extent (how many people it benefits)

Two things are clear. First, it is *impossible* to look at that list and not make jokes about utilitarianism being like sex. I mean, come on. "Intensity," "how long it lasts," "how much other pleasure it can lead to"—if you read that section and did not immediately make a joke about Jeremy Bentham being history's horniest philosopher, you're a better person than I am. But second: this calculator stinks. How are we actually supposed to apply these scales to the things we do? How can we calculate the "fecundity" of loaning a coworker twenty bucks, or the "purity" of eating a fried turkey leg at a state fair? Bentham even suggested new terminology for our measurements: "hedons" for units of pleasure, and "dolors" for units of pain. This dude wanted us to walk around and say things like, "By my calculation, buying produce from a local farmers market instead of a large national chain creates 3.7 hedons and only

1.6 dolors, and thus it is a good action." Doesn't seem plausible. But Bentham—who, it should again be noted, had his skeleton stapled to a chair and permanently displayed in a famous university—clearly believes in his system, and writes about it with great conviction. He even made up a cute little rhyme to help guide us:

> Intense, long, certain, speedy, fruitful, pure—
> Such marks in pleasures and in pains endure.
> Such pleasures seek if private be thy end:
> If it be public, wide let them extend.
> Such pains avoid, whichever be thy view:
> If pains must come, let them extend to few.

And you know what? Despite all of the problems we've already noted with the greatest happiness principle, that ghoulish human taxidermy experiment had a point. If you knew nothing about morality and all you did was follow Bentham's little rhyme, you'd be a pretty decent person. When we create pleasure or pain, he says, those sensations can be defined by how intense, long, certain, speedy, fruitful, and pure they are. If you're acting only for yourself, go ahead and seek pleasures however you want—but if you're acting publicly, aim to spread as much pleasure around as you can.[7] Avoid causing pain whenever possible, but if you can't, do your best to limit the amount of pain people experience. That ain't half bad. The main thing Bentham and the other utilitarians have going for them is their overriding concern for other people, and their belief that all people's happiness matters equally. *My* happiness is no more special than *anyone else's*, they said, which essentially eliminates the concept of elitism. The utilitarian cruise ship has no first class section reserved for the wealthiest passengers—everyone's room is the same size, and everyone eats from the same buffet.

So . . . is utilitarianism the answer?

---

7 If you restrained yourself before, I bet you're making the jokes now, aren't you?

No. Utilitarianism Is Not "the Answer" (in Many Situations).

Unfortunately, any stress test that we perform on utilitarianism can reveal crucial weaknesses in its central tenets. If all that matters is maximizing happiness and minimizing pain, we quickly arrive at some gnarly conclusions—like, say, that a doctor could go ahead and strangle an innocent custodian in order to hand out his organs to five needy patients. Bentham's greatest happiness principle also suggests that if a pig has enough pig slop and mud to roll around in, the pig is "happier" (and thus, more "successful" in its life) than, say, Socrates, who was maybe a brilliant thinker but also annoyed everyone in Athens so much that his government threw him in jail and made him drink hemlock and die. Any ethical theory that suggests a muddy pig had a happier and better life than one of humanity's greatest thinkers is in trouble right off the bat, probably.[8]

Indeed, ever since Bentham introduced utilitarianism to the world, philosophers have delighted in designing thought experiments to reveal how flimsy it can be. Here's one I like:[9] Imagine there's an electrician (let's call him Steve) working on a transformer at ESPN during a World Cup soccer match. Steve slips and falls behind the transformer—just gets really wedged in there—and the electrical equipment starts repeatedly jolting him. We could get Steve free, but doing so would require that we shut the transformer down for a few minutes, interrupting the broadcast. The strict consequentialist makes an easy call here: tens of

---

8 Mill devoted a lot of time to correcting the more basic problems in Bentham's work, including this one. "Few human creatures," he wrote, "would consent to be changed into any of the lower animals for a promise of the fullest allowance of a beast's pleasures. . . . It is better to be a human being dissatisfied than a pig satisfied."

9 This is a reformulation of a thought experiment invented by T. M. Scanlon in his book *What We Owe to Each Other* that I've tinkered with a little because I'm using it in a slightly different context. We'll meet Scanlon in chapter 4.

millions of people would be *so sad* if the feed gets cut, so, sorry, Steve, you'll just have to stay there and get continuously zapped until your bones are visible through your skin like in cartoons. But that answer leaves us cold. It feels wrong to let poor innocent Steve suffer so others can be happy. That's what a lot of the problems with consequentialism boil down to, really—sometimes it simply *feels* like the conclusion we come to, when we tally up the total "pleasure" and "pain" resulting from a decision, just can't be right.

Now, utilitarians had a clever response to this: If we conclude that some action created more good than bad, but it seems like this action can't possibly be morally permissible, well . . . that just means we did the calculation wrong. When we're totaling up the good and bad of the action, we have to consider the entire picture; that is, how much pain would be caused not just to the one innocent person who suffered, but to *all* people, who now know that this has happened *and* that our society has deemed it permissible—which means the same thing could theoretically happen to them. Hearing that we let Steve get zapped like the robber in *Home Alone 2* when he touches Kevin's booby-trapped, electrified sink just so we could watch a soccer match would thus make *a lot of people* at least *a little bit* miserable, so we have to add their psychological and emotional pain to Steve's actual physical pain, which makes the total amount of "bad" far greater than we at first thought. This is both a brilliant defense and a total cop-out, because anytime a utilitarian calculation leads to an unpleasant conclusion, the utilitarian can just tell us we did the math wrong.

And even if we do factor in the nebulous amount of pain/sadness caused to the world at large by letting Steve be zapped, a consequentialist might *still* let it happen. I mean, sure: Theoretically, everyone now knows that our society permits such things and is thus aware that it may happen to them someday . . . but honestly, what are the chances this *would* happen to any of us? We're not electricians, we don't work at ESPN—we might (correctly) write this off as a freak accident. Plus, Steve must have understood the risks when he took the job of "transformer fixer"—*all* jobs carry *some* risk. So the strict consequentialist might do a thorough calculation of hedons and dolors and *still* decide that it's cool to just leave Steve there, vibrating like a tuning fork, so we can all watch the last eight minutes of the Brazil-France semifinal. Sorting out these broader, secondary pleasure/pain implications can be a maddeningly inexact science.

Another problem: determining the results of our actions requires that we understand the link between those actions and their results— that we actually *did* what we think we did—which is frequently not the case. If there's one thing people are bad at, it's drawing the correct conclusion from a given result.[10] Often we do things whose consequences we can't determine for a long time. Sometimes we can't tell the difference between causation—we did *this thing*, which caused *that result*—and correlation—we did *this thing*, and also that other thing *happened*, but they're not related. (Sports fans, for example, often wear a certain jersey or sit in a specific viewing location in their living room because at some level they think it helps their team win—which of course it does not.[11,12,13]) It's awfully hard to determine how much good or bad we've created if we don't even truly understand what we've "done."

---

10 Well, if there's *one* thing people are bad at, it's "maintaining composure during minor delays in air travel." But drawing correct conclusions is a close second.

11 And yet I've engaged in those superstitions literally thousands of times. I forced my wife, J.J., to sit immediately to my right for nearly every game of the 2004 baseball play-offs, because the first time she sat there (American League Championship Series, game 4), the Red Sox won. They ended up winning every game thereafter, and thus claimed their first World Series in eighty-six years. So, you know: It worked!

12 Note from Todd: It was 1996, I believe, when I saw a bunch of Knicks shave their heads before the playoffs and so I shaved mine. It *didn't* work.

13 Follow-up note from Mike: As we were editing this book in 2021, the Knicks made the playoffs for the first time in forever. You think it's a coincidence that this happened *exactly twenty-five years* after Todd shaved his head? No way. It was because of Todd. Congrats, Todd!

Here's an example. Let's say we're trying to achieve some kind of good—we're teachers, and we want our students to get better test scores. To increase their motivation, we tell them that if the average grade on the next math test is above an eighty, we'll give them each a prize: one big puffy marshmallow! Some of the kids like marshmallows, so they study harder. Some hate marshmallows, and they study less. Some are indifferent, so they study the same amount. And some are so incredulous at how boneheaded an idea this is, they conclude that their teachers are irredeemable goobers and they need to transfer to another school—so they study harder than they ever have before, and all ace the test. At the end of the day, the average grade is an eighty-two, and we high-five each other because we think we've solved the problem of student motivation: offer everyone a marshmallow! Our findings are published in *Awesome Teacher Magazine* with a picture of us holding a bag of marshmallows under the headline: "What's Their Sweet-cret?! These Teachers Know How to Get S'more out of Their Students!"

We just learned a bad lesson from a good outcome—we think offering our students marshmallows helped to achieve a greater good, but in fact they largely achieved the intended result *despite* our action, and we're now inclined to continue doing something that actually makes us *worse* teachers. The great majority of human actions involve incomplete information, either on the front end (before we do it) or on the back end (when we observe the results), so determining the moral value of an action based on the results seems like a risky proposition. (And worse, a true consequentialist might not even care that the result was achieved in an unintended way—we got the result we wanted, so who cares how it happened?) If we're declaring an action "good" or "bad" based on its results, and results are often impossible to fully understand . . . where does that leave us? And doesn't "pulling the lever" on the trolley seem a bit riskier now?

Two More Problems for Utilitarianism:
Hedonists and Murderous Sheriffs

Let's head back to the Trolley Problem, to better understand why we *feel* differently as we make our way through the variations, even when the big-picture utilitarian calculation keeps spitting out the same instructions. Remember that when we approach the original question, we unconsciously respond as utilitarians: saving more people = good. But should we shove Don the weight lifter off a bridge to stop the train? Well, no, say most people. "Why not?" ask the knowing Philosophy 101 professors, springing their trap—"You're still choosing to kill one person to save five." "Because it just *feels* different," we reply weakly. What about killing one healthy person and harvesting his organs to save five people who need organ transplants? "No way," we say. Doing that would make us feel like we're not even *ourselves*—like we're the bad guy in a movie starring Don Cheadle and Rachel McAdams as detectives in search of the infamous "Utilitarian Killer."[14] I suspect the reason for the inconsistency is somewhat related to those teachers and their marshmallow experiment; the utilitarian answering the "Trolley Problem Classic" might arrive at the right answer for the wrong reason. Maybe it *is* morally correct to pull the lever and save the five people . . . but not just because "five is greater than one."

As I mentioned, when Mill and Bentham brought utilitarianism into the world in the eighteenth and nineteenth centuries, it drove philosophers batty—much of the academic world angrily rejected the idea that ethics could be a results-only enterprise. Their critiques are really fun to read, because they're as close as philosophers get to trash-talking.[15] In

---

14 Cheadle plays Detective "Steady" Eddie Gray, six months from retirement. McAdams plays Joelle "Joey" Goodheart, whose impeccable detective instincts mask a troubled past as a teen runaway. Admit it—you'd watch that movie.

15 If they talked about them at all. Will Durant's seven-hundred-page opus *The Story of*

1945, Bertrand Russell[16]—who as it happens was J. S. Mill's godson—published *A History of Western Philosophy*, an impressive survey of everything from the pre-Socratic Greeks to twentieth-century logicians. Although Russell was fond of his godfather and found both his intellectual prowess and his deeply moral life admirable, the section Russell wrote on the utilitarians oozes disdain. "There is nothing new in this doctrine," he sniffs, and later adds that "the influence of the Benthamites on British legislation and policy was astonishingly great, considering their complete absence of emotional appeal." Among his other thoughts:

There is an obvious lacuna in Bentham's system.

and

His optimism was therefore perhaps excusable, but in our more disillusioned age it seems somewhat naïve.

and

John Stuart Mill, in his *Utilitarianism*, offers an argument which is so fallacious that it is hard to understand how he can have thought it valid.

Philosophy, published in 1926, doesn't contain so much as a paragraph about utilitarianism. Bentham and Mill are mentioned in passing, mostly only in footnotes. That's some hard-core academic shade.

16 Russell has the distinction of being one of the most British people who ever lived. His full name is Bertrand Arthur William Russell, Third Earl Russell, OM FRS ("Order of Merit, Fellowship of the Royal Society"). He was born at Ravenscroft in Trelleck, Monmouthshire—an extremely British-sounding place—into an aristocratic family, including his grandfather Lord John Russell, who'd been the dang prime minister of the whole dang United Kingdom. Bertrand also married four women: Alys Pearsall Smith, Dora Black, Patricia Spence, and Edith Finch, which are all deeply British names for women. The dude was *British*.

and

> Jeremy Bentham was an ignorant fool and should I ever visit University College London I shall rip off his wax head and fling it into the Thames.

Fine—he didn't write that last one, but you get the idea. He didn't like utilitarianism. He summarizes his displeasure this way:

> Anything whatever may be an object of desire; a masochist may desire his own pain. . . . A man may desire something that does not affect him personally except because of his desire—for instance, the victory of one side in a war in which his country is neutral. He may desire an increase of general happiness, or a mitigation of general suffering. . . . As his desires vary, so do his pleasures.

Russell, whom I imagine writing this section of his book while clenching his fountain pen so hard it eventually snaps in half, touches on a decent point here. The utilitarian focus on total amounts of pleasure or pain makes us think about the potentially massive differences among the people who are experiencing the pleasure and pain. Remember earlier when I mentioned that some people, like me, are normal and well-adjusted, and other people, who are not, enjoy Hawaiian pizza (which, if you don't know, is topped with pineapple and ham)? Well, what if I'm running a pizza shop and encounter you, a weirdo who loves Hawaiian pizza—in fact, you love it *so deeply and thoroughly* that the amount of pleasure you get from it is just off the charts? One slice of Hawaiian pizza sends you into an orgasmic reverie—just buckets of hedons dripping off your forehead—so that the "total pleasure" of you eating one slice of Hawaiian is greater than the total pleasure of everyone else eating normal pizza. If I'm being a good little utilitarian, shouldn't I stop making normal (good) pizza in order to devote my life to making

Hawaiian (crime against nature) pizza, solely to benefit you and cre
more pleasure?[17]

Utilitarianism often runs into problems like this, because human
beings, it turns out, are *weird*, so searching for actions that create the
most "total happiness" can create bizarre situations. It doesn't seem
fair to prefer a ton of pleasure for one Hawaiian pizza–loving sociopath
over smaller pleasures for a large number of more decent and stable
people, who understand that the proper places for ham and pineapple
are in sandwiches and fruit salads, respectively. Other times, utilitarians do the reverse, making rules that seem to eliminate the peculiar-
ities of each individual and congeal all human happiness or sadness
into giant clumps. That's hard to swallow too, given that the differences
in what makes people happy are beautiful and interesting—they're the
very things that make us *us*. To some of its critics, utilitarianism isn't
really even ethics—it's math. And if someone complains about the
result, a utilitarian points to the fact that more people are happy than
sad and yells, "Scoreboard!" like a drunk football fan whose team is
winning.

One of my favorite anti-utilitarian thought experiments—the one
that really helps explain the Trolley Problem weirdness—comes from
Bernard Williams (1929–2003), another British[18] philosopher, who designed the following (paraphrased) scenario. It's a close cousin of both
"Steve the Zappee at ESPN" and the Trolley Problem, but his analysis
puts an even finer point on Russell's critique:

---

17 Of course, there would be other calculations here . . . Would my other customers be
sad if I did this, and if so, how sad? . . . Would my pizza place shut down, thus making
me and my family sad? And so on. But the important part is: Don't put pineapple on
pizza. It's wet and juicy! Nothing wet and juicy should go on pizza! Honestly, if that's the
only thing you take away from this book, I'll feel like I've done my job.

18 Williams wasn't quite as British as Bertrand Russell, but he was born in Westcliff-
on-Sea, Essex, which is so deeply British it makes "Monmouthshire" sound like Akron,
Ohio.

Jim is vacationing in a small town in some distant part of the country, and he happens upon the local sheriff, Pete, who is pointing a gun at ten residents.[19] Pete tells Jim that here in this town they do a super-fun thing to maintain law and order: every so often they kill ten people at random, just to remind everyone who's boss. But now that Jim is here, it's a special occasion, so if Jim agrees, he—Jim—can shoot just *one* of the locals, and that will serve as the weekly "lesson." (Before you ask, it's also clear that Jim can't like grab the gun and pull some cool Jason Bourne moves on Pete and let everyone go free.) For the utilitarian, the solution is obvious: Jim should kill the one local and save nine lives. But the problem, for Williams, is that this utilitarian answer ignores *Jim*. What becomes of a man who was out for a nice walk and then stumbled into a situation where he was forced to murder an innocent person in cold blood, simply to achieve some kind of maximal hedon/dolor ratio? How does Jim just go back to his normal life?

Williams uses the word *integrity* to attack the utilitarians—less in the sense of "honesty and moral uprightness" than "wholeness," or "un-dividedness." He says that their worldview causes a crack in the basic foundation of an individual's being—the sense that "each of us is spe-cially responsible for what he does, rather than for what other people do." Ten people might die because Sheriff Pete thinks mass murder is a good way to maintain law and order—but that's on Pete. If Jim kills a guy, *that's on Jim*, even if he does it for the sake of some kind of "greater good." Jim's integrity has to matter, at some level—his sense of being a holistic entity who's not required to compromise himself by acting in a way that divides him into parts, some of which he won't recognize as his own. Jim has to think it's permissible *for him*—not just for "someone"—

---

19 Williams actually uses the pretty-standard-for-1973 but very-offensive-for-2022 term "Indians," so I changed it. It's also pretty offensive that he originally set this scene in a village in South America. A lot of things in the culture become offensive very quickly! (More on this later.)

to shoot an innocent person if it saves nine others, or to shove a weight lifter off a bridge if it stops a runaway trolley. It might be that the morally right thing to do is in fact to kill the one local. But in the utilitarian's mind, it's simply a numbers game, and for Williams, numbers can't be the only factor.

We'll come back to the Trolley Problem in the next chapter (and get more explanations for our inconsistent responses), but for now, let's just be content with this notion: when we're confronting moral dilemmas, especially ones where serious pain and suffering result from our actions, relying solely on utilitarian accounting is bound to cause significant problems—there are other factors here, not least among them our *integrity*, and ignoring those factors may result in our doing things we really don't feel are the right things to do. And even if our personal formulation of the right action happens to line up with a utilitarian worldview, that doesn't necessarily mean the utilitarian worldview is the *reason* it's the right action.

Enough Picking on Utilitarians—Let's Focus on the Positives!

Most of the thought experiments invented to attack consequentialism involve having to do something awful to prevent something *more* awful from happening; the best way to exploit the flaws in a "numbers game" theory is to design scenarios where people suffer no matter what you decide to do. But to let the utilitarians off the hook a little, we should note that their theory often holds up far better when we're simply trying to maximize good. Put runaway trolleys and murderous sheriffs aside for a second and consider a more common real-life situation: a hurricane damages a city, and a food bank containing one thousand meals needs to decide how to divide them up. The utilitarian would simply aim to spread the food around to as many people as possible, starting with those who had been hurt the most by the storm or were in the greatest need—because we'd create more pleasure by giving those people food than if we gave it to people who were only lightly inconvenienced. That's a pretty good system! The complications arise when you run into those weird pleasure-monster requests; like, maybe there's one guy named Lars who claims he should get one hundred of the meals for himself, because he's composing an emo-rock opera based on the movie *Avatar* that will take months to complete, so he needs a lot of food to keep his creative juices flowing. Well, this is just great—now the utilitarian has to calculate how much pleasure Lars will get from completing his emo-rock opera, and how much pleasure other people will get from hearing it.[20] Suddenly, what seemed like a straightforward distribution model gets all gunked up. It's unlikely (absent other factors)[21] that giving one-tenth of the available food to some James Cameron–worshipping Fall Out Boy superfan is ethically preferable, but if we're being good little utilitarians, we have to go through the process of thinking it all through and recalculating, which is difficult and annoying.

Consequentialism has recently seen a resurgence in the world of moral philosophy. This may be due to something endemic to the mod-

---

20 Likely answer: Not much. But even if it were a *lot* of pleasure, like if Lars is some kind of Philip Glass–type genius whose emo-rock opera based on *Avatar* is going to sweep the world *Hamilton* style, one of Bentham's questions relates to *how quickly it would bring pleasure*. Emo-rock operas probably take a long time to write and rehearse, so the utilitarian likely concludes that the *immediate* happiness created by allowing more people to, you know, *eat*, is still the right move.

21 If you want to go down another utilitarian thought-experiment rabbit hole, imagine if the dude weren't some amateur emo opera composer but were instead a farmer who himself grew food he could give to others. Or a doctor who made vaccines. Or a climatologist working on a plan to reverse global warming and thus prevent more hurricanes in the future—should *she* get more food? Those answers I'll leave to the reader to decipher on her own.*

  * This is a *classic* philosophy trick—you just lob huge questions out there and then say, "The author leaves it to the reader to determine the answers on her own." Philosophy teachers do this all the time. I think it's totally unfair, and a complete abdication of their responsibility as educators. So why do they do it, then? The answer to that I will leave to the reader to determine.

ern world, like income disparity hitting all-time highs, which has refo-
cused academic attention on the misappropriation of capital. Or maybe
the world's problems have just become so massive, the population so
enormous, and the questions of how we treat each other so urgent, a
philosophy that simply aims to help as many needy people as much as
we can makes more sense in moral terms than it did in simpler, less
populous times. Quite literally *as I write this*, governments everywhere
are deciding how to administer the various Covid-19 vaccines, which (at
least at first) are in limited supply. Those calculations are indisputably
utilitarian—they prioritize those most likely to get very ill or die, as well
as people whose jobs put them at higher risk. The "good" of each dose
is therefore maximized, because each one alleviates the most potential
pain and unhappiness—we'd be hard-pressed to find a school of philosophy that could describe a better way to vaccinate the public against
this disease. While a purely results-based philosophy can create a lot of
problems, there are clearly situations that greatly benefit from caring
only about how much pleasure we can create[22] and how little pain.

But we also saw that determining the moral value of our actions
based solely on their results can be impossible, or misleading, or hard
to calculate, or all three. So . . . what if we ignore the results? What if we
can determine the moral worth of what we do *before* we do it? What if,
faced with a choice between killing one person or five, there were some
kind of rule we could follow that would guarantee we acted correctly
regardless of the result? And what if we could go back to that Universe
Goodness Accountant from the introduction, who tsk-tsked us for all the
bad results we got, and say, "Hey, lady—we don't care if our day of good
deeds got all screwed up, because we *meant* to do good things and only
our *intentions* determine our moral worth"? Wouldn't that feel good, to
rub it in her face a little?

Buckle up, people. It's Kant time.

---

22 Still making the jokes in my head. Can't stop won't stop.

CHAPTER THREE

Should I Lie and Tell My Friend I Like Her Ugly Shirt?

Which of these false excuses have you used to avoid an annoying social obligation?

- "Sorry, I didn't get your text. My phone's been weird lately."
- "I can't make dinner tonight—our babysitter dropped out at the last second."
- "I would *love* to attend your daughter's middle school orchestra concert, but my lizard is depressed. She isn't sitting on her favorite rock, and she won't eat lettuce, and I just need to be there for her."[1]

"Should I tell the truth?" is one of the most common ethical dilemmas we face. Most of us don't *enjoy* misleading people, but the gears of society do mesh more smoothly if we grease them with white lies. It certainly seems easier (and maybe even more polite) to tell someone we have to look after our sick lizard, rather than saying, "I do not want to go to your kid's concert, because it will probably suck and be boring," or worse yet *actually going to the concert*. However, we also sense that there must be some ethical cost when we lie. We know we're not supposed to do it, and every

---

1 This isn't verbatim, but a girl once told me something very similar when I asked her out on a date in ninth grade, and it took me like a week to realize it was probably not 100 percent true.

time we do, we feel a twinge of wrongness; it feels *bad*, or at least *iffy* . . . but the feeling usually fades quickly, we just go about our lives, and in most cases, no one seems the worse for wear. So . . . is it actually bad?

When we're first confronted with one of these situations—a friend bought an ugly shirt to wear to a job interview, say, and asks us for our opinion—we might do a couple of consequentialist calculations:

Good Things About Lying and Saying We Like the Shirt

1. We don't hurt our friend's feelings.
2. In fact, we make her *happy*.
3. We don't seem like a jerk.
4. Our friendship continues apace.

Bad Things About Telling the Truth and Saying the Shirt Is Hideous

1. We make our friend sad.
2. We may have to have a difficult conversation and argue that true friendship means always being honest, which can be a tough sell when someone is upset at you for being honest.
3. We seem like a jerk.
4. Our friend may react badly, double down on her own opinion in order to prove us wrong, wear the ugly shirt to the interview, fail to get the job because the interviewer questions the decision-making ability of someone who would buy such an ugly shirt, fall into a deep depression, sever ties with her friends and family, turn to a life of violent crime, and spend twenty-five years in a maximum-security prison.[2]

---

2 Admittedly, a worst-case scenario.

If we are being good little consequentialists, we might also try to anticipate the larger, broader set of consequences—what will be the effect of
living in a world where our closest friends don't always tell us the truth?
We may then conclude, correctly, that such a world *already exists*, and it's
not so bad, really, so maybe we should just avoid any conflict and proclaim that the lace collar really pops and the oversize neon green buttons
are a cool conversation starter.

But as we've seen, consequentialist accounting is fuzzy and impre-
cise. Not to mention that this experiment seems a bit tainted, because
the benefits we identified are largely to *ourselves*—*we* will either avoid
some pain (the tough conversation with our friend, hurting her feelings)
if we lie, or feel that pain if we tell the truth, and since people generally
try to avoid pain whenever possible, our judgment may be skewed here.
Generally speaking, the best ethical decision is probably not "take the
easy route out of self-interest." It would be awesome it if were! But it's
probably not.

We should also acknowledge that when we made these consequentialist calculations, we only went halfway: we thought about the good/
pleasure that comes from lying and the bad/pain from telling the truth,
but did not try to calculate the good/pleasure that comes from telling the
truth or the bad/pain from lying. We don't think about those sides of the
equation as much because they're more nebulous—how do we calculate
the societal *benefit* of truth, or the societal *ill* of a white lie? It only seems
possible if something tangible results from those actions—say, if we
falsely proclaim that we like the ugly shirt, and our friend, brimming
with confidence from our compliment, wears it to the interview, doesn't
get the job because of how ugly the shirt is, falls into a deep depression, turns to a life of violent crime, and spends twenty-five years in a
maximum-security prison.[3]

There's a whole bunch of "what-ifs" involved with ethical calcula-

---

3 Admittedly, another worst-case scenario.

tions, which is partly what makes utilitarian accounting feel shaky. So maybe there is some other ethical system we can use—one that promises hard and fast rules we can follow to *guarantee* moral success. Perhaps what we need is a real stickler. A stern hardass who crosses his arms disapprovingly when we equivocate. A no-nonsense Germanic dad who will look at our moral report card, see five A's and one A-minus, and ask: "What happened with the A-minus?"

We need Immanuel Kant, and the philosophical theory known as deontology.

The Categorical Imperative: The Most German Idea Ever

Deontology is the study of duties or obligations. If you've heard the term before, you either (a) studied philosophy or (b) had a very annoying conversation at a cocktail party with a grad student, probably named Jonas, who drank Japanese whiskey and talked way too much about David Foster Wallace.[4] Immanuel Kant (1724–1804), primarily responsible for bringing deontology to prominence, believed that we should discern rules for moral behavior using only our ability for pure reasoning, and then act out of an unflinching duty to follow those rules. Some situation presents itself, we tease out the specific "maxim" we have to follow, we follow it, and we're done. Since the only thing that matters is our adherence to the duty to follow whatever rule we came up with, the *results* of our actions are irrelevant. Following the right rules = acting morally. Not following them = failing to act morally. End of story. No leeway, no loopholes, no excuses.

It's a pretty rigid system, and as you might expect, Kant was a pretty rigid dude. As legend has it, his routines were so predictable and exact

---

4 I *love* David Foster Wallace, but even I'm annoyed by how much I talked about him from 1995 to . . . like, March of last year.

that local shopkeepers in East Prussia would set their watches based on when he walked past their stores. That's most likely apocryphal, but it speaks to the myth that built up around him based on his hard-core view of morality and his scholarship in general; I mean, anyone who built an entire ethical theory on the back of "pure reason" is bound to be an intensely scholarly fellow. Before he delved into moral philosophy, he was a lover of history and science, as Bertrand Russell tells us:

> After the earthquake of Lisbon he wrote on the theory of earthquakes; he wrote a treatise on wind, and a short essay on the question whether the west wind in Europe is moist because it has crossed the Atlantic Ocean.

There isn't a ton of humor to be found in the writings of eighteenth-century philosophers, but honestly, nothing is funnier to me than imagining Immanuel Kant's "treatise on wind." I mean, picture the most boring text you can imagine. The 1976 Caldwell, Idaho, business registry, or a nine-hundred-page history of the garden hose. I guarantee you they are not one-tenth as boring as Immanuel Kant's treatise on wind. But once he moved past his fascination with . . . air that moves around, he focused his considerable intellect on morality, and even today is held in extremely high regard among Western philosophers. Probably because none of them ever had to read his treatise on wind.

Kant's explication of deontology is famously difficult to read—much harder, I think, than utilitarianism or Aristotelian virtue ethics.[5] Jeremy

---

5 For me, Kant isn't as hard to read as some, like Georg Hegel (gave up after two minutes) or that fascist Heidegger, but it's still hard, and I'd recommend reading an annotated edition if you decide to dive in. This is a good chance for me to plug the online *Stanford Encyclopedia of Philosophy*, which has well-written and pretty clear explanations of just about everything that's ever happened in the field. And it's free! The *Good Place* writers used it all the time, whenever we got lost or needed a refresher course on something (which was: frequently). For the record, the hardest thing I've even attempted to

Bentham may have suffered from a creepy postmortem scarecrow fantasy, but at least he included fun little poems in his ethical writings. Kant never composed any fun little poems. Kant's writing is the *opposite* of fun little poems. Kant's writing looks like this:

> A completely isolated metaphysics of morals . . . is not only an indispensable substrate of all theoretically sound and definite knowledge of duties; it is also a desideratum of the highest importance to the actual fulfillment of its precepts.

I picked that chunk at random, but they're all like that. Not a great beach read. However, the most important idea in Kantian ethics *is* fairly simple to understand. It's called the categorical imperative, which he introduced in his not-at-all-intimidatingly titled *Foundations of the Metaphysics of Morals*:

> Act only according to that maxim whereby you can, at the same time, will that it should become a universal law.

We need to really take that in, because it's arguably the most famous sentence in Western philosophical thought. The only others that really come close would be René Descartes's *Cogito, ergo sum* ("I think, therefore I am"), Thomas Hobbes's "The life of man [is] solitary, poor, nasty, brutish, and short," and of course the Insane Clown Posse's "Water, fire, air, and dirt / Fucking magnets, how do *they* work?"

The categorical imperative states that we can't just find rules that tell us how *we* ought to behave—we have to find rules *that we could imagine*

---

read is Ludwig Wittgenstein's *Tractatus Logico-Philosophicus*, which, like, don't even *try*. Wittgenstein is largely thought of as a genius even by professional philosopher standards, and that seventy-five-page-long migraine is the only book he ever published in his lifetime. Imagine being so brilliant that you only write one seventy-five-page book and the smartest people who ever lived are all like, "Man, that guy is a *genius*."

everyone else following too. Before we do something, we have to determine what would happen if *everyone* did it; and if a world in which everyone did it would be all screwed up, that means *we're* not allowed to do it. So, should we lie to our friend? No. Because first we have to imagine a world where *everyone* lies—and in such a world, we'd realize, no one would ever trust each other, human communication would cease to function, all interactions would become suspect, and even lying (the thing we're thinking about doing) would lose its point. So: we can't lie to anyone, ever, for any reason. (See? The dude is hard-core.)

And when we tell the truth, we have to do so not "because we care about our friend" or "we're afraid we'll be caught in a lie" or something— we tell the truth only out of a duty to follow the universal maxim we have reasoned out. Giving money to charity because, say, "we feel sad about the state of the world" might be a nice thing to do, but the action has no moral worth. It *only* has moral worth if we're adhering to a maxim— perhaps "When we are able, we ought to help those less fortunate"—that we can imagine *everyone in the world* following. In order to be good little Kantians, our motivation in any action cannot stray one inch from "Act out of a duty to follow a universal maxim." No exceptions!

Basically, Kant wanted to differentiate between humans using their pure reason (thus confirming our specialness, as the only creatures who can do that) and the rest of the beasts in the lower, animal world, where emotions and feelings reign supreme and events unfold due to these baser passions. That's why things like happiness and fear have to be taken out of the equation when we're looking at motivations—I mean, cows and porcupines can feel happiness or fear, and we've gotta be better than some dumb porcupine munching on a twig. This explains why Kant thinks giving to charity out of sympathy or sadness might be *praiseworthy*, but not *moral*. His esteem for the human ability to use our brains makes him a bit of a snob—and that snobbery puts him in good philosophical company. Most schools of thought both ancient and modern spend a decent amount of time extolling the most brilliant and educated among us, and affirming that humans are better than other creatures because we can think and reason and philosophize. Those arguments make sense until you see a bunch of kids on a speedboat during spring break chugging vodka from an ice luge shaped like a shotgun, and then you start to think maybe otters and butterflies have it more figured out than we do.

But Kant's strict system also provides a form of comfort. Since moral "success" comes only from acting out of duty to follow a universal maxim, if something "bad" happens as a result of whatever we do, it ain't on us—we acted correctly! In that sense, Kantian deontology is the exact opposite of utilitarianism;[6] to that point, while all of utilitarian ethics was based on maximizing happiness, Kant thought "happiness" was irrelevant.

> There can be no imperative which would, in the strict sense, command us to do what makes for happiness, because happiness is an ideal not of reason but of imagination, depending only on empirical grounds which one would expect in vain to determine an action through which the totality of consequences—which in fact is infinite—could be achieved.

That's how Kant explains my "Hawaiian pizza and Red Hot Chili Peppers" problem. There's no followable maxim involving the creation of "happiness," because "happiness" is something subjective that we can only define for ourselves. Nothing in the world, no matter how simple, will make everyone happy—my own daughter, Ivy, doesn't like *cake*, and my son, William, doesn't like *ice cream*—so we cannot possibly design a rule involving "making people happy" that we would want everyone to

---

6 Seems important to note that Kant and Bentham were roughly contemporary, and Kant entirely pre-dates Mill, so it's slightly more accurate to say that utilitarianism was a response to deontology and not the other way around, even though we discussed utilitarianism first in this book.

follow. What makes me happy will make someone else deeply sad or indifferent or maybe happy but in a different way or to a different degree. So, if Kant *had* written a fun little poem to explain his philosophy, like Bentham did, it would look like this:

Act only out of duty to follow a universal maxim
Derive these maxims using your pure reason
Happiness is irrelevant
End of poem

Not quite as catchy.

Categorical Imperative 2:
The Rare Sequel That's Better Than the Original

So, Kant doesn't care what you think of the world versus what I think of the world—he wants to take feeling and sentiment out of the equation. This is Kant's calling card: the insistence that morality is something we arrive at free of our subjective feelings or judgments. None of that Aristotelian trial and error, or consequentialist happiness/sadness guesswork—we have to use our rational brains, and *only* our rational brains, to create rational rules that lead to rational conclusions about rational actions. Whether you agree or not, Kant's hard-core brain-based theory was a seismic event in Western philosophy; his monumental influence can be understood only when you see how many contemporary philosophers worked from his source material. He's sort of like Hitchcock in film, or maybe Run-DMC in hip-hop: he had a *massive* influence on those who came after him.

But deontology also creates new problems for us. Chief among them: when we replace feeling and individual judgment with strict universal laws that we have to discern and then follow, it can take a very long time to figure out what the hell to do. Sometimes, behaving ethically can be a "trust your gut" type of exercise, and Kant is here to tell us our guts are stupid and we shouldn't listen to them. This is a frequent criticism of Kantian theory: trying to obey it is a purely intellectual exercise, and it's *really goddamn hard*. The character Chidi Anagonye in *The Good Place* is a strict Kantian, and he's so concerned with formulating precise Kantian maxims that he essentially paralyzes himself with indecision, struggling to act in even the simplest of circumstances. At one point, Chidi is so desperate to avoid lying, in order not to violate the categorical imperative, that he struggles to lie to actual *demons* who want to destroy him and his friends. (After suffering Chidi's tortured internal debates for the millionth time, Michael, Ted Danson's character, asks him, "Has anyone ever told you what a drag you are?" His reply: "*Every*one. *Constantly*.") There are many other criticisms, however. One I personally like comes from nineteenth-century German grump Friedrich Nietzsche, who found Kant overly moralistic and schoolmarmish:

> Some moralists want to vent their power and creative whims on humanity; some others, perhaps including Kant, suggest with their morality: "What deserves respect in me is that I can obey— and you *ought* not to be different from me."

Or, to paraphrase, "Ugh. Get over yourself, Kant."[7]

But there's a second formulation of the categorical imperative, some-

---

7 The irony, of course, is that Nietzsche and Kant certainly have things in common, not least of which is that Nietzsche was an *inveterate* snob. His entire worldview is based on the idea that most people are weak and dumb, and a very small number are incredible and brilliant, and *those* people should be allowed to do whatever they want. This is another case—like the Greeks celebrating "wise men" while they cleared their throats and pointed to themselves—of a philosopher essentially arguing that we ought to revere people who are suspiciously like the philosopher himself. Also, if you're scoring the philosophy fight between Kant and Nietzsche, at least Kant's snobbery didn't accidentally help create the Nazis.

times called in translation the *practical imperative*. It adds a rule to Kant's philosophy that isn't nearly as difficult to follow:

Act so that you treat humanity, whether in your own person or in that of another, always as an end and never as a means only.

In other words: don't use people to get what you want. Lying to our friend does just that—we're doing it *in order to* avoid a difficult conversation, or *in order to* avoid seeming like a jerk. She's not an end in herself, she's a means to an end. This formulation of the categorical imperative also retroactively gives a new explanation as to why we felt so queasy about poor Steve, the ESPN engineer. If we let him get zapped so we could watch the World Cup, we'd be (literally) using him as an object that absorbs pain so that we can experience pleasure. As technical and brainy as Kantian theory is, I find there to be something sweetly humanistic about the second formulation. Kant holds humans in the highest possible regard and rejects any action that demeans them or turns them into tools used to achieve some other goal. I'm not saying you'd want him to be your dad and comfort you after you strike out in Little League, but I think this iteration of the categorical imperative means there's a beating heart under all that pure reason.

Finding the Right Maxim: It's Nearly Impossible!

Let's now look at the Trolley Problem through Kant's eyes. He obviously rejects the coarse utilitarian results-based calculation: *kill 1, because 1 < 5*. Since the results of an action are irrelevant, the "We saved four people!" refrain bounces harmlessly off the imposing Germanic fortress of deontological theory. Kant only asks: When considering our options, what maxim could we will to be universal, and what action will obey our duty to follow it? Maybe we could reason out a maxim that says "We should always try to spare the lives of our fellow humans," which could certainly be universalized—the world in which everyone follows that rule seems like a pretty good world. So, then, should we pull the lever? I mean, we'd save lives . . . but we would also be *causing* that one other worker to die, which seems to betray the maxim . . . so actually, hang on a second—maybe we could design a different maxim that says "We should never *intentionally* cause an innocent person to die"[8] (again, easily universalized), and since pulling the lever does in fact *cause* a person to die, maybe we *don't* pull it? I mean, if we do nothing, *we* wouldn't be causing five people to die—the failed trolley brakes would cause that, right? Or, but hang on, because maybe the second the brakes fail the "thing that's causing something to happen" transfers from the trolley brakes to us, since we are the only ones with the ability to affect the trolley, which means "doing nothing" *is* actually us *causing* five people to die. But hang on again, because by pulling the lever we would *definitely* be causing the one other guy to die, and he never would've died without us pulling the lever, so how is that okay?!

See how hard this is? Even though Kant promises clear answers to moral problems, when you apply his reasoning to the Trolley Problem, it seems like we're in trouble. (We're *always* in trouble with Kant. He's

---

8 In classic "philosophy is impossible" fashion, I have to make this an "innocent" person to avoid counterarguments about self-defense, and also Todd points me to something called "just war theory," which is a collection of arguments about the specific set of criteria necessary to justify war—because in some extremely constrained circumstances, it turns out, killing an innocent person may in fact be permissible. Again, we're in one of those *but although however* spirals where you can't even say "Let's agree that there are things" before some philosopher raises her hand and points out twenty-six reasons why we can't actually declare that there are things. Several times over the course of *The Good Place* we had someone say, to Chidi, "This is why everyone hates moral philosophers." I never truly understood why that's funny until I began writing this book.

always standing right behind us, clucking his tongue, pointing out how badly we're blowing it.)

Now, again, most situations are not as death-soaked as the Trolley Problem. Most situations are far more mundane—like, should we lie to our friend and say we like her ugly shirt?—so we can more easily tease out the right Kantian move. But the Trolley Problem does reveal a lot of what is frustrating about deontological theory: the maxims take time to formulate, and acting out of a duty to follow them sometimes still seems wrong, and then we have to start over and come up with a new maxim. For better or worse, the strict utilitarian can just lightning-quick say "Five is more than one!" and yank the lever. The Kantians have to use their pure reason to draw up a universal rule and act only out of a duty to follow that rule, and in this instance, they have to do that while barreling down the tracks on a runaway trolley with screaming passengers and scared old ladies and the lives of six somehow-still-unaware-of-their-impending-doom construction workers at stake. How the hell are they gonna pull that off, in real time?! I mean, we've been mulling this over for ten pages and we *still* don't have a clear answer for what we're supposed to do.

But let's put practicality aside for a second. There must be some way to create a maxim we can follow that (a) we could will to be universal, and (b) leads to saving the five lives (which our guts kinda told us would be the better outcome). Remember, our intention is all that matters here. We just need a maxim that means we're *intending only to save five people* who would be smooshed if we did nothing, which would mean that the smooshing of the one other guy wouldn't be morally weighing on our shoulders, because we didn't *intend* to smoosh *him*. So, let's return to the maxim "We ought to spare the lives of innocent people whenever possible," but modify it slightly to say: "We ought to spare the lives of *as many innocent people as we can*, whenever possible." (Now, this is obviously sending us back toward utilitarian math. Put a pin in that, we'll return to it in a second.) Since five innocent people are about to die, we conclude that the action that obeys our duty to that maxim is: "Pull this lever." We can reasonably argue that we would have pulled that lever if *no one* were on the other track, so if the result of following our maxim is "one guy gets smooshed," well, that sucks, but it was not our *intention*.

Philippa Foot was actually addressing this exact point in her original paper—it has to do with the doctrine of double effect, a philosophical idea that goes all the way back to Saint Thomas Aquinas in the thirteenth century. Basically, it means that an outcome can be more or less morally permissible depending on whether you actually *intended* it to happen when you acted—like, when we kill someone in self-defense, we *intended* only to save our own innocent life, and the *result* was that someone else died. If we pull the lever *intending* to deliberately smoosh a guy . . . not so great. But if the guy *got smooshed* because we were *intending* to save the lives of five guys, we're off the hook. This may all seem like semantics—or worse, a loophole—but since intentions are all that matter to Kant, if we pull this off we can maybe eat our cake (saving more lives) and have it too (not disappointing Immanuel Kant).

One aspect of Kantian reasoning actually makes the Trolley Problem clearer and not murkier; it helps explain—even better than Bernard Williams's "integrity" argument—why our gut reactions to its different versions varied from example to example. Remember how most people feel like pulling the lever is okay, but shoving the weight lifter off the bridge is not? Until now, we could only explain this by saying "It feels wrong," or maybe "Our integrity has to matter." Those are *decent* explanations, but Kantian deontology gives us a much sharper knife, and we can now slice this baloney really thin. A second ago I mentioned that we were drifting back toward utilitarian accounting by adding "*as many innocent lives as we can*" into the maxim, which feels like we're stirring some utilitarianism into the deontological stew. We might wonder, if utilitarianism and Kantianism kind of merge here, why we need the annoying, difficult-to-follow Kantian rulebook at all. Can't we just use the easier-to-understand greatest happiness principle?! This all goes back to the idea that sometimes, if we use utilitarian methods, we arrive at the right moral answer but for the wrong reasons.

Viewing the original Trolley Problem from a deontological standpoint, we decided to follow the maxim "We ought to spare the lives of as many innocent people as we can, whenever possible," and the action we took out of a duty to obey that maxim was: pulling a lever. Pulling a lever is a pretty neutral action—it isn't inherently "wrong" or "bad." In the "shove a weight lifter off the bridge" version, our action is certainly *not* neutral—we're straight-up murdering a guy. So while a duty to follow the maxim "We ought to spare the lives of as many innocent people as we can, whenever possible" might seem like just a fancy way of a utilitarian saying "Five is more than one!" that similarity dissolves when we add in the second formulation of the imperative: that we should not use people as a means to an end, but rather as ends in themselves. Shoving Don off the bridge certainly counts as using him as a means to an end— he would cease to be a person, and *literally* become a tool (in this case, a "human trolley stopper") that allows us to achieve some other goal. In the Trolley Problem Classic, utilitarian accounting and deontological duty overlap—whichever one we use, we're likely to arrive at the same result (pull the lever, save the five people). But utilitarian accounting isn't as finely honed as Kantian reasoning. As the details of the problem shift and change, strict utilitarianism keeps telling us to "kill one and save five,"[9] even when we start to feel queasy about the way in which

---

9 A philosopher named John Taurek wrote a paper on this issue, essentially tearing utilitarianism a new one, called "Should the Numbers Count?" Taurek is flabbergasted at the notion that you would ever make a life-or-death decision based on how many people are on one side of the equation and how many are on the other, because doing so ignores the fact that each person's life is maximally valuable *to that person*, and just mathematically adding the values of five lives together doesn't give you some kind of "greater total value" than the value of one life. He essentially argues that if you have a choice between saving a million lives (with, say, a million doses of lifesaving medicine) or one life (giving all million doses to one person who needs that much medicine to be cured), you should . . . flip a coin. It's pretty intense. His dedication to this idea is admi-

we're carrying out the "kill one" part. Deontology, however, draws important lines of distinction between acceptable and unacceptable "kill one" actions. Again, we should note that utilitarians might claim we're calculating wrong here—that living in a world where anyone could be shoved off a bridge in order to stop a careening trolley would cause so much widespread psychic agony, the "pain" of doing it would outweigh the "pleasure" of saving more lives. But it's hard not to see that Kant's more meticulous playbook gives us a better, sturdier reason not to shove Don off the bridge.

We Can't Even Lie . . . to Murderers?

Part of Kant's enduring appeal, it seems to me, is that he promises a foolproof how-to guide for living a moral life. He's telling us that we can—if we stick with his program—get an A on this test. But just like with the thought experiments designed to show the limits of utilitarianism, we can find some hypotheticals that seem to poke holes in deontology. Here's a fun one:[10] Let's say a murderer wants to kill your brother, Jeff, who is hiding upstairs in your house. The murderer knocks on the door (he's a polite murderer; he doesn't just barge in) and says, "Hello, I am a murderer. I am trying to kill your brother, Jeff. Is he home, perchance?" Our natural inclination would be to say, "Sorry, Polite Murderer, he's not here." But remember: Kant tells us that *we are not allowed to lie*, because lying can't be universalized, because if everybody could lie it would render all human communication

---

rable, but I feel like it would be awfully hard to give a million doses of medicine to one person while a million other people died. I also feel like, were I that one guy, I'd maybe think: "Yeah . . . go ahead and save a million people."

10 The irony of this thought experiment, which seems to find a crucial flaw in deontological reasoning, is that it comes from Kant himself. It's what the kids would call a "self-own."

meaningless, etc., etc. And so, absurdly, Kant tells us *we're not allowed to lie to a murderer*, even when he has flatly stated that *he is there to murder our brother*. If Kant is our guide, Jeff is doomed. Sorry, Jeff. I hope you understand—we just can't violate a universal maxim. Thanks for taking such good care of us all those years after Mom and Dad got divorced. Sorry you're gonna be murdered.

But maybe we can finagle a different maxim out of this situation (as we did with the Trolley Problem) and find a little escape hatch, which may in turn help us with the problem of our friend and her ugly shirt. What if we respond not with a lie, but with a *true* statement that doesn't help him find Jeff? What if we say, "You know, Polite Murderer, I saw my brother earlier today at the grocery store . . . and I know on Tuesdays he likes to go to the park and feed the ducks." If those statements are true, and we are good enough actors to hide our nervousness, and the murderer doesn't ask any follow-up questions, and Jeff doesn't step on a creaky spot of the upstairs floor at the exact wrong time like in a horror movie, the murderer may go and check the duck pond instead of, you know, going upstairs and murdering our brother. This little hedge allows us to avoid disobeying a categorical imperative, and also saves Jeff's life. Sometimes with Kant it feels like a game where we have to find either the right way to phrase the maxim we will follow, or a way to avoid *not* following it, in order to achieve the result we want without running afoul of his rules.

Stuff like this is where Kant loses me, honestly. If a murderer is at our door trying to kill our brother, we don't really have a lot of time for adherence to universal maxims other than "Don't let anyone murder our brother." Of course, this is Kant's whole point: they're not universal maxims if you can pick and choose when to follow them. (That's why they're not called "mostly-universal-but-if-you're-in-a-tough-scrape-they-don't-have-to-be-*totally*-universal" maxims.) Still, I bristle at Kant for not allowing us to use our judgment here. It just doesn't feel very . . . human. Aristotle, in contrast, allows us to seek virtue in a more experiential way—by trial and error, essentially—which strikes me as more compassionate. It feels like he *trusts* us, and has more tolerance for the mistakes we're bound to make. Universally mandated duties are good in theory, but I wonder how Kant would feel if *he* were hiding in our attic and the polite murderer came looking for *him*. Maybe he'd hope we had ignored his writings and read more Aristotle. (Though he was so hardcore, he'd probably be perversely psyched to die because we followed the categorical imperative.)

In the case of our friend and the ugly shirt, then, we might find a way to be good little Kantians and still not cause our friend pain or sadness by straight-up saying "That shirt is butt-ugly." Ideally, of course, we have the kind of friendship where we can say "Honestly, that's not your best look," and our friend will receive that comment with equanimity. But if our friend is more sensitive, or more nervous about her interview, perhaps we could say "You know, I really like that blue shirt you have—you should wear that one." Or perhaps we say that this interview is so important, we should go shopping and pick out a shirt she looks even better in. Or maybe, if we see that she really loves the shirt, and wearing it seems to be giving her confidence heading into this job interview, and we get the sense that her wearing the shirt isn't going to ruin her life or cause her any exquisite pain or suffering, we could simply say that we generally think she always looks good, and that if the interviewer has half a brain she'll give our friend the job no matter what shirt she wears.

With these first chapters, we've learned about the three main globs of secular ethical thought in the Western world over the last 2,400 years: Aristotelian virtue ethics, consequentialism, and deontology. But sometimes, in our everyday lives, we encounter a mundane little question about what we ought to do in some basic earthbound scenario, and we don't want to have to employ a huge all-encompassing moral theory to make sense of what's right. We just want someone to tell us—quickly— what we should do. We want *rules*, like the ones Kant offers us, but, you know, *simpler* rules. Really we just want someone to explain, for example, whether we should return our shopping cart to the rack by the grocery store entrance, or whether it's okay to leave it in the parking lot. Can someone just tell us whether we should do that, without a complicated universal maxim derived from pure reason or a multitiered hedon/dolor utilitarian calculation?

Is that too much to ask?

Do I Have to Return My Shopping Cart to the Shopping Cart Rack Thingy? I Mean . . . It's All the Way Over *There*.

What's the smallest nice thing you do for other people on a regular basis? Not "other people" like your best friend or sister, but people you don't know—the individual faceless dots comprising the mass of humanity you're aware of but never really think about, unless one of them talks too loud in a movie theater or throws a fit in a Jamba Juice because there's not enough mango in her smoothie. Maybe when you park on the street you try to leave a full car-length of space between your car and the car in front of you, so that someone else will also have a spot to park in (instead of an awkward half-spot's length, which, when you come upon it, boils your blood). Or maybe if you're walking on the street at night and there's a woman walking alone a few yards ahead, you cross to the other side of the street so she doesn't have the unsettling sound of footsteps behind her. You do these things, maybe, because your grandfather taught you to be considerate, or because someone once did a similarly nice thing for you and it made you feel good. And when you do these things, these little basic "other people" things, you get a twinge of happiness. "I'm a good person," you think. "I did my 'good thing' for the day." But what you didn't know, is that all of those things are *very bad*.

I'm just kidding. Of course they're good! Why would they be bad? They're warmhearted and thoughtful and nice. Just thought it would be funny to make you sweat a little.

I love those little kindnesses—the almost imperceptible improvements on the world we live in, done solely for the benefit of other people. When I'm the recipient of these courtesies—when someone stops and waves me out in a moment when I have to take a difficult left turn across two lanes of traffic, say—I get disproportionately happy. It means that the people around me are considering the lives and feelings of others, and I believe that consideration to be the glue that holds society together. And when the opposite occurs—when someone in rush hour decides to ignore the NO LEFT TURN 4–7 P.M. sign and just sit there in the left lane, waiting to turn down a side street, utterly disregarding the hundreds of cars grinding to a stop behind him—because apparently *his* desire to make a left at this exact street is *far more important* than *everyone else's* desire to get wherever they're going *combined*—I dream of shooting fire from my eye sockets and melting his car into a puddle of smoldering metal.

The thing about these nice little gestures is: they're essentially free. We have to park *somewhere*, so why not park in such a way so as to allow for other people to park too? You have to walk *somewhere*, so why not relieve a fellow pedestrian's potential anxiety by popping over to the other side of the street and signaling that you're not a threat to her safety? These tiny decisions don't cost us anything except the ounce of thought needed to execute them, and they're helpful for other people. But what about when it *isn't* free—when it requires a little extra effort? What about, say, after we unload our groceries into our car, and our empty cart is sitting there in the parking lot, and the cart rack is *over there*, forty yards away, and we just want to get home . . .

I mean . . . do we *have to*?

Come On. Be Reasonable.

When I began working on *The Good Place*, literally at square one of trying to figure out what made someone "good" or "bad," I figured that learning the answers would be way easier if I had some actual philosophy experts to help me. (Aristotle was right, it turns out—everybody needs a teacher.) I emailed a UCLA professor named Pamela Hieronymi and asked her to meet me for coffee one afternoon, where I was hoping she could explain all of moral philosophy in a tight ninety minutes so I could beat the traffic.¹ When I explained the show's premise and asked her for some guidance, her first recommendation was that I read a book called *What We Owe to Each Other* by T. M. Scanlon. So I did. Well, more accurately, I read the first ninety pages, got lost, put it down, picked it back up a month later, got lost again, tried one more time, gave up, and haven't looked at it since. But I feel like I got the gist. And Pamela explained it very thoroughly. Whatever. Don't judge me.²

Scanlon calls his theory "contractualism." It's nowhere near as central to the history of philosophy as our Big Three, but its core tenet really appeals to me. It provides a reassuring ethical baseline—a kind of standardized, universal rulebook that we can all thumb through for guidance as we wander around in the world bumping into people on the street and getting caught in awkward interactions at Jamba Juice. Scanlon's work comes out of Kantian "rules-based" ethics, but it isn't as demanding. You know how when you buy something electronic, like a dishwasher or Bluetooth speaker or something, there's a three-hundred-page manual printed in fifty different languages . . . and then there's a two-page "Quick-Start Guide" that tells you the basics of how to turn it on and plug it in and stuff? In rules-based ethics, Kant wrote the three-hundred-page manual. Contractualism is the Quick-Start Guide. Now,

---

1 When I arrived, she . . . wasn't there. An hour went by. I emailed her and asked if I'd gotten the date wrong, but it turned out she was just so deeply lost in her own research and writing that she'd forgotten about the meeting entirely. Which delighted me. I mean, that's *exactly* what you want out of your philosophical advisers.*

    *Hilariously passive-aggressive subnote from Todd: Sorry about my prompt responses to your emails, Mike.

2 In the series finale of *The Good Place* I had Eleanor finish reading the book after (quite literally) an eternity of trying.

while it's true that we can get a decent handle on Kant through his relatively pithy imperatives, he still requires us to use our pure reason to abstractly formulate those thorny universal maxims, which as we've seen can be tricky and time-consuming. For me, Scanlon's process for determining ethical rules is much easier to grasp and deploy.

Hieronymi, who'd been a student of Scanlon's at Harvard, described contractualism to me this way: Imagine our crew has been at war with another crew for years, just slugging it out in a dense forest, firing on each other from trenches a hundred feet apart. It's an absolute stalemate. Neither side has any advantage over the other, and no hope of ever gaining one. Exhausted and weary, we call a temporary truce and decide we somehow need to design and describe a mutually livable society; we need a set of rules that can be accepted by both sides, no matter how wildly different our views are (and we obviously hold *very* different views, hence the endless trench warfare). Scanlon's suggestion: We give everyone on both sides the power to veto every rule, and then we start pitching rules. Assuming everyone is motivated to actually find some rules in the first place—that everyone is *reasonable*—the rules that pass are the ones no one can reject. This means we'll all design our rules in such a way that they can be justified to other people, because if we don't, they won't become rules. It's a simple, elegant way of finding the basic bucket of societal goo that holds us together.

Now, it makes a big assumption—that everyone is going to be "reasonable." This is definitely one of those moments in philosophy where we have to back up and define something in order to feel like we know what the hell we're talking about. Scanlon doesn't give a quick, pithy definition of "reasonable," in part because . . . there isn't one. But in essence he says this: I'm reasonable if, when you and I disagree, I'm willing to constrain or modify my pursuit of my own interests to the same degree that you're willing to constrain or modify *your* pursuit of *your* interests. When we come together to suggest our rules, then, we aren't just "looking out for number one." Rather, we *both* want to design a world where we accommodate each other's needs, so that when we don't see eye to eye on something, finding a way to coexist in some kind of harmony becomes our top priority. Scanlon is after "a shared willingness to modify our private demands in order to find a basis of justification that others also have reason to accept." It's a contract he wants all of us to sign, giving us all the same exact motivations.

Importantly, this doesn't mean we always have to defer to other people in every conflict—because in Scanlon's world, *they're* approaching the conflict with the same intention to modify *their* interests in order to justify them to *us*. It creates a kind of dynamic tension, where we all regard everyone else's interests as equal to our own—not *more* important, but *equally* important. We can now better understand why Hieronymi explained this to me by setting the scene of endless, miserable, stalemated war—both sides' weariness and desire for a path forward help us believe that everyone *will* be reasonable, because we're all motivated to find a way out of this quagmire, and we all recognize that everyone else is motivated in the same way.[3]

When we apply Scanlon's theory to the world we live in—the world comprising thousands of small moments and decisions and interactions—contractualism makes a pretty good divining rod for bad

---

3 Obviously, we might wonder what happens if some people *aren't* reasonable. Simply: they don't get to weigh in. Pamela described the cases of "the doormat" and "the asshole." When we pitch rules to the doormat, he agrees to everything, because he undervalues his own interests. When we pitch rules to the asshole, she agrees to none of them, because she *overvalues* her interests. So, neither of these unreasonable people gets the chance to sit at the metaphorical table where we're coming up with our rules. More important: if we're not at a metaphorical and imaginary table but rather out in the real world interacting with real people, it can sometimes be up to us (when we encounter a person like this) *to project reasonableness onto them*. We can't take advantage of the doormat, for example, by realizing he will just agree to whatever we propose and then proposing a bunch of rules that serve to benefit ourselves at the doormat's expense; instead, we need to keep *ourselves* in check by recognizing that there is a disconnect between the way these doormats/assholes are acting and the way a reasonable person would be acting, and only propose rules they'd follow if they were, indeed, reasonable.

or unjust behavior. For example: If someone proposed a rule that said, "No driver should use the breakdown lanes on any highway unless there is an emergency," no one could reasonably reject that rule. This rule, properly applied, would treat everyone the same[4] and serve public safety. But if Wayne the Lamborghini Driver said, "Hey, I got a rule: no one can use the breakdown lanes *except* for Lamborghini drivers, who can drive wherever they want, because Lambos rule," someone *could* (and likely would) reasonably reject that rule. Scanlon's theory allows us to quickly identify behaviors that feel unjust or selfish, like when you're stuck in heavy traffic and a rich dope in the obvious throes of a midlife crisis pulls his yellow Lamborghini into the breakdown lane and whizzes past you.

And when we apply contractualism to any of those little "free" decisions from earlier in this chapter, we'll get the answers we'd expect: Would anyone veto a rule that says, "We should park our car, whenever we can, in a way that allows other people enough room to park"? No. Why would any reasonable person veto that? How about: "We can park wherever we want, and everyone else can go to hell"? Well, now, that's definitely getting vetoed. Scanlon isn't trying to turn us into flourishing, virtuous super-people. He just wants us all—no matter our personalities or religious beliefs or political bents or pizza-topping preferences—to be able to look each other in the eye and justify our basic rules for how to live.

That's partly why contractualism appeals to me more than Kantian deontology. Kant wants us to encounter a problem, press pause, enter some kind of solitary meditation zone, use our pure reason to discern and describe a universal law that applies to the problem, and then act out of a duty to follow that law. Scanlon wants us to figure this stuff out

---

4 This is assuming *the governing body* treated all people the same—traditionally not the case, in most countries, but we're creating an imaginary and fair society here, so just go with it. If we were actually designing rules for our society, we'd probably want to start with some rules for the governing body itself, like "No racism" and "All people have equal rights regardless of gender," and a bunch of other basic stuff that was left out of the founding documents of almost every nation on earth.

with each other—to sit across from one another and simply ask: "Do you agree that this is okay?" He puts his faith not in abstract reasoning, but in our necessary relationships with other people. Now, this can seem dicey too—I'm guessing that for many of us, leaving our fate in other people's hands doesn't seem like the safest possible bet. It's hard enough to figure out rules for how we ought to live, and now this guy tells us our choices could be vetoed by Cindy, our next-door neighbor who talks to squirrels like they're people, or by our cousin Derrek, who jumped off a diving board into a swimming pool that was frozen solid and broke his tailbone? Perhaps more relevantly, here in 2022, we'd be depending on the "reasonableness" of people with whom we vehemently disagree, like conspiracy-theory-spouting Facebook trolls or racist great-uncles. You're telling me *those* people can reject our rules for permissible behavior? Well . . . yes, *as long as their objections are reasonable,* and they constrain their own desires to the same degree we constrain ours. (And remember, many of their more extreme views would be rejected *by us* as unreasonable.) As odd and annoying and unpredictable as the people around us can be, given that *they're the people we have to live with,* I think it's often a better idea to design the moral boundaries of our world with their cooperation than it is to do it abstractly, in their absence. And I further think it's a better idea for *them* to do so with *our* cooperation.

Okay, I Get It, Just Tell Me If I Have to Return the Damn Cart to the Rack, Please, I'm in a Hurry

Again, the previous examples (like where to position our car when we park on the street) are the sort of "free" decisions where we have to do *something,* so it's no skin off our backs to do the best version of whatever the thing is. But what about when the decision *does* cost us something— some amount of time, or effort, or energy, or sacrifice? Like, say, the question that started this chapter: Should we return our shopping cart to the shopping cart rack?

A bunch of new complications make this . . . more complicated. First, the rules of shopping cart replacement have never been clear to me. Are we *supposed* to bring them back, or is the store cool with us leaving them in the parking lot? Some grocery stores have employees who collect them, which seems to imply that it's okay to leave them near our cars . . . or maybe they *have* to hire those employees because people are selfish jerks and leave carts in the parking lot even though the store would prefer we didn't. Also, maybe it's *better* to leave them in the parking lot, because then people just pop out of their cars and *bam*, there's a cart right there waiting for them! But then again, sometimes people pop out of their cars and *bam*, their car door hits a stray shopping cart, which stinks. Plus: We go to the grocery store, approach the door, get a cart from the rack, go shopping, bring it to our car . . . and then just leave it there? There's something slightly off about that. It seems like we ought to return it . . . but returning it requires one last little bit of effort on our part to close that loop—one forty-yard jaunt back across the parking lot, the wobbly wheels of the cart grinding unpleasantly on the asphalt while our groceries wilt a little in the hot car,[5] then a tricky final push as the cart jangles awkwardly back into its stationary nesting-doll column, and finally the reverse jaunt: forty yards *back* to our car, dodging traffic, fumbling with our keys, unlocking the door again, and settling into the seat where we could've been three minutes ago, in a better mood, if we'd just decided to tell ethics to screw off.

So what would Scanlon say about all this? The rule we're proposing seems something like: "After using a grocery cart, return it to its rack so the next person can use it." No reasonable person rejects that rule, in all likelihood. But what if it's "After using a grocery cart we should return it to the rack, unless the store has a dedicated employee whose job it is to collect carts from the parking lot, in which case it's fine to leave it in

---

5 The car might not be hot. But I live in Los Angeles. It's always hot here. I hate it.

the parking lot"? That also seems unrejectable. So, I guess . . . if there's a dude in a reflective vest wandering around the parking lot gathering carts, we can leave ours at the top of our parking space and head on home. That action would be allowable.

So . . . is that it? Are we done?

Contractualism has a ceiling—it sets in place only the rules we'd all live by if we were each motivated to find a minimum standard for co-existence. Scanlon is looking around at a world full of very different kinds of people and trying to establish certain baselines of behavior we will all follow. His theory is designed to stop people from doing something obviously crappy and disagreeable—like *stealing* the shopping carts, or damaging them so no one else can use them, or getting *in* one that we find on the street when we're drunk after a wedding and having our friend Nick push us down the sidewalk really fast until we wipe out (because Nick is also drunk and loses control) and go tumbling onto the street.[6] All of *those* rules, if they were suggested as allowable uses for shopping carts, would reasonably be rejected.

So, although Scanlon's rules create this minimum basis for a livable society, that might not be the only tool we want to use when we make ethical decisions. We don't only want to meet some kind of "minimum requirement"—we don't just want a passing grade on this test! We want to clear the bar described by "rules we all agree to" with room to spare, and become the ethical rock stars we know we can be. This means that while we *have to* follow whatever contractualist rules we all agree to, maybe we *should* do more. Maybe we *start* with contractualism, and then keep going . . .

---

6 This is purely theoretical. I myself never did this, in 2005. Because if I had, I would've torn a huge hole in the only suit I owned and had to buy a new one for another wedding I had to attend the following month, and that would've been stupid. And I *definitely* didn't immediately get up after wiping out and then offer to push Nick in the shopping cart, causing him to also wipe out and bruise his shin. None of that happened. I was thirty years old in 2005! That would be a ridiculous thing for a thirty-year-old man to do.

So let's play this out. Let's say we're at a grocery store that does, indeed, hire people to sweep the parking lot for stray carts and return them to the rack by the front door. After unloading our groceries, we decide—as we're wont to do—to formulate our next action using T. M. Scanlon's theory of contractualism. Given that we don't believe anyone would reasonably reject the rule "We can leave our shopping cart in the parking lot if the store has an employee whose job it is to collect it," we decide to do just that. But then we think about a few other things. We think: "It's not *that* far back to the rack." And we think: "I *did* just use this cart, and my dad always told me to put things back where they belong after I use them." And then we think: "Someone else will need to use this cart, and if *all* shoppers just leave our carts in the parking lot, the employees who collect them might fall behind and then future customers might approach the rack and find no carts there, which is annoying when it happens to us."[7] And then we think: "Letting the carts drift free in the parking lot can be irritating, because they sometimes wobble into people's cars, or partially block parking spaces, or I bang my door on them when I'm getting out of the car." And then we think: "Yes, there are employees tasked with collecting the carts from the lot, but that work is boring and physically tiring and repetitive, and the people who do it are outside in the heat or cold and they aren't paid very much, probably, so yes it's their job, but also I have the chance to make their job a little easier." The overall amount of "good" we can do by just running the cart forty yards over there and putting it back where we got it is small, but it's real, and it may slightly improve the lives of a lot of people: the employee (who doesn't have to clean up our mess), future shoppers (who find carts waiting for them in the rack by the front door, where they

---

7 This notion—that if *everyone* did it, things would go haywire—is of course the essence of Kantian theory, as we saw in the previous chapter. Kant really does pop up a lot—no matter how you slice and dice ethical dilemmas, you're sure to eventually hear a deontological echo.

are most convenient), and future car parkers (who don't get their cars dinged by drifting carts or slam their doors into them or have parking spaces blocked). That's so many people! For so little effort!

So. Do we *have to* return the cart to the rack? No. Probably not.

But should we? Yeah, I think we probably should. If we're able, we should move beyond the "minimum requirements" of contractualism and do that small amount of extra work.[8] (And I say this as a guy who frequently does not do that extra work, because: who wants to do extra work?) It requires a fairly negligible amount of effort and consideration from us, and has the potential to create a decent amount of happiness and convenience and stress-reduction for some number of other people. It can *help* other people. That ought to be a goal we all share.

"Helping other people" is a big, nebulous idea, but there's no such thing as "ethics" without it, so we'd better figure out what we mean, exactly, when we decide to move beyond contractualist minimums and declare "helping other people" as our new goal. We can easily imagine *literal* ways of helping other people—carrying boxes up a flight of stairs when our friend moves, or donating fifty dollars to a soup kitchen. But what about, just, the ethereal ideas of "treating other people well" or "being considerate" or "behaving unselfishly"? It's hard to pin down, at least in a practical way that will help us figure out *what the hell we're supposed to do* as we mill around the earth and bump into people. But just because it's hard to describe doesn't mean we should give up trying to describe it. In fact, one of the best explanations of why "other people"

---

8 Predictably, as soon as we come to this conclusion, we may run into new problems—those unintended consequences rearing their ugly heads. What if we all decide to start returning the shopping carts to the rack, and the grocery store employees' union gets mad at us because they represent a thousand workers whose jobs are now obsolete? The answer, basically, is: We take a deep breath, remember that we didn't intend this harm, and we stop. We fall back to the contractualist minimum of the rule we settled on as unrejectable: that we return the carts to the rack if the store does not have people who were hired to do that job.

matter isn't really an "explanation" at all, but rather a worldview: it's the southern African concept of *ubuntu*.

"I Am, Because We Are"

Explaining ubuntu will take a second, because there's not really (as far as I've found) a perfect encapsulation, and since I don't speak Zulu or Xhosa or any other African language, all I have to go on are somewhat murky English translations. A lot of the explanation of ubuntu is done through aphorisms, anecdotes, and proverbs, though the South African political philosopher Johann Broodryk defines it this way:

> A comprehensive ancient African world view based on the values of intense humanness, caring, sharing, respect, compassion, and associated values, ensuring a happy and qualitative human community life in the spirit of family.

Broodryk anticipates our next question: "It may be asked whether this notion is unique," he writes, "since all cultures ascribe basically to these positive values." He's right, of course—if we think of ubuntu as, say, "human interconnectedness," there are parallels in Buddhism, or the Hindu concept of dharma. The difference, he says, is that in Africa "these values are practiced on a much deeper level. It is about a real passionate living of humanity, as if humanity is the primary reason for living above all other concerns." Another writer, Mluleki Mnyaka, further interprets ubuntu as an actual ethical system, which plays "a determining factor in . . . [the] formulation of perceptions . . . of African society about what is good or bad behavior." Okay, we might be thinking, it's the root of an African philosophy, a worldview related to the ways humans are connected to each other, a humanistic ethos that describes values and good behaviors . . . but what does the word "ubuntu" actually *mean*?

The answer seems like a bit of a cop-out: "ubuntu" means a lot of different things, no one of them directly or easily explicable in translation. In fact, because it encapsulates a community-specific set of ethical guidelines, it may even have different meanings depending on who you are and which African language you're speaking; Broodryk notes that the word itself varies—in Zulu it's *ubuntu*, in Swahili it's *utu*, in Shona it's *unhu*, and so on. But the central idea remains the same—it's always related to *humanness*, or "the ideal of being human." I first heard of it in a decidedly nonacademic context—after the Boston Celtics (my favorite basketball team) won the 2008 NBA championship, their coach Doc Rivers said that he used ubuntu as a way for a group of individual star players to focus on a collective goal (a team championship) instead of personal glory. Rather than getting hung up on what the word actually "means," it's better to focus on the essence of the concept. Here's a proverb that I think comes close to encapsulating the whole idea:

A person is a person through other people.

Ubuntu is Scanlon's contractualism, but supercharged. It's not just that we *owe* things to other people—ubuntu says we *exist through them*. Their health is our health, their happiness is our happiness, their interests are our interests, when they are hurt or diminished *we* are hurt or diminished. The virtues that political scientist Michael Onyebuchi Eze cites as being characteristic of ubuntu ring an Aristotelian bell—"magnanimity, sharing, kindness"—but the emphasis is now on the *communal* instead of the individual. In 2006, Nelson Mandela was asked to define ubuntu and said this:

In the old days, when we were young, a traveler to our country would stop in our village, and he didn't have to ask for food or for water. Once he stops, the people give him food, and attend to him. That is one aspect of ubuntu, but it [has] various aspects. . . . Ubuntu does not mean that people should not enrich themselves. The question, therefore, is: Are you going to do so in order to enable the community around you to be able to improve?[9]

So. Why should we return the shopping cart to the shopping cart rack? Because it helps other people, and *we* are only people *through other people*. Living in our world, going about our days with our own problems and annoyances and issues to deal with, it's easy (and tempting) to remain trapped in our little brains and to only do stuff that improves our lives or eases our own pains. But . . . come on, that stinks. We're not alone here on earth. We're one tiny part of a much larger whole, as the Kenyan philosopher and theologian John S. Mbiti wrote:

> The individual does not and cannot exist alone. . . . He owes his existence to other people including those of past generations and his contemporaries. He is simply part of the whole. . . . Whatever happens to the individual happens to the whole group, and whatever happens to the whole group happens to the individual. The individual can only say, "I am, because we are; and since we are therefore I am."

---

9 Mandela doesn't elaborate on what he means here. I choose to see "enabling the community to improve" as a nonmaterial kind of thing; meaning, like, when we enrich ourselves, we shouldn't do so *at the expense* of the community, or in such a way that those around us suffer. Instead we should do so in a way that keeps the overall health and flourishing of our community as our priority. Another possible interpretation would be that he's more literally saying, in essence, "We can make money only if everyone else makes money too." In a later chapter we'll meet John Rawls, who dealt with this idea in different terms; Rawls called society a "cooperative venture for mutual advantage," and aimed to figure out how to divide up limited resources (like those in any society) not *evenly*, exactly, but in such a way that if one person gets a little more, it also benefits the people who have the least.

We don't just owe *things* to people—we owe *our whole freaking existence* to them. And when we think of "other people" *that* way, well, we're not going to stop at the minimal amount that we "owe to each other"—we're gonna damn well return the shopping cart to the rack if we think it eases the burden of those around us. All we're really doing here is making sure the checklist we run down anytime we're deciding what to do puts "community health and happiness" as its primary concern, not just as a pleasant potential by-product.

This has been a core tenet of Southern African philosophy for centuries, but in Western philosophy the contractualist idea that our moral lives are dependent on our mutual relationships with other people is more of an outlier. We're not really going to discuss René Descartes, but consider for a second his famous Enlightenment formulation *Cogito, ergo sum*—the aforementioned "I think, therefore I am"—which, again, is one of the very foundations of Western thought. When we place it next to this ubuntu formulation—"I am, because we are"—well, man oh man, that's a pretty big difference. Descartes saw his own singular consciousness as proof of existence. Practitioners of ubuntu see our existence as conditional on *others'* existence. Someone could write a very interesting book on the sorts of civilizations and laws and citizens that emerge from each of these two utterances. Not me, though—it sounds really hard. But *someone*.

The point is, I've been describing contractualist theory in a pretty dry, intellectual way, as like a board meeting where we're soberly pitching rules and voting on them. But as Hieronymi pointed out to me, there's a warmer, fuzzier way to look at it. Scanlon asks us to approach the people we share the earth with and declare the following: "I know you treat me as someone who matters, who has a veto in our system, and you know I treat you in that way, and we each know that the other knows this." He wants us to create an ethical system in which "mutual respect can be mutually recognized." That reorientation of morality doesn't go quite as far as ubuntu, but it does place a check on our inherent egoism, and puts our relationships with those around us—both the people we know and those we don't—at the center of our personal goodnessometers. Once we assume that position, it gets really hard to be, for lack of a better word, a jerk.

Doing the Bare Minimum:
Still (Apparently) Too Much for Some People

For the first year-plus of the Covid-19 outbreak, there was one persistent and harmful issue: No one wanted to wear masks. Or, more accurately: no one *wanted* to, but millions of dopes actually *wouldn't*. Scanlon published his book in 1998, but if he were writing it now, I bet he'd have a lot to say about those dopes. Wearing a mask is roughly as annoying as returning a shopping cart to the rack after we've unloaded our car—it takes more effort than just doing nothing, but *barely* more effort, really, and when we run through the pros and cons of mask-wearing it becomes ludicrous not to do it. Here's what was asked of us: buy a two-dollar face covering and use it when you go outside. Here's who would benefit: everyone, everywhere on earth. Here's how they'd benefit: *society returns to normal much faster, and everybody doesn't get sick and die.* A global pandemic is, oddly, an ideal scenario to illustrate contractualism—what we owe to each other in this case is both easy to identify and infinitesimally small, and the benefits are *astronomically huge*. I said before that contractualism can quickly and effectively identify behavior that feels unreasonable or selfish—well, every time I see a video where someone screams that wearing a mask in this Taco Bell is a form of oppression, my first thought is: "You're being unreasonable, and I reject your rule." (For someone practicing ubuntu, of course, suggesting that we don't all have to wear a mask would be ludicrous; the main function of these masks is not to keep ourselves safe, but rather to keep *other people* safe if *we* happen to be sick. Masks are physical incarnations of ubuntu.)

Scanlon's book may be a slog, but his theory is not—it's elegant and simple. In fact, the theory is so simple that Scanlon told me, when I met him,[10] that his mentor Derek Parfit didn't find it very convincing. Parfit, perhaps the most important philosopher of the last fifty years, had been badgering Scanlon to write a book. When Scanlon finally showed him his initial writings on contractualism, Parfit responded, "Tim, this is not a moral theory. It's just a description of your personality." (Philosophers can be jerks[11] sometimes.) But I disagree—I find contractualism to be a reliable ethical guide when I'm weighing my decisions and my responses to other people's. Remember, though, that it gives us only a minimum baseline for creating a livable society. Once we determine that baseline, it's up to us to exert a little more effort, to try a little harder, if we really want to improve both ourselves and our world.

We now have a lot of arrows in our quiver—virtue ethics, deontology, utilitarianism, contractualism, ubuntu . . . this quiver is jam-packed, baby! But so far we've been asking pretty simple questions: Should we be violent for no reason? Should we lie? Should we put things back where they came from? The next batch of questions will be trickier and more nuanced. We're going to need all of the big theories we've already learned, and a bunch of new ideas we'll pick up along the way, and it's *still* going to get harder and harder to come up with answers.

But, I mean, we gotta *try*, right?

---

10 Is philosopher name-dropping grosser than Hollywood name-dropping? Hadn't occurred to me until now, but I think it's possible. I'm leaving this in, though, because I got to meet T. M. Scanlon and it ruled. Sue me.

11 Note from Todd: Parfit was an objectivist about morality: he believed there is an objective right or wrong that doesn't depend on our reactions to things. Scanlon, as a contractualist, believes that rightness or wrongness is rooted in our (reasonable) judgments. So from Parfit's point of view, Scanlon is rooting morality in something too subjective. Still jerky, though.

PART TWO

In Which We Take Everything We've
Learned, and We Start Asking Some
Tougher Questions, and We Use the
Stuff We've Learned to Try to Answer
Them, and We Also Learn a Bunch
More Cool Stuff

CHAPTER FIVE

Should I Run into a Burning Building and Try to Save Everyone Trapped Inside?

Jack Lucas was thirteen when the United States entered World War II. Two years later he lied about his age, forged his mom's signature, and enlisted in the Marine Corps, joining a unit that landed on Iwo Jima in 1945. Less than a week after he turned seventeen, he was in a trench when two grenades landed nearby. Since he was the only one who saw them, he shoved his fellow soldiers out of the way, jumped on one grenade, and *pulled the other one underneath him.* The explosions sent him flying through the air; he landed on his back and was left for dead. Except somehow he wasn't dead, despite having 250 pieces of grenade shrapnel lodged in his body. He eventually recovered and received the Medal of Honor for his bravery.[1]

As amazing and heroic as that story is, tales of military heroism have a way of affecting us . . . only so much. Soldiers exhibiting extraordinary combat bravery don't *seem* like regular people—even though they frequently *are* regular people who've been placed in impossible scenarios we can't imagine ever facing ourselves. But we've probably seen other

---

[1] A bunch of other wild stuff happened to him too. In 1961 he was on a paratrooper training mission when both of his parachutes malfunctioned, and in 1977 his wife hired a hit man to drug his beer so she could show up with Lucas's gun, kill him, and make it look like a suicide—but the police were tipped off and Lucas switched the drugged beer, foiling the plot. Somehow he survived it all and died in 2008 at the age of eighty.

stories about someone who *is* like us, and who acted heroically within a general space we *do* inhabit—jumping onto subway tracks to rescue someone who'd fallen, maybe, or running into traffic to save a wayward turtle that was trying to cross the freeway. We may chew on these stories a bit longer, and they may affect us more deeply, because they're closer to our own experience. We may wonder whether we could or would do the same thing in the same situation. We may secretly think, "Man, I'm glad *that* lady did that, because no way I'm risking my life for some dumb turtle with no sense of direction," and then we might feel a little bad about ourselves, because we've realized we wouldn't be as brave. And then, eventually, we may forget about the whole thing and watch a YouTube video of a cool Rube Goldberg contraption that some teenager constructed in her house during the Covid-19 quarantine.[2]

Part of the wonder of being human is that we get to learn about the extraordinary levels of virtue of which other humans are capable. We hear stories of courageous London shop owners during the bombings of 1940, keeping a stiff upper lip and marching through rubble to open their stores. We watch video of an anonymous man in Tiananmen Square standing alone in front of a tank, and read about women who expose horrifying abuses while risking their careers and mental health in order to prevent the same awful things from happening to others. So we know these things are possible—this level of courage, bravery, fortitude, generosity, and empathy is *achievable*, in the same way that a four-minute mile is achievable, or free-solo-ing a cliff face is achievable. Most of us, thankfully, will never be in one of these situations. Most of us will never even have to decide whether to save a turtle from a freeway. But if we want to be good people, we still need some theoretical understanding of how we *ought* to react in extreme situations, should they arise—and more to the point, we need to know whether being good people *requires*

---

2 And then we may feel bad about ourselves again, because *we* could never design that thing! How does anyone design those things?!

us to act the way those heroes did. Understanding the limits of required virtue can give us a North Star by which we can navigate: Exactly how good do we have to be, practically speaking, before we've achieved our goal of becoming good people? Which human actions define *necessary* goodness, and which ones are like "That's amazing that you did that, but if I *don't* do it I'm not necessarily a bad person"? I mean, it can't be true that if we don't rush into a burning building to rescue everyone inside, we're *bad*, right? The jokey title of this book aside, in order to be *good* we don't have to be *perfect*, right?

. . . Right?!

Moral Perfection: A Cautionary Tale

We sort of know the answer already, if we're aspiring Kantians: our actions do, in a way, have to be "perfect." Kantian deontology is the most all-or-nothing of these schools of thought, because he's an absolutist; we don't even need to pose a theoretical extreme outlier like the burning-building scenario in order to know whether we'd fail Kant's test, because no matter how mundane or crazy the situation, if we don't discern a universal maxim and then act out of a duty to follow that maxim, we've failed, and Kant will shake his perpetually disapproving head at us. But let's consider the burning building anyway. Again, depending on how we phrase the maxim, we may feel as though Kant requires different levels of valor; for example, if the maxim is "We should always sacrifice our own safety if we have the chance to save other people"—well, put a handkerchief over your face and storm inside. But if the maxim is "We should act swiftly and decisively in order to save human lives," we might only be required to call 911 and alert professional rescuer-type people of the emergency. But what if we know that the nearest firehouse is an hour away? Does the maxim have to include the either/or forking path regarding proximity of a professional rescue squad? Or any other variable?

Predictably, we find ourselves confronting the same criticism of

Kantian thought we discussed earlier: the formulation of these stupid maxims he wants us to devise through pure reason can be damn near impossible. To me, a key part of any ethical system has to be that it *can actually work in real life*. And while there are plenty of scenarios where we have the time and patience to engage in Kantian reasoning, there are also plenty where we don't. If a building is on fire and we have to tease out the proper universal maxim that applies, I mean . . . those poor people. I can imagine them now, yelling from the windows:

"Help us! We're trapped!"

"Okay, hang on," we yell back. "It's unclear to us whether we are morally required to attempt to rescue you!"

"We totally get it! Just make sure you act out of your duty to follow a deontological maxim!"

"Thank you for understanding! Should have an answer in the next thirty to forty minutes!"

Since extreme situations, for Kantians, don't require any different moral reasoning than boring everyday situations, and both can be really hard, let's approach this from a utilitarian's perspective and see what happens. As we've seen, utilitarian actions can be easy to determine in simple situations but harder in complicated ones, and this one's on the complicated end of the spectrum. It's about saving lives, like the Trolley Problem, but now with an added wrinkle: we don't *know* whether we can succeed in rescuing these people. In the Trolley Problem the results were definite and baked into our calculation—one dies or five die—but now . . . who knows? Maybe we save everyone. Maybe they all die. Maybe we save some, but *we* die. Maybe we save *no one* and we die. That would suck. And yet, from a strict utilitarian position, if we have the chance to save multiple lives we should do it . . . right? More happiness would be better? Even if we might die? Even though this burning-building situation is really scary, and we don't know anything about how to assess danger from structure fires, and also maybe we haven't been working out a lot recently and aren't in great shape and got winded yesterday trying to open a jar of mayonnaise so it seems pretty goddamn unlikely that we'll be able to pull off a heroic lifesaving rescue? Well, too bad, says the strict utilitarian rulebook—we ought to risk one life (our own) to try to save however many lives are threatened by this towering inferno. And if that's true, then shouldn't we—if we want to be good little utilitarians—buy a police scanner and listen for other burning-building scenarios and then rush over to try to help save *those* people? I mean, how can whatever we're doing right now create more happiness than saving lives?

Here we find a new criticism of utilitarianism: when we follow consequentialist theory out to the far end of the bell curve—reaching the inescapable terminus of a life where we act *only* in order to maximize happiness—we fall into a big ol' booby trap: the "happiness pump."

Let's say we adopt a purely consequentialist worldview. One day we find a five-dollar bill on the street, and since we don't really *need* five extra bucks, we decide to make the world a little better. We go online and find a highly efficient charity that for five bucks can purchase a mosquito net and get it to sub-Saharan Africa, where it can prevent a kid from contracting malaria and maybe dying. Five bucks to save a human life?! Easy call. Flush with success, we look at our bank account and see a balance of $3,000. We've already paid our rent this month, and we have a steady job and no immediate health crises, so that money isn't *vital*, right now. Three thousand dollars would buy six hundred more mosquito nets—that's six hundred more human lives! So we give it all away. Then we look around our house and see a bunch of old clothes and books and furniture we don't need, so we sell them and donate all the money to buy more mosquito nets. Then we figure we don't technically *need* a car, because we *could* walk to work and take Lyfts everywhere else we need to go, and why should we drive around in a car we don't *really* need when kids are dying of malaria? How is that fair? It isn't. So we sell our car and give the money to the mosquito net charity. Then we sell our house, donate the money, and move in with our friend. And then we realize: "Hey, I have *two* kidneys, and I only *need* one . . ."

You get the point.

Classic utilitarianism gives us a simple rule for how to be good—

create more happiness and pleasure than pain and suffering—but it doesn't really suggest at what point we are allowed to put restraints on our goodness-creating actions in order to just maintain our basic lives. In *The Good Place* we invented a character named Doug Forcett, who had taken the idea of maximizing happiness to the extreme—he ate only lentils he grew himself, because they required very little water. He allowed himself to be pushed around by a teenage bully who'd realized that Doug would do whatever dumb thing the bully wanted him to do, and since doing those things made the bully happy, Doug obliged. If we adopt a utilitarian worldview wholesale and follow it to the end of the line, we risk becoming this kind of "happiness pump"—a battery, essentially, powering the happiness of other people at the expense of our own. Any limits we put on utilitarian actions are arbitrary and self-defined, which to me dents its usefulness as a guiding principle. If the people who invented utilitarianism never told us when we could stop . . . when should we stop?

The contemporary philosopher Susan Wolf wrote about this in a paper called "Moral Saints," in which she questions the very idea of what it would mean to be "morally perfect." She writes:

> For the moral saint, the promotion of the welfare of others might play the role that is played for most of us by the enjoyment of material comforts, the opportunity to engage in the intellectual and physical activities of our choice, and the love, respect, and companionship of people whom we love, respect, and enjoy. The happiness of the moral saint, then, would truly lie in the happiness of others, and so he would devote himself to others gladly, and with a whole and open heart.

This is that "happiness pump" idea, rephrased: Wolf describes it as a person whose default setting is not "self-preservation," but rather "other-preservation." It's the ego turned inside out. When we think of it that way, it doesn't sound *so* terrible—it even echoes ubuntu—but in order to achieve this moral sainthood we'd have to do this *all the time,* in every scenario, which essentially renders the idea impossible. If we were having lunch with our best friend, Carl, and across the street a woman got frustrated by a malfunctioning parking meter, we would have to leap up and rush to help her . . . unless doing so made Carl upset, because he was right in the middle of an emotional story about his ongoing troubles with his sister, and thus the act of helping the parking meter lady would cause *him* more *unhappiness* than the happiness we would create by helping the woman with her parking meter troubles . . . but then as we're making that calculation we happen to overhear someone talking about a flood in Missouri that displaced thousands of people, all of whom are more in need than Carl *or* Parking Meter Lady, so we rush to the airport . . . This constant and endless utilitarian calculation makes it impossible for us to live anything approaching a normal life.

And what becomes of such a person? How would we be, for lack of a better term, *people,* if our only goal were moral sainthood? Wolf worries about that too.

> If the moral saint is devoting all his time to feeding the hungry or healing the sick or raising money for Oxfam, then necessarily he is not reading Victorian novels, playing the oboe, or improving his backhand. . . . A life in which *none* of these possible aspects of character are developed may seem to be a life strangely barren. . . . An interest in something like gourmet cooking will be . . . difficult for a moral saint to rest easy with. For it seems to me that no plausible argument can justify the use of human resources involved in producing a *pâté de canard en croute* against possible alternative beneficent ends to which these resources might be put.

The moral saint can't go see movies, or play tennis, or learn Arabic, or cook whatever the hell a *pâté de canard en croute* is, because doing so robs her of valuable moral saint activity time. And without any of these life-enriching activities, the moral saint becomes *super boring*. "A moral saint will have to be very, very nice," Wolf writes, drily. "It is important that he not be offensive. The worry is that, as a result, he will have to be dull-witted or humorless or bland." Right! A person who self-abnegates to the point where he cannot risk laughing at something that others might not find funny, or who can't risk making an observation about the world out of the fear that someone else might not share a similar view, is a *snooze*.

Not to mention that no one wants to hang out with a person who has only one interest—whether that interest is being morally perfect, or swimming, or playing the bagpipes. The idea of individuality, of being a living entity with dimension and specificity, frees us to pursue things we love and want to experience, and without caring to fertilize those seeds unique to our little human gardens we're not really *people*. In other words: Not *everything* can or should be about morality. ("There seems to be a limit," says Wolf, "to how much morality we can stand.") Human accomplishment is cool, and valuable, and admirable, and when we realize that those valuable accomplishments are incompatible with moral sainthood, we can let go of moral sainthood as a reasonable guide for how to live our lives. If we don't, we become dull, dimensionless batteries, doing nothing but powering the rest of the world.[3]

---

3 Wolf is a great writer, and this part of her argument is really elegant: She describes two sorts of moral saints, the Rational Saint (a Kantian approach) and the Loving Saint (a utilitarian approach). She then very neatly dismisses both as self-defeating, by saying that the Rational Saint could not universalize the maxim "make everyone else as happy as possible," because if everyone tried to do that, we would all just stand in a big circle, waiting for everyone else to have a problem we could fix, and thus no one would do anything. (Also, remember that Kant himself dismissed the idea of universal maxims regarding happiness, because of my "Hawaiian pizza and Red Hot Chili Peppers" problem—that different people are made happy by different things.) And if we all became utilitarian Loving Saints, denying our own happiness for the sake of others, we'd all become deeply *unhappy*, and thus could potentially *reduce* the total happiness in the world, which is the opposite of what we'd be aiming for.

The question we're trying to answer—"What's the upper limit of required goodness?"—seems like a job for virtue ethics; because again, while Kant and Mill ask *What should I do?*, Aristotle is asking *What kind of person should I be?* The first question aims to be more practical, I suppose—those guys are trying to give us actual instruction manuals that we can break open whenever we are faced with a tough choice. But in certain situations those rule-based theories break down, or suggest that we do outrageous or absurd things. Aristotle suggests that if we can focus on becoming virtuous people, we will then make good choices. His "practice makes perfect" approach (or, more accurately: "continual practice brings us asymptotically closer to perfection"—but that's not as catchy) contains a key to answering the question: "Just how good do I have to be in order to be good?"

By definition, the golden mean provides for every virtue both an upper and a lower limit—those vices at either end of the seesaw. The soldier with *too much* courage will become rash and stupid, charging over a hill and trying to take on an entire army by herself, while the one with *no* courage will wet his pants at the first sign of trouble and abandon his fellow soldiers. The ideal amount of every virtue, again, is that theoretical perfect balance between excess and deficiency. So now, instead of a seesaw, let's think of this as a tug-of-war. You know how there's a flag at the center of the rope, and the flag drifts a little this way and then back the other way as one side or the other gains the upper hand? The teams are vices—like cowardice and rashness—and the flag is the golden mean of courage. If everything is in balance, the flag remains at the very center of those two vices, thanks to the equal tension from each side. But if one or the other vice starts to pull harder, the flag drifts a little bit toward that vice and needs to be pulled back the other way *by the opposing vice.* So the golden mean actually *demands* that we exhibit some amount of mildly "vice-like" behavior in order to maintain our virtuous balance. The person seeking the golden mean of courage, for example, *has* to occasionally stir in a little cowardice, because if she doesn't, she may become too rash.

Edith Hall, a professor of classics at King's College London, excellently explains this angle on Aristotelian means:

> I believe my own worst faults are: impatience, recklessness, excessive bluntness, emotional extremes and vindictiveness. But Aristotle's idea of . . . "the golden mean" explains that all these are fine *in moderation*—people who are never impatient don't get things done; people who never take risks live limited lives; people who evade the truth and do not express pain or joy at all are psychologically and emotionally stunted or deprived; and people who have no desire whatsoever to get even with those who have damaged them are either deluding themselves or have too low an estimate of their own worth.

In other words, Aristotle doesn't demand that we be perfect little moral saints, smiling all the time, never losing our tempers, and polishing apples for our teachers. In fact, such a person is *failing* at finding the Goldilocks bullseye for whichever virtue he's attempting to exhibit. And he's also super annoying. And boring. Who wants to hang out with *that* guy? Just sitting there, being all perfect all the time, lording it over us—or worse, *not* lording it over us, because he's so perfect he would *never* lord anything over us. How *dare* he not lord it over us?! That guy is the *worst*!

Sorry. The point is, we *need* "imperfect" qualities, as long as they are exhibited only in the correct amount to be useful—by keeping us from tilting too far into excess or deficiency—and not harmful. For Aristotle, all of this *doing* and *searching* and *orienting* has one purpose: to approach a state of "flourishing." But to me, there's a sort of adjacent, and more pragmatic, benefit: the allowance for, or even *need for*, some amount of vice-like behavior as we search for virtue takes the pressure off us. To use yet another leisure time–activity metaphor, virtue ethics functions like those bumpers that bowling alleys put up for kids, to prevent the balls from rolling into the gutters—if we drift too far in one direction, the search for the golden mean nudges us back onto a better trajectory.

Knowing we don't have to be *completely* courageous or *utterly* kind or *perfectly* generous makes the arduous project of becoming better people seem less impossible.

Don't Sacrifice Your Entire Life for a Random Violinist

One thought experiment we might explore here is Judith Jarvis Thomson's "Violinist." Thomson (1929–2020), whom you may remember from her contributions to the Trolley Problem, imagines a scenario in which a woman we'll call Meg wakes up back-to-back with a famous violinist named Armando, whose kidneys are failing. Meg apparently has the only compatible set of kidneys around, and the Society of Music Lovers has kidnapped her and medically connected her to Armando in order to save his life. The Society of Music Lovers tells Meg she must remain connected to Armando for some indeterminate amount of time, because he's a world-class violinist and his music makes a lot of people happy, so . . . sorry, Meg—your only job now is to serve as a sedentary blood-cleaner for this diseased violin maestro.[4] Is this a reasonable request? Most people would say no. Most people would also start keeping an eye out for members of the Society of Music Lovers, who apparently are a lot more dangerous than their name would suggest.

But a strict consequentialist might say that Meg should submit to this new life as a human blood-cleaner. Armando has millions of fans! His music brings so much joy to so many. And what have you ever done, Meg? Oh, you're an HR rep for GEICO. Big deal. Have you ever played Dvořák's Violin Concerto in A Minor with the London Philharmonic?

---

4 Thomson does not make it clear how Armando's going to continue to play the violin while he's in this hospital bed getting his blood cleaned by someone else's kidneys, but we'll let that slide.

Because Armando has, and it was *incredible*. Suck it up and clean Armando's blood. (Though again, yes, the strict consequentialist has to add in the pain caused by people knowing this could happen to them, etc., etc.)

A Kantian would of course turn up her nose at this—you want to talk about treating someone as a means to an end instead of as an end in herself? Armando is literally using the entirety of Meg's existence to stay alive. Meg is a human crutch for Armando. Bad bad bad. The Kantian would also have some words for the Society of Music Lovers, and the doctor who performed the surgery, and the orderlies who clean the room, and the guy who filled the vending machines in the hospital. Kantians have a few words for everyone.

Aristotle would agree with Kant that Meg is not required to unwillingly donate her kidneys to Armando in perpetuity, but for a different reason. He might say that there is a limit to self-sacrifice, because someone who tilts too far toward helping others to flourish—a happiness pump, essentially—may be unable to flourish herself. There is some amount of "selfishness" that's appropriate and even *good* for us to have, because without it we aren't properly valuing our own lives. If *flourishing* is the ultimate human purpose, it requires us to protect ourselves a little from suffering. "I don't have to loan my renal system to a random violinist at the complete unending expense of my own life and happiness" certainly falls within the bounds of the reasonable amount of "selfishness" a person should exhibit.[5]

It may seem like I am nudging us toward choosing Aristotle as our official guide in the quest to become better people. I'm really not—I believe that each of these schools of thought has something useful to offer

---

[5] At the risk of drifting into the thorny world of politics, Thomson designed this thought experiment to discuss the issue of abortion, in the case of unwanted pregnancy. It's not hard to guess what her conclusion was. Foot was also discussing abortion in the 1967 paper that started it all—the title was "The Problem of Abortion and the Doctrine of Double Effect."

us. (Also, Aristotle had his problems—for instance, he was *very* into slavery. He 100 percent thought slavery was cool. I know it was 2,400 years ago, but still—don't be so into slavery, Aristotle!) No matter which school of thought we're talking about, while it's obviously courageous to run into a burning building and try to save everyone, it's not ethically *required*, especially if the chances for survival (for you and the people inside) are impossible to calculate.[6] We wouldn't universalize a maxim that said, "We must *always* risk our lives to save other people," because doing so would cause people to constantly intervene in situations where they're unlikely to survive. It's also hard to claim that we are "maximizing good" by making a very risky bet that we—who are not in any way qualified to assess the dangers of a fire and then navigate the situation in order to save others—can succeed. And just like Aristotle's overly courageous soldier taking on an entire army himself, recklessly charging into a burning building may certainly be labeled an *excessively* courageous act, tilting over into rashness. Like anything else, it's a calculation: brave is good, foolish is not.

So, ultimately, there *are* limits on what's required of us—moral perfection is impossible, and it's unwise to think of it as any kind of reasonable goal. But what if we *did* storm into the burning building, and rescued the people inside? We either formulated a universal maxim in record time and followed it, or we hold the concept of maximizing happiness in such high regard that we decided to risk our own safety, or we felt as though rescuing those people was not exhibiting an excess of courage . . . and we freakin' did it! Everyone pats us on the back, in awe of our bravery (and possibly the speed with which we formed a universal maxim and then followed it). Someone snaps a photo of us emerging

---

6 Like everything else in ethics, the calculation changes with the circumstances. Are we paid firefighters who are on duty? Well, yeah, now we should charge in there, because it's the job we signed up for. Just like with the Trolley Problem variations where we're either a professional trolley driver or a bystander, the specifics of our role in the situation matter a great deal.

from the flames, and we look super badass—modern-day superheroes, risking life and limb to save others. As we consider the picture, flush with the endorphin rush that comes from an act of heroism, our Instagram account starts calling out to us . . .

"Post it . . . You'll look so cool . . . Post iiiitttt . . ."

CHAPTER SIX

I Just Did Something Unselfish.
But What's in It for Me?!

A few years ago, I caught myself doing something embarrassing. There's a Starbucks near my house, and I got the same thing every time I went in: a medium coffee. The price was $1.73, I paid in cash, and when I got my change I would toss it into the tip jar by the register. Except . . . I *didn't* just toss it in. After handing me my change, the barista would turn around to get the coffee, and I would wait until he had turned *back* around before I graced him with my generous tip of twenty-seven U.S. cents.

When I suddenly realized that I was doing this—after maybe the hundredth time I did it—so many questions popped into my head at once: Why did I need that person to see me perform such a minuscule act of kindness? Did I crave some kind of *ethical credit* for tipping this guy twenty-seven cents? Or was it perhaps the fear that if he *didn't* see me do it, he'd think I was the kind of person who *didn't* tip? What did this mean for the (different but related) act of charitable giving—is there a greater moral value in donating anonymously? If so, isn't that annoying? I mean, if you don't let them include your name on the donor roll, then no one will know what a good person you are!

Whatever the reason, one thing became clear: I was being super lame. Tipping twenty-seven cents was pretty lame, and doing so only when I knew I would be seen doing it was *doubly* lame. (The only real good that came out of the whole episode was that pondering it led directly to creating *The Good Place*.) It made me wonder (again) what the hell I was doing, and why the hell I was doing it. I poked around to research why exactly I was being so lame, and came upon the concept of moral desert.[1]

Humanity's Unquenchable Thirst for Gold Stars

In philosophy, "desert" deals with figuring out what people are owed, or in some cases what they're *entitled* to, based on different actions in different scenarios. *Moral* desert is the idea that if we do good deeds, we should be rewarded for them—sometimes in like a cool spiritual way, where our souls become enriched by the cosmic positivity we've created, but sometimes in a literal, "big shiny trophy!" way. There's a lot of writing about the morality of people getting what they deserve, and our duty to give people what they deserve (or at least nudge them further toward what they deserve), and it can get really hairy and difficult to understand; a lot of it becomes mathematical, with charts and graphs and logic matrices, and we'll just skip right over that stuff and talk about the most basic question: Do we "deserve" some kind of bonus if we act with virtue? In my case, when I tipped the barista, some part of me felt like I was owed the gratitude he would display when he saw my generosity—I was inverting the very idea of a tip, because the purpose of the action became a reward for *me* instead of the guy who'd earned it. And when you put it like that . . . I mean, that can't be right. Right?

---

1 Confusingly, the "desert" here isn't the dry, sandy place where camels roam around; nor is it dessert, like ice cream, though that's how it's pronounced. It's etymologically linked to the concept of *deserving* something. I do X, so I *deserve* Y. The "ice cream" version also kind of works, in the sense of: "If you finish your green beans you get dessert," but that's not actually where the philosophical term comes from. One notable book on the subject is Shelly Kagan's *The Geometry of Desert*, which sounds like a book written by a cool math teacher who uses stacks of Oreos to teach you about cylinders.

I was heartened to discover how widespread this feeling is. The desire for others to recognize our goodness has been discussed for centuries, and when I did an informal survey of my friends and colleagues, many of them copped to the same foible: When we do something good, we want credit, dammit. We want a little gold star. We want to be seen as good people—and I mean *literally* seen—which I think is both completely understandable and deeply embarrassing. (Side note: *So much* of philosophy involves investigating embarrassing human activities and inclinations. We really are weird little creatures.) Why do we so intensely crave recognition for our good deeds, even if those deeds are minuscule?

There's a couple of ways to look at this, and they cover ground that stretches beyond what we might traditionally think of as "ethics," at least in the Western philosophical sense. When I caught myself doing this silly, borderline-pathetic thing—craving twenty-seven cents' worth of moral desert—I asked myself the question we talked about in the introduction: "What am I *doing?*" Up to that point in my life, I hadn't often interrogated myself that way, especially in mundane situations like buying coffee. But I've since come to believe that making better decisions requires that we do so routinely. That belief led me to the writings of Thich Nhat Hanh.

Thich Nhat Hanh (1926–) is a Buddhist monk from Vietnam who was nominated for the Nobel Peace Prize in 1967 by Martin Luther King Jr. Take a second and reread that sentence. Have you ever heard anything more impressive than "he was nominated for a Nobel Peace Prize by Martin Luther King Jr."? But here's the important part: instead of doing what everyone else would've done—put on a T-shirt that says I WAS NOMINATED FOR A NOBEL PEACE PRIZE BY MARTIN LUTHER KING JR. and stand on the corner waving a flag that says I WAS NOMINATED FOR A NOBEL PEACE PRIZE BY MARTIN LUTHER KING JR.—Thich Nhat Hanh just kept advocating for peace in Vietnam and trying to help people. That's how good a person he is. In perhaps his most famous book, *The Heart of the Buddha's Teaching*, he shares this story:

Emperor Wu asked Bodhidharma, the founder of Zen Buddhism in China, how much merit he had earned by building temples all over the country. Bodhidharma said, "None whatsoever." But if you wash one dish in mindfulness, if you build one temple while dwelling deeply in the present moment—not wanting to be anywhere else, not caring about fame or recognition—the merit from that act will be boundless, and you will feel very happy.

Mindfulness is the core of Buddhist philosophy; Hanh defines it as "the energy that brings us back to the present moment." This may seem like more of a religious idea than an ethical one, but when you apply it to my lame quest for moral desert, it takes on an ethical dimension. Some part of my action—waiting until my "good" deed could be recognized before I did it—came from the desire to have the deed function as something other than what it was. I cared about the *reaction to* the deed, and how *I* might benefit from it. Tipping ceased to be simply the action of tipping—it became a means to an end, and the end was selfish. Buddhist philosophy suggests that true happiness comes from remaining focused on the things we do, and doing them with no purpose other than *to do them.*

Giant chunks of Western philosophy are captured and elegantly reformulated in this one beautiful idea.[2] For example: by succumbing to this desire to be thought of as people who do good, which leads us to do things with the intention of receiving praise or some other moral desert, we're also running afoul of our stoic[3] Prussian watchdog Immanuel

---

2 Thich Nhat Hanh also wrote the passage that inspired the metaphor for death that Chidi gives Eleanor in the series finale of *The Good Place*. He describes a person's life as analogous to a wave forming—with specific dimensions and properties and qualities—and then returning to the ocean whence it came. The water is the constant—the wave is just a different way for the water to be, for some amount of time, so when it ceases to be a wave and returns to the ocean, we should be happy, not sad. It's beautiful and peaceful and makes me cry a little every time I think about it.

3 The Stoics were a group of ancient Greek, Roman, and Syrian philosophers who

Kant. He'd chastise us for not acting out of duty to follow a universal maxim *and* tell us we are using the recipient of the small gesture as a means to an end—making ourselves feel good and receiving praise or recognition. (A Kantian double whammy! He'd probably be so psyched about how bad we're being, that freak.)

A utilitarian, on the other hand, might say that it's better to make two people feel good than one, so it's actually *preferable* to make sure the barista saw the tip—that way he feels good, and I feel good too because I get recognition for my (twenty-seven cents' worth of) generosity. Now, the utilitarian might note that the tip will *eventually* be noted and counted, so the happiness of the *barista* will wind up being the same no matter what,[4] and thus *I* can feel roughly the same amount of happiness that I'd feel in the moment of instantaneous acknowledgment. But there is still the extra happiness I get from *seeing the barista see me*—so in total, tipping in view of the tippee slightly increases the total happiness.

And Aristotle? I'm honestly not sure what he'd say. This action doesn't fall neatly into a "virtue" category. It's a slight excess of pride, maybe? Or possibly a deficiency of humility? (The one thing I know for sure is that an Aristotelian would definitely say twenty-seven cents is a crummy tip. Chip in a buck and let's get closer to that golden mean of generosity, bud.[5]) Aristotle might also ding me for exhibiting my old

---

worshipped Socrates and attempted to free people from what Russell calls "mundane desires" (like the desire for material possessions) in order to achieve greater freedom. I mention this only because I am using the word "stoic" here in the dictionary sense, meaning "indifferent to pleasure or pain," but anyone reading this who knows a lot about philosophy might see the word "stoic" applied to Kant and immediately begin a lengthy refutation of the entire book based on my flawed understanding of the capital-*S* Stoics. Although now that I'm rereading Russell's section on the Stoics I see that he says Kant "resembles them," so I take this all back; I meant it as a sly little philosophy reference because I'm super smart and well-versed in this topic.

4 Though again, "propinquity" mattered to Bentham, so the faster the barista sees the tip, the better. More on this in a second . . .

5 Important to note the role that context plays in situations like this. I'm a well-paid TV

peccadillo: excessive dutifulness. I eventually concluded that while I was indeed seeking some kind of praise or "hat tip" from the barista, I was *more* motivated by the fear that he would think I *hadn't* tipped him, since tipping is a "rule" (or generally agreed-upon practice) in American restaurants. I came to that conclusion after my wife, J.J., reminded me that when we were in Paris on our honeymoon, despite having read about the European system wherein service gratuity is not required in restaurants (but is instead wrapped into the price of the meal), I still left tips for our waiters everywhere we went. In that case I was worried about two things: (1) being seen as a boorish, selfish American, and (2) breaking a rule, even though I had ample evidence that the "rule" in question was not being broken. (I did this so consistently that as we got off the plane at the end of the trip, J.J. looked at me and said, "Did you tip the pilot?" Which was an excellent burn.) Same deal with the Starbucks tip—I needed the barista to tick a little box next to my name on an imaginary "good customer checklist." Remember how I said my excess of dutifulness can be kind of annoying? There you go.

But let's return to this (pretty compelling) utilitarian counterargument, which I noted above: the "added good" caused by the barista seeing me tip him, and thus feeling pleased because he's being recognized for doing a good job. Again, granted, he'd also feel this at the end of the day when he counts up his total tips, but the small, mutually acknowledged in-person human interaction is a little bright spot in his day, and mine, and there is value there. This argument was made to me by a friend I was hashing this out with, and it started me thinking about the concept of one-way monetary transactions in much larger realms—like charitable giving. That's obviously a different sort of transaction than a

---

comedy writer, married to another well-paid TV comedy writer, so for me, twenty-seven cents is a bummer of a tip. Someone in a different socioeconomic position might be quite generous in tipping that amount. We'll deal with this further in chapter 12.

gratuity, but the ethical questions around moral desert pertain to both—in each case, we are giving money to someone (or something), and in each case we want to be rewarded for what we've done. We feel that we're *owed* a moral pat on the back, and even though it's shameful to admit it, that feeling is powerful. We want the credit!

In his twelfth-century magnum opus, the Mishneh Torah, the Jewish scholar Maimonides lays out eight levels of charitable giving. One of the highest is to give money anonymously to people you don't know (assuming they need the money and are worthy of the gift). A little farther down on the list are things like giving anonymously to people you *do* know, and giving to people before you're asked. At the very bottom, essentially, is rolling your eyes, grunting, "Ugh, FINE," and tossing a quarter at a starving kid. When I tipped my twenty-seven cents, I was just one level above that: "When one gives inadequately, but gives gladly and with a smile." (Again, the Starbucks tip wasn't "charity," but the specifics of the action here are less important than the desire for credit.)

If one of the highest levels of charity is "anonymous giving to anonymous people," that means that if we give a large amount of money to, say, a group fighting poverty in rural Arkansas, we ought to do it anonymously. However, the anonymity (morally good for us, maybe) also affects other people, who see only "Anonymous" in the donor list. Maybe that's a good thing. Maybe the anonymity sends a message that this donation was, in Thich Nhat Hanh's words, *mindful,* and people will be inspired by the act of giving purely for the sake of giving, and not for recognition or pride. But many others—I'll speak for myself here—look at "Anonymous" and can't help but think: *Who is that?!* There's a museum in Los Angeles we used to take our kids to when they were driving us nuts and we were totally out of ideas for how to entertain them, and a list on the wall shows gifts of *tens of millions of dollars,* some of which are anonymous. I can't help it—I want to know who the donors were! I don't know why, really—partly suspicion, maybe, that the gifts came from people L.A. museumgoers would find objectionable . . . partly low-level gossip-seeking about who ponied up that kind of dough . . . and partly a moral curiosity. *Who did this good thing?*

That's the crux of this counterargument to donating anonymously: How much *extra* good has come from famous people—George Clooney, or Oprah, or LeBron James—publicly announcing their charitable giving? How much more attention has been brought to those causes because of the public nature of their gifts? Certainly: a *lot*. And it doesn't have to be famous people—if we give $1,000 to fight poverty in rural Arkansas and our friends and coworkers and family see what we've done, perhaps they'll be inspired and decide to give themselves. There's gotta be some golden mean here between "total anonymity" and "post a selfie while cutting a huge check, with hashtags #ImAwesome, #BetterThan You, and #GenerousAF."

Score One for the Utilitarians!

We can't deny there is something good, pure, and *mindful* about giving anonymously, which strips away everything surrounding the act other than the act itself. Honestly, I am more drawn to that humanistic Buddhist explanation of why anonymity is good than Kant's "rules and regulations" approach. But after mulling this all over for a good long time, my inner utilitarian takes over and wins the day. (See? Told you I wasn't in the bag for Aristotle!) The goal of charitable giving is to maximize the transfer of money from people who have it to people who need it. Often, the circumstances are dire—the money will be used for emergency disaster relief, to provide food, shelter, or medicine. Requiring a purity of motivation seems like a limiting demand in a realm where we shouldn't impose any limits. In other words: I don't really care why you're giving money, as long as you're giving it. (Within reason, of course—more on this in a second.) The utilitarian drive to maximize good takes the pole position, for me, in this race.

As an example: I once attended a fancy charity event that honored

one Hollywood mogul type per year. The point of honoring these mo-
guls was not to reward them for their excellent service to the cause—
many of them had nothing to do with the charity in question before they
were chosen as the honoree—but rather to get them to use their power
and influence to force other people in Hollywood to give money. If Scott
Powerbroker calls people on the phone and says, "I'm being honored at
a charity dinner, would you like to buy a table?" everyone says yes, because they are flattered that Scott Powerbroker is calling them, and also
they want to brag to their peers that they and Scott are *old, old* friends.
("We've known him forever," they want to say. "Actually, we're going to
see him this weekend at a charity thing.") The year I went, a powerful
talent agent was being honored—let's call him Josh. I asked a friend
who worked closely with the charity why Josh was the honoree, and he
explained that the year before, they had honored Josh's longtime rival,
Greg, who had raised an all-time-record amount of money. They figured
if they honored Josh, his lizard-brain competitive instinct would kick in,
and he would try to outdo his rival. "Did it work?" I asked. My friend
laughed and said that when they called Josh, before they could even get
all the way through the request, he barked, "How much did Greg raise
last year?!" He promptly accepted the honor and set out to raise more.
Which he did.

Now, in terms of motivations to raise money for charity, "Vanquish
my rivals and establish alpha male superiority in Hollywood" is . . . not
ideal. That's probably pretty low on Maimonides's list, it certainly fails
Kant's test, and it's verrrrrrrry far away from a Buddhist state of mindfulness. But also, I think: Who cares? Josh raised millions of dollars for
a good cause, and if his ego was inflated as a by-product, so be it. Charitable giving in the modern world is a numbers game—there are billions
in need, and money is concentrated in the hands of very few. And when
we're talking numbers games, utilitarianism has a massive leg up on
every other ethical theory. If ignoring everything (within reason) except
the results—the total money raised—gets the world to become a more
equitable place, that's fine with me.

Now, a lot of ethicists will scoff at this. "Scoff!" they'll say. The whole point of ethics is to draw lines of distinction between better and worse kinds of actions, and if you ignore the reasons people do things, you're not really even "doing ethics." So let's draw a distinction here: when it comes to charitable giving, I'm just less concerned with people's motivations for giving than I am with *how we judge those people.* And to those scoffing ethicists, I offer as philosophical backup to my view: the writings of William James.

A Philosophical Jambalaya

James (1842–1910) was a sort of nineteenth-century Aristotle—he wrote about psychology, philosophy, education, religion, and a bunch of other stuff. He's sometimes called the "Father of Modern Psychology," which is a very cool thing to be called, and there's a huge building named after him at Harvard that he didn't even have to pay for. Do you know how impressive and academically influential you have to be to get a Harvard building named after you without donating a ton of money?[6] James's main philosophical contribution is in the theory known as pragmatism. In a series of lectures from 1906, he describes it as "a method of settling metaphysical disputes that otherwise might be interminable," and man oh man, does *that* seem like it could be useful to us.

The anecdote he uses to begin his lectures involves an argument his friends were having about a squirrel on a tree. A person on the other side of the tree keeps running around it, trying to see the squirrel, but the squirrel is too fast and keeps scrambling around in the same direction, so the tree is always between the squirrel and the would-be squirrel-seer. The question is, did the person "go around" the squirrel?[7] James's re-

6 Extremely.

7 Brief aside that may be of interest only to me: What James describes here is nearly

sponse: It depends on what you mean by "go around." If you mean "the person was at various points located to the north, east, south, and west of the squirrel," then yes, of course he "went around the squirrel." But if you mean "was the person in front of the squirrel, then to one side, then behind it, then to the other side," then no, the person didn't "go around the squirrel," because the squirrel always kept his belly pointed toward the person (with the tree between them). The larger point James makes here is: *What difference does it make?* We can accurately describe

---

precisely the way in which Earth and its moon relate to each other. The moon slowly rotates as it revolves around Earth, and thus the same side of the moon is always facing us. Hence "dark side of the moon"—that's the side we never see. I'm a bit surprised that James uses the squirrel and the tree instead of the moon and Earth, because James's whole philosophy is inexorably and sort of beautifully tied to science and seismic changes in scientific theory. There's a cool historical thing going on here, where James is speaking in the immediate aftermath of a massive shift in the way people understood the universe. The year preceding these lectures, 1905, is sometimes called Albert Einstein's *annus mirabilis*—"year of miracles"—because the papers he published on special relativity and the particle theory of light blew the world of physics to smithereens, and all scientists everywhere had to basically start from scratch. Imagine how hard it would be, intellectually and emotionally, to have based your entire worldview on a set of seemingly provable theories, and then one day find out that they were *all wrong*. Imagine being a sixty-eight-year-old physicist in 1906, having to suddenly junk all the lectures you've been giving for four decades. Oof. So here comes William James, philosopher and (not inconsequentially, I think) psychologist, who explicitly designs a theory that can help move people away from old, inferior ways of thinking and toward new and better ones. He writes about the process of forming new opinions, how "a new experience puts them to a strain," causing an "inward trouble . . . from which he seeks to escape by modifying his previous mass of opinions." Against a backdrop of recent scientific breakthroughs, he's addressing the flexibility we need to absorb new truths, and not to reject them on the basis of a previous truth we believed in but that is no longer relevant or even accurate. (We'll deal with this a lot more in a later chapter.) The point of all of this is, I wish he used the moon rotating and revolving around the Earth instead of the squirrel thing, because I think employing a scientific analogy would be a better thematic link to the point he is trying to make. Counterpoint: it's kind of cute, imagining that little squirrel scampering around the tree. So. Either way works, I guess.

the event, the results of either explanation are the same in terms of what occurred, so the rest is just semantics. That's what pragmatism asks:

> What difference would it practically make to any one [*sic*] if this notion rather than that notion were true? If no practical difference whatever can be traced, then the alternatives mean practically the same thing, and all dispute is idle. Whenever a dispute is serious, we ought to be able to show some practical difference that must follow from one side or the other's being right.

James's pragmatism "look[s] away from first things, principles, 'categories,' supposed necessities" and toward "last things, fruits, consequences, facts." It's simply concerned with truth and uses every method at its disposal to find it. The metaphor James uses for pragmatism is a "corridor in a hotel," with a lot of doors branching off it. Behind one door is a religious man; behind the next is an atheistic woman; then a chemist, a mathematician, an ethicist, and so on—each one offering a possible way to arrive at some kind of fact that we can rely on. The pragmatist can, at any moment, open any of those doors and use what she finds to arrive at truth. It's the jambalaya of philosophy.

So we can see the point here, right? In the case of the poorly intentioned charity honoree, we can wander down the corridor and hear a lot of yelling from behind the doors: *The method he used to raise money was not based on a universal maxim! It doesn't represent a golden mean of generosity! It doesn't attain Maimonides's ideals! It's not mindful!*[8] We listen to all of these protestations, take them in, consider them . . . and then we hear a utilitarian say: *But . . . his little ego trip did maximize the amount that was donated, without causing any tangible harm.* And, to the pragmatist, this indisputable fact would probably outweigh all those other opinions.

---

8 I'm enjoying imagining the extremely peaceful Thich Nhat Hanh behind one of these doors, just absolutely screaming this at the top of his lungs.

So, while pragmatism isn't itself "utilitarian," in this case it may employ utilitarian thinking to get to an answer that seems best—just as it might align with Kant or Aristotle in some other instance.

Now, there's a trap here that we need to recognize and sidestep. Remember earlier when I said that I was fine ignoring everything "within reason" except the good result (that the donations were maximized)? That parenthetical "within reason" is doing a *lot* of work. It's easy to think of a situation where the motivation for charitable giving would *not* be ignorable, and a pragmatist would conclude that there *is* a practical difference between two different sorts of donations. Maybe someone donates to charity because he's a criminal, and uses the foundation to launder money, or to achieve social status that cloaks his criminal activities. Think of notorious sex trafficker, pedophile, and all-around nightmare person Jeffrey Epstein—he donated tons of money to dozens of causes as a way to maintain access to influential people and power-wash his reputation. So if we're talking about Jeffrey Epstein, well, yeah—now there's a definite "practical difference" between his donation and that of someone who's less, you know, horrifying. But the case of the egotistical Hollywood mogul contains no criminal activity (that we know of), no harm to another person . . . *no real practical difference* in how the money got to those in need. The guy and the squirrel both ran around the tree— who cares how we describe it?

James called pragmatism "a mediator and reconciler" that—and I love this phrase—" 'unstiffens' our theories." Pragmatism, has, in fact, "no prejudices whatever, no obstructive dogmas, no rigid canons of what shall count as proof. She is completely genial. She will entertain any hypothesis, she will consider any evidence"—as long as its reasoning is tethered to the right facts. In this case, the fact is: more money was raised for people in need than might have been otherwise because of an egotistical guy's ego, and no recognizable harm came to anyone else because of that fact. So be it.

It should be noted that Thich Nhat Hanh would probably disagree with James (and me) here, because he cares more about the person doing the thing than what happened when he did it. The Buddhist view of happiness requires that it be the *right* happiness—the mindful happiness that comes from devotion to the Buddha's teachings. As Hanh says,

> Everyone wants to be happy, and there is a strong energy in us pushing toward what we think will make us happy. But we may suffer a lot because of this. We need the insight that position, revenge, wealth, fame, or possessions are, more often than not, obstacles to our happiness.

We have focused mostly on the results of charitable giving (or tipping), and we ended up in a pragmatic/utilitarian conclusion that if good is maximized, motivation of the giver is secondary. But much like Kant, Hanh wants us to think about the act itself. If we give money to charity for *our own* happiness—if the goal is to be showered with praise and admiration—we are violating both Kant's universal maxim and Hanh's (or Buddha's) view of what brings us *actual* happiness instead of a false equivalent. The mindful action—the doing of a thing with no intention but to do it—provides greater calm and joy. Hanh would not have felt satisfied watching that Hollywood fundraiser unfold, because despite all of the money that was flowing to those who needed it, he would have thought the honoree to be a deeply unhappy person. Also the meal was flank steak and Hanh is a vegetarian, so that would've bummed him out too.

Perhaps a pragmatist wouldn't care one way or the other whether we pat ourselves on the back after doing something good—self-aggrandizement is less an ethical issue than a "good taste, bad taste" one—but Immanuel Kant would, and Thich Nhat Hanh would (for a different reason), and it's not hard to imagine a bad motivation for a good act causing us actual moral trouble at some point. We may start to see the external "rewards" for good deeds as more desirable than the acts themselves, which might then lead to us doing things just for clicks and likes and faves and flattering interviews. That's what plagues the character Tahani Al-Jamil in *The Good Place*—her desire for fame and attention overwhelms her, taking her to some dark places as a result. (She was so jealous of her more famous, more successful sister Kamilah, she literally died after toppling a statue of Kamilah, which crushed her.) Although I'm arguing for some pragmatism here, we probably don't want to stray too far away from a mindful life of good and pure intentions. At the far end of the spectrum, way past "donating so we can brag about it on Twitter," we find some truly harmful acts of fake altruism done for bad reasons or in conjunction with other, despicable behavior—wealthy people giving money to a university in order to buy a spot for an undeserving child, or the Sackler family donating to museums while Purdue Pharma, a company they founded, peddles (and lies about) their highly addictive prescription drugs. Those are hardly the sorts of moral acts we want to venerate.

Pragmatism asks us to be moral referees, watching the action unfold and determining whether there is any difference between one outcome and another—and thus whether the dispute is idle or meaningful. Of course, if we're playing referee, a new question arises: When do we blow the whistle? If someone does something bad, something that we believe has a tangibly negative effect on the world, should we say so? When, if ever, should we not only determine that someone is acting immorally, but actually call them on it?

Well, let me tell you about the time my wife bumped into a guy's car at 1 mph and our whole life was turned upside down.

CHAPTER SEVEN

Yes, I Bumped into Your Car. But Do You Even *Care* About Hurricane Katrina?!

In 2005, J.J. (then my fiancée) bumped into a guy in very slow-moving traffic. A nearby police officer looked everything over and said he didn't see any damage. Nonetheless, they exchanged information and went on their way. A few days later, we received a claim for $836. The entire fender, said the man, needed to be replaced.

It's important to note that this took place during Hurricane Katrina. New Orleans was literally underwater, and I—like everyone else in America—watched in horror as thousands of people's lives were destroyed and a great city nearly disappeared forever. A friend of mine who'd grown up there had just lost his father; very soon after the funeral, which was difficult enough, their family home was badly damaged.[1] Just awful, in every direction. In the midst of that turmoil, I went and examined this man's car, and if I strained *very* hard, I could *barely* discern a six-inch pencil-line crease along his rear bumper. In a fit of pique, I told him that although we didn't dispute the events that led to this tragic disfigurement of the rear bumper of his Saab sedan, I found it absurd that this blemish was worth $836. I told him that things like this were why car insurance in Los Angeles is so expensive. And I made him an offer: I would donate

---

1 This friend wants me to add that his home was not nearly as damaged as many homes and buildings in the city. (Because he's a good person who cares about other people.)

$836 to the Red Cross's Katrina relief efforts in his name, and he would go on living with damage to his rear bumper so minimal you needed a high-powered microscope to notice it. He said he'd think it over.

Convinced that I commanded the moral high ground, I angrily shared this story with my friends and coworkers, and the snowball started rolling down the hill very quickly. Many of them joined my cause—they started pledging more and more money to the Red Cross if this guy would agree not to fix his bumper. (The guy, it should be noted, was unaware any of this was happening.) Soon I had promises of $2,000 . . . $5,000 . . . In less than forty-eight hours, thanks to the early days of internet virality, hundreds of people had pledged upward of $20,000 if this unsuspecting Saab driver would agree not to fix his car. I started a blog to keep track of all of it and posted regular updates. I got media inquiries from several major news outlets. I had dreams of rescuing New Orleans all by myself, armed with nothing but a keyboard and a brilliant masterstroke of moral reasoning.

And then I started to feel sick.

So did J.J.—and at exactly the same moment. We were excitedly discussing the most recent events, and pledges, and media requests, and we looked at each other and instantly read on each other's faces the same queasy feeling: there was something very *wrong* about what we were doing . . . though we couldn't pinpoint what it was. The little voices in our heads were chirping at us, and we finally started listening to them. If I'm carbon-dating my own personal journey through moral philosophy, I'd mark that conversation, late at night on the front stoop of our first jointly rented house in Los Angeles, as the point of origin.

Having no better idea of what to do, I started reading articles and sections of books on ethics. I cold-called philosophy professors, many of whom were kind enough to talk it through with me. (Philosophers, it turns out, *really* enjoy talking about philosophy.) I might have wanted a definitive take on whether what I was doing was ethical, but as these things usually go in philosophy, the people I consulted gave me a wide range of answers. Publicly decrying this man's behavior might be *good*, because it could call attention to more important matters and effect change. No: publicly decrying his behavior was *bad*, because it was unfair to force him to choose between something rightfully owed to him and a societal good that has nothing to do with the accident. One professor scoffed at the idea that this was even a moral question—he just said I was being kind of a jerk to the guy, and you don't need moral philosophy to tell you not to be a jerk. Fair enough.

Though these conversations led to contradictory conclusions, they also helped me see that there was an actual philosophical explanation for why we felt queasy: I was *shaming* this guy. Naming what was problematic about my actions both provided some relief and caused some new pain. It was like sensing that something is wrong in your abdomen, and then having a doctor tell you your appendix has burst—a real good news (you were right!) bad news (go to the hospital!) situation. The moral repercussions were complicated and hard to parse. But generally speaking: J.J. *did* bump into him, and although $836 is a crazy amount of money to replace a fender, he didn't set that price, so he hadn't really done anything wrong. Whatever nuances and shadings and complexities needed to be teased out, I clung to that as a baseline to guide myself: shaming someone when he did nothing wrong (or, at least, shaming him to a degree far out of proportion with his action) felt like a bad thing to do.

So ultimately, I bit the bullet and called the guy. I told him everything that had happened, copped to my mistakes, and apologized. I also let him know I had already cut him a check, which was en route. He was pleasant and forgiving, and said he might give some of the money to the Red Cross. Then I wrote a note to all of the people who had pledged money and asked them to donate anyway, because giving money to hurricane victims is a good thing to do. People generally (but not unanimously) felt like this was a happy outcome, and at the end of the saga, more than $27,000 went to Katrina victims.

But don't celebrate this utilitarian victory just yet. Much like those goofball teachers and their dumb marshmallow experiment, this has the distinct feeling of a good result from a bad action.

Fine, I Screwed Up. But What About All the Times *You* Screwed Up?!

Something I'd never pondered before my wife creased that guy's bumper was the difference between shame and guilt. In its most basic form, guilt is the internal feeling that we have done something wrong—it's our own icky, private sense of personal failure. Shame is humiliation for *who we are*, reflected back at us through other people judging us from the outside. (In a memorable scene from *Game of Thrones*, the diabolical character Cersei, after a lifetime of unpleasant medieval royalty–type actions, is forced to walk naked through the streets while people yell, "Shame! Shame!" at her. Thanks to her many private monologues, viewers know that she feels exactly zero *guilt* about her many transgressive actions, and after her literal walk of shame ends, she sets about destroying everyone who has wronged her.) I was shaming the Saab driver for what I saw as his misaligned value system—how can you possibly care about this crease on your bumper when New Orleans is drowning?! Then I invited everyone to shine a spotlight on him and judge him for his choice. What made J.J. and me feel icky was guilt stemming from our behavior (really, mostly *my* behavior)—the nagging internal feeling that we were doing something wrong, even if we couldn't put a name to what it was.

We can certainly imagine situations that call for shame to be deployed. A daily perusal of American newspapers reveals dozens of shame-worthy activities: corruption, rampant hypocrisy, using power for personal enrichment, dereliction of duty, racism and dishonesty.[2] We instinctively feel

---

2 I'm writing this the week of Senator Cruz's "I only flew to Cancún during this deadly winter storm to drop off my daughters and then I was just gonna fly right back the next morning—you know, as people do—and please ignore the large suitcase I packed, and also please ignore the group text that someone leaked where my wife was inviting people to the Ritz-Carlton in Cancún for a week; all of that is irrelevant; what is definitely true is that I always intended to just pop down to Cancún for one night to drop off my kids—it's

that shaming people for their misdeeds serves an important purpose: to make those bad people feel bad for the bad things they did, or at least to make *good* people realize that the people who did the bad things are bad. But in order for shame to work as a moral deterrent, there has to be a causal link between the thing they did and the shame we intend them to feel. In the case of the Saab bumper, there . . . wasn't. The creasing of his bumper had jack squat to do with Hurricane Katrina, except that the two events occurred at the same time. Is the destruction of a city more important than a crease on a bumper? Of course. No one in the world would disagree.[3,4] But the problem with what I did—well, *one* of the problems; there were several—is that it's simply not fair to launch that sort of random moral attack. There will almost *always* be something more important going on in the world than whatever it is two people are beefing about. Let's say we borrow fifty dollars from our sister and agree to pay it back in a week. If she comes back a week later and asks for her money, we could simply glance at the news, find an unfolding calamity, and say, "How dare you ask me for the money when children are starving in South Sudan!" Shaming someone for caring about Thing X when unrelated Thing Y is far more dire just doesn't hold water. The common modern-day term for this is "whataboutism."

Whataboutism is most commonly deployed as a defensive strategy. Someone is caught doing something bad—anything from an actual crime to saying something mildly offensive on the internet—and

---

really all their fault, if we're being honest—and then I had planned to fly right back to help my desperate constituents, which I will now do by loading bottled water into people's cars in front of a photographer. See? I'm helping!" scandal of 2021, which might be forgotten by the time this book comes out, but which is maybe the best example I have ever seen of the modern American Politician Shame-Demanding Cocktail.

3 Note from Todd: Weirdly, the Scottish philosopher David Hume would raise a question about it. He thought there was no such thing as an irrational desire, so that it wasn't irrational to value a hangnail removal more than the survival of the world.

4 Note from Mike: This is why everyone hates moral philosophy professors.

then instead of owning up to it, he says, "Well, what about [Way Worse Thing X]?!" or "What about that bad thing *you* did?!"[5] or "What about the fact that I also did [Good Thing Y]?" It's a way to throw sand in the eyes of the people making the charge, blinding them momentarily and giving the accused a chance to wriggle free. Nearly all whataboutisms are indefensible, because by definition they fail to address the moral shortcoming the bad actor has exhibited. Let's say Tim makes a misogynistic joke. His friend Joe calls him on it and says Tim should be ashamed of what he said. Then Tim responds, "Oh, like you're so perfect? You once stole an alpaca from a petting zoo!" Even if this is true, it has nothing to do with Tim's behavior. Tim is using a moral wrong committed by his accuser to insinuate that his accuser's charge has no merit or is compromised. Which is stupid. Two things can be true: Joe shouldn't have stolen that alpaca, and also Tim's comment was misogynistic. And most importantly, the fact that Joe once stole an alpaca does not mean he forfeits the ability to point out that Tim said something offensive.

Here's another varietal: In the aftermath of 9/11, a controversy arose over the proposal to build a mosque near the Ground Zero site in New York. A common refrain among those opposed was *We'll build a mosque at Ground Zero when they build a synagogue in Saudi Arabia!* Which leads one to ask: Why would the American people base *any* decision on what Saudi Arabia does, given their . . . let's call it "iffy" record on human rights? When it comes to religious liberty, shouldn't the U.S. be aiming *considerably higher* than Saudi Arabia? It was a flatly disingenuous argument, linking one country's actions to another's for no good reason. Any parent will surely recognize this strategy—we tell our kids to stop watching TV, and they fire back that Madison's parents let her watch TV fifteen hours a day! Well, we respond, Madison is a disaster, and her parents got so drunk at the school fundraiser that at the end of the night

---

5 You Latin nerds might think of this as *argumentum ad hominem*: attacking the person making the argument instead of the merits of the argument itself.

they had to be fireman-carried to an Uber. (We don't say this, really, though we want to—we just say, "You're not Madison, and we're not her parents.") "Somebody else did something bad, so *we* should be able to do something bad" is a flimsy moral argument.

When we screw up, deflecting attention onto a completely unrelated action utterly misses the point, which is: *that we screwed up.* Despite their fundamental differences, the philosophical theories we've discussed all agree—on like a "this is so obvious we shouldn't have to say it" level— that each of us is responsible for our own actions. They might differ on the moral accounting we do once we've decided to act, but none of them suggests that our actions should be judged based on *other people's actions* that have nothing to do with ours. It's plainly obvious, and yet here we are, in the year 2022, surrounded by people who try to get away with stuff because of other stuff that has nothing to do with their stuff. Which leads us all the way back to my own whataboutism—using a hurricane to shame a guy who just wanted his damn car fixed.

Anyone Want to Defend Me Here?

The concept of public shame has been around at least since biblical times—people would be fastened in pillories or stocks and ritually abused, screamed at, tickled,[6] whatever—to punish them for their sins and perhaps to vent some puritanical revenge energy. The stocks fell out of favor in the nineteenth century, but have come roaring back in a new form: the social media "dragging" (as the kids say) that comes roaring through our devices every day, when someone with even a modicum of fame does something offensive. Now, it should be noted that the people being dragged frequently deserve what's happening— the person in question has said or done something bad, has been

---

6 Yeah. Tickled. Weird, right?

exposed, and is now paying the price. There is public good here, without question—some awful people have been called to the mat for their awful behavior in a way they never could have been before. In my opinion, the modern system of radical exposure has done more good than harm. But there's a larger question here, which is whether shame is a productive way to achieve an ethical outcome. For one thing, when people are shamed, they may not want to change their behavior—often, their defenses go up and they dig in their heels, which can have the opposite effect that we want it to have.[7] What we want, ostensibly, is for them to not only suffer consequences for what they've done, but also *change* their behavior going forward. That's hard for people to decide to do when they're reeling backward and getting publicly pummeled like a speed bag.

I had, in the early stages of my crusade, made a few good decisions—I didn't publicly name the Saab owner, or publish a photo of his license plate. I remember thinking clearly that we shouldn't do those things—maybe the little voice in my head managed to eke out those small victories. (It's impossible to know what the guy would have felt if we *had* done that, but I imagine it would've been a cocktail of anger and shame, and I sure don't think that would've helped.) But I made several terrible decisions too. So let's conduct a little debrief on the Fender Fiasco (or Saab Story?) through the lens of our three ethical schools of thought.

If I'm looking for a philosophical defense, my best bet is through consequentialism. After all, I turned a minor fender bender into a massive redistribution of wealth to people in tremendous need—whatever sadness I caused the guy by shaming him, the increase in happiness I

---

7 We're obviously drifting into psychology here, but there's some cool research into a phenomenon called the "backfire effect," which shows that when people are confronted with information that contradicts their core beliefs, even if the evidence is both demonstrably factual and overwhelming, they're much more likely to double down on their original beliefs than they are to accept the new ones. The human instinct to avoid shame is very powerful.

created through pledged donations more than made up for it. However, the consequentialist would also have to include in her tally the societal damage of my actions: everyone now has to live in a world where every minor transaction could result in a public referendum on the importance of that transaction. That doesn't seem like a generally happy society. Remember Steve, the ESPN transformer fixer? When we were trying to recalculate and add the extra pain caused by everyone now living in a world where they knew the same thing could happen to them, we figured it wouldn't be *that much* pain, really, because most people would know they'd never be in Steve's position, so they wouldn't really fear such a world. That's not the case here. Most people would realize that they *will* at some point find themselves in a situation where a minor dispute could become garbled and derailed due to some other, larger issue—*everyone* has minor disputes with other people, and there are *always* bigger problems unfolding somewhere else. This utilitarian "recalculation" isn't nearly as hard to execute—we have to add a ton of dolors to the total.

And how would a Kantian be disappointed in me? Let us count the ways. I'm pretty sure that "we should force people involved in minor traffic incidents to weigh the relative importance of their car repair against the needs created by national catastrophes before receiving restitution" violates the categorical imperative. Could we will that rule into existence, to be used by everyone all the time? No. That way madness lies. But the Kantian doesn't stop there. She also certainly says I violated the second formulation of the imperative, because I used the guy as a means to any number of ends: helping people who had nothing to do with the accident . . . mollifying my own anger at the treatment of New Orleans hurricane victims . . . making a statement about the absurdities of Los Angeles auto insurance. I mean, if you're a Kantian and you want to find a way to criticize my behavior, the world's your oyster. (I don't even want to think about how a contractualist would react to what I did. T. M. Scanlon would be so disappointed in me if he ever heard this story. No one tell him.)

Aristotle might applaud me—in like a quiet, golf-clap sort of way—for the *aftermath* of my initial decision, the part where I felt guilt over what I'd done. A person who's *deficient* in guilt may never change his behavior, becoming callous to the effects of his actions. A person who feels *excessive* guilt might develop low self-esteem or become a recluse out of a fear of harming others. Somewhere in the middle would be the mean—let's call it "self-awareness." So . . . good work, Mike, on the aftermath, in which a healthy dose of guilt pulled me away from my deficiency and back toward that mean. But what about the shame that I made the other guy feel for *his* actions? Will Aristotle applaud me for that too? Hopefully?

No. No he will not.

Again, there may be some amount of shame we should make other people feel when they do something bad. Shame has a function in a healthy world, because it gives us a weapon in the war against bad behavior. If people were incapable of feeling shame, they would do whatever they wanted to with impunity, never worrying that their reputations might suffer in the public square. The act of lightly shaming our fellow citizens for unvirtuous actions or beliefs may therefore be okay; this isn't guesswork on my part—Aristotle actually says that while shame is not a virtue, per se:

> The person excessively prone to shame, who is ashamed about everything—is called excessive; the person who is deficient in shame or never feels shame at all is said to have no sense of disgrace.

But remember how we described Aristotle's approach to mildness—the golden mean represents an *appropriate* amount of anger, directed only at *people who deserve it*. That's the key to my own blunder regarding the Saab guy. He didn't *deserve* the tornado of shame I whipped up and sent at him. I might take issue with how much he cared about his car, but by bringing Hurricane Katrina into the equation—an entirely asymmetrical and unrelated disaster with massive human pain and suffering attached to it—I obliterated the calculation he and I were trying to make over how to handle the minor accident. It was a massively unfair act, which explains my sudden feeling of guilt when it exploded into the public sphere. Were he around to witness all of this, I think Aristotle would've said: "Dude. You *super* blew this."[8]

If there's some amount of guilt that might help us or shame that could be helpful to other people, I'd wager that the amount of guilt that can be helpful is far higher than the shame. Guilt comes from reckoning with ourselves, and we're probably more likely to pay attention (and react well) to our own little voices, rather than other people's. Sometimes I wonder what would've happened if instead of concluding on our own that we were screwing this up, J.J. and I had been yelled at by someone else for what we were doing—if *we'd* been shamed for the act of shaming someone. (A meta-shaming!) Would we have responded calmly and re-examined our behavior? Or would we have dug in our heels and fought back, highlighting the money going to charity and the absurdity of an $836 bumper crease? If we'd been called out and our defense mechanisms had kicked in, I might be writing a very different book right now, called something like *How to Be the Ultimate Judge of Everyone Else's Actions with #NoRegrets*.

The problem, of course, is that we can't always count on our little voices to create the feeling of guilt that made J.J. and me course-correct so dramatically—especially when the thing that's happening is nuanced and complicated and messy. Looking back, I think that what helped us the most wasn't anything philosophical or theoretical. J.J. and I realized we were screwing up because we were *talking about it*. The simple act of speaking out loud about what we were doing led us to conclude that

---

8 It helps me to understand philosophy if I imagine the philosophers talking like my friends.

what we were doing was problematic.[9] At the time, of course, we had no real understanding of moral accounting—at the risk of sounding like a bad rom-com movie trailer: we only had each other.[10] When we're trying to become better people, we should remember how powerful the simple act of conversation can be, to help us navigate these choppy waters.

Revisiting the incident, I also better understand the true power of Julia Annas's quote: "The result [of practicing something] is a speed and directness of response comparable to that of mere habit, but unlike it in that the lessons learned have informed it and rendered it flexible and innovative." Now we get it, right? I blundered into a situation I did not understand, thanks to a combination of not having ever studied philosophy before and how straight-up weird the situation was. In a flash, we were wrestling with issues of legal ethics, car insurance rates, duty, responsibility, hurricanes, shame, guilt, and the economics of fender repair in late-model Saab sedans. Who could possibly know exactly what to do in that moment? Well . . . maybe someone who is so practiced at various virtues that she can approach new and thorny situations calmly and knowledgeably. J.J. and I might have saved ourselves a lot of guilt—and spared others a lot of shame—if we'd already put in the time toward cultivating virtue, to the point where we were flexible and innovative. (Or maybe we still would've blown it. But we would've had a better shot at getting it right.)

At the end of the day, that fender bender did a lot of good. For one thing, it kicked off my personal interest in moral philosophy. It raised

---

9 This is essentially what therapy is, and it's why I highly recommend therapy to anyone who can afford it.

10 Pamela Hieronymi related an anecdote about J. S. Mill, who attributed his ability to rebound from depression not solely to reading Romantic poetry but also to the love of his life, Harriet Taylor. When they met she was married with two children, but they developed a close friendship, and twenty years later Harriet's husband passed away. She and Mill were married soon after, and Mill credited her with influencing and improving his writing (she was a writer as well). I guess what I'm saying is, J.J. and I are like the Harriet Taylor and J. S. Mill of our time. Except, obviously, our contributions to philosophy will be far more important.

a bunch of money for charity, which the utilitarians among us will applaud. It forced me to reckon with my own actions and apologize, a thing I think we should all do a lot more often. (More on this in chapter 13.) I remember thinking that my life had in some big, messy way . . . *improved.* I was a better person on the other side of the whole thing.

That's a good feeling—that we're a little better today than we were yesterday. It buoys us, sends us about our day with a smile and a little wind in our sails. So what if, feeling those lovely feelings, we decide to go knock off some errands we've been ignoring, head to the grocery store, and after returning a few stray carts in the parking lot to the rack on our way in (that's right, that's how good we are now—we're returning *other people's carts*), we see a plate of free cheese samples with a sign that says LIMIT ONE PER CUSTOMER. And man oh man, if it isn't smoked gouda—our favorite cheese. So even though it clearly says LIMIT ONE PER CUSTOMER, a thought occurs to us:

"I'm a good person. There's a higher balance in my moral bank account than there was just a week ago. I've *earned* the right to break this little rule. I'm gonna take *three* pieces of smoked gouda from this tray, instead of one."

That's okay, right?

We've Done Some Good Deeds, and Given a Bunch of Money to Charity, and We're Generally Really Nice and Morally Upstanding People, So Can We Take Three of These Free Cheese Samples from the Free Cheese Sample Plate at the Supermarket Even Though It Clearly Says "One Per Customer"?

My dad used to have a theory. After my parents divorced, he got really into live music (as forty-year-old bachelors are wont to do) and started amassing an enormous CD collection. He would buy two to four CDs, two to four times per week. He wasn't exactly rich, and when I would comment on how much money he was spending on music he would say something like: "Think about it this way: I don't like the band U2. They have like ten albums. I'm not going to buy *any* of their albums—which means I've *saved* a hundred and fifty bucks, so the next hundred and fifty I spend on other CDs is essentially free!"

Now, he was kidding, obviously, but it always stuck with me as a fun financial loophole: imagining that we have some kind of "reserve" of money built up, resulting from things we *didn't* buy, which we can then spend without consequences.[1] Some people hold a related view of moral respon-

---

1 This silly example is only slightly kookier than the actual practices of corporate financial accounting—which is among the least ethical arenas in our culture. Some compa-

sibility. They believe that doing a bunch of good stuff gives them a kind of bank account balance of moral currency, which they can then withdraw and "spend" if they want to do something . . . not so great. Essentially: "I know I shouldn't eat hamburgers because the beef industry is destroying the environment. But, whatever, I drive an electric car. Fire up the grill!"

Our lives are filled with thousands of rules—in school, at work, in traffic, in society, at home—and at times, for one reason or another, we feel we're allowed to break one. Maybe we think the rule is dumb or outdated, or maybe we think of ourselves as good people whose other good deeds have earned us a free pass. No one—not even excessively rule-following dorks like me—follows *every* rule. It's impossible. But if we're trying to be good people, we should know how to deal with the moments when we actively choose not to be.

Moral Exhaustion:
The Most Important Term You'll Learn from This Book

Thinking that our past good deeds give us an excuse to occasionally break rules (or make choices that contradict our general moral worldviews) is an understandable position. I often *hold* that position, and again, I'm a hard-core rules nerd. Recently, I realized I didn't really know anything about the bank I use for my checking account. Out of curiosity, I poked around and read about the founders, the current CEO, and various board members. My shocking conclusion: they're monsters. (At least, to me they are.) Their sociopolitical positions are callous and borderline cruel. They've donated millions of dollars to politicians and causes I find re-

---

nies, for example, use what's called "mark-to-market" accounting, in which they can project future income or asset valuations as if they are certain and not hypothetical, in order to inflate their stock price. If you're wondering how that usually works out, do a quick internet search for "Enron."

pugnant. In some cases, they actively funded the people responsible for the seditious insurrection at the Capitol on January 6, 2021. They have publicly said things that if my children ever say will lead to extremely unpleasant Thanksgiving dinners. Well, okay, I thought, time to shift my checking account to some other bank.

Then the reality of what that would mean began to sink in.

First of all: *Every* multinational bank is full of (in my eyes) monsters. A quick round of research about the equivalent people at other banks revealed that these dudes (and they're basically all dudes) are essentially interchangeable. Was I really going to find an American bank CEO who sides with me on the need for campaign finance reform? Also, there is no reasonable alternative to keeping one's money in a bank. We're not really living in a "hole in a mattress" world anymore. Plus: Moving my checking account would be *annoying.* I have checks, and auto-withdrawals for monthly bills, and an ATM card, and the whole deal. Picking it all up and relocating it and transferring everything *sounds so hard and irritating,* and it makes me sleepy.

So . . . maybe I just leave my checking account where it is? I mean, I'm generally a good dude. Can I just . . . let this one go?

Here we're confronting a condition I think of as Moral Exhaustion.[2,3] Trying to do the right thing all the time is—and I'm going to use a fairly wonky, technical philosophy term here, so bear with me—*a huge pain in the ass.* Every day we are confronted with dozens of moral and ethical

---

2 Okay. So. I am capitalizing "Moral Exhaustion" because I really hope it becomes a thing people attribute to me. All the great philosophers have cool-sounding terms they're credited with—Kant's categorical imperative, Aristotle's golden mean, etc. I figure this is my only shot to get my own cool, pithy, philosophical idea out there into the world. Let's make this happen, people!

3 And then Todd immediately brings up the fact that there is already something called "compassion fatigue," which according to the American Psychological Association "occurs when psychologists or others take on the suffering of patients who have experienced extreme stress or trauma," and "can result in depression and anxiety." To that I say, "Todd, please just let me have this."

decisions—which products to buy or use, which political candidates to support, how to simply exist in and move about the earth—and some options are certainly better than others. There's an environmentally "best" toothpaste we should buy, an "ideal" length of time we should leave the water running when we shower, a "most ethical" car to drive, and a "better" option than driving at all. There's a "most responsible" way to shop for groceries, a "worst" social media company we definitely shouldn't use, a "most reprehensible" pro sports franchise owner we shouldn't support, and a "most labor-friendly" clothing company we should. There are expensive solar panels we *should* put on our roofs, low-flow toilets we *should* install, and media outlets we *shouldn't* patronize because they stiff their journalists.

What makes it doubly exhausting is that we also—and again, sorry for the overly academic terminology—have our own crap to deal with. Family logistics, romantic entanglements, school meetings, secrets we should or shouldn't keep from our friends, cars that need to be fixed, toasters that need to be fixed, door hinges that need to be fixed—why does everything break all the time?!—and so on, to infinity. And that's if things are going *well!* We'll also at some point face far more serious problems: illnesses, job losses, family crises, toasters we didn't fix that malfunction and start fires—*there is so much going on, all the time.* Those daily annoyances, and larger, more serious problems, make the work of being alive incredibly difficult even for the luckiest among us, to say nothing of those in poverty or other distress. So if we want to be good, by the time we deal with all the crap we *have* to deal with and finally decide to try to achieve that goal, our internal battery is at about 5 percent. (Oh, that's another thing we have to deal with—the batteries in literally every device we use are always about to run out.[4]) Now add to this cocktail of stress the fact that very often, doing

---

4 I was recently awoken at 3:00 a.m. by a smoke alarm "Battery low!" beeping alert and I just ripped it off the wall and threw it in the trash can and even if my house someday burns down because of that decision I will still feel like it was the right move.

the "right" thing is harder and requires more intestinal fortitude (and money!) than doing the lazier/worse thing. And the capper—the rotten cherry on top of this turd sundae—is that, as we saw in the introduction, even if we scale the triple-peaked mountain of Daily Stress, Serious Problems, and Circumstance, and (running on 5 percent battery power) try our very best to do the harder/better thing, *we often fail miserably* despite our best intentions.

It. Is. Exhausting.

So . . . *not* doing the "right" thing once in a while feels like a little present we can give ourselves, saving us the time and effort we know it would require to research and act and change and improve. It might also feel like a luxury we've *earned* through other good actions. Should we continue to use Facebook, even though we know about the horrifying spread of misinformation it facilitates? No, we probably shouldn't. But dammit, it's a nice way to keep up with our family—and we just gave a hundred bucks to a friend's 5K Irritable Bowel Syndrome Run for the Cure, so give us a break, man. We're good people!

And then there are other situations where we're tempted to break the rules because *the rules stink*. Two years ago, my family adopted a very sweet, very sickly stray dog we named Henry. Henry is an adorable twenty-pound mutt, who's loving and affectionate despite his rough first year of life. After we adopted him and nursed him back to health, we began taking him on walks around our neighborhood and discovered that being on a leash turns him into a *monster*. He barks, he snarls, he growls, he wrenches out of his harness—it's bananas. Off a leash? Delightful dream pup. On a leash? The predator, from *Predator*.[5]

---

5 Some of you, right now, are thinking, "Oh yes, 'leash aggression,' he should try *this*," or, "I know a woman who can cure Henry by doing *that*," and I politely invite you to save it. We tried everything. Trainers, therapy, a pet psychic—you read that correctly—and nothing worked. Henry is a lovable lost cause. Also, my daughter, Ivy, just found out I mention Henry in this book and not our other dog, Louisa, and she thinks that's unfair, so I am hereby extending this footnote in order to officially mention the existence of Louisa.

So, whenever one of us takes Henry on a walk, we have to make a choice: leash or no leash—which, in our neighborhood, would be against the rules. I, being the Rules Dork, always press for "leash." But I also have to admit: following the rule makes us miserable. It makes everyone else miserable. It makes Henry miserable. It scares children. And given all that . . . shouldn't we break the rule?

Two cases of potential rule-breaking. In the first, we have a sort of fun-house mirror reflection of moral desert—instead of doing something good and feeling like we ought to be rewarded, we feel like we *can* do something *bad*, because of other good things *we've already done*. There's no real logical or ethical basis for thinking this way, but it's tempting—because again, life is hard, and maybe we deserve a hiatus from moral calculations once in a while. In the second case, we're staring at a rule we know to be silly, or wrong, or harmful, so we reasonably feel like we should ignore it. Yet even as we're tempted to dismiss a rule for either of these reasons, we can feel the cold, unforgiving stare of Immanuel Kant boring a hole through the backs of our skulls. Rules are rules, he says, in his characteristically flat, emotionless German.[6] If something is wrong, it's wrong. If everyone could pick and choose her own rules to follow, the world would be lawless! *Keine Ausreden!*[7]

Moral Jaywalking

I'll risk the back of my head and disagree with Kant here, because of what I think of as the Hot Day Jaywalking rule. Let's say we need to cross the street to get to a store on the other side. The crosswalk is a block south of us. It's 103 degrees, and we just drove here in a car whose interior

---

6 I have no idea what his voice sounded like. But I bet it was flat and emotionless.
7 According to Google Translate, that means "No excuses," which I assume is engraved on Kant's tombstone.

was 200 degrees, and there's no traffic . . . so we jaywalk. It's technically a crime, but it's *barely* a crime, and utterly understandable, and it saves us some misery. Would Kant let us do it? No. Categorical imperative, universal maxim, blah blah blah. But you know what? Shut up, Kant. *It's so hot out here* and we just need to pop into CVS to pick up a prescription, it'll take two seconds, and we're sweating buckets, and *shut up*. We're not perfect. Sue us. In moments of exhaustion, when the act we'd be committing is so infinitesimally "bad" it barely even registers as "bad" (or it's only "bad" in a fuzzy, complex way), I think it's okay to break those small rules.

Maybe this sounds self-serving. Maybe I want to make an argument for moral jaywalking (under the right circumstances) just to create a reasonable defense for my decision to walk my Jekyll-and-Hyde dog without a leash, or to not switch banks (which, again, *how annoying does that sound?*). But I don't think it is self-serving. For one thing, as we learned from Susan Wolf's "Moral Saints," and from the case of that annoying guy who allowed his dutifulness to run amok (me), following *every* rule *all the time* in *all scenarios* isn't necessarily good. In fact, the political scientist James C. Scott actually thinks breaking a rule every once in a while is morally necessary:

> One day you will be called upon to break a big law in the name of justice and rationality. Everything will depend on it. . . . How are you going to prepare for that day when it really matters? You have to stay "in shape" so that when the big day comes you will be ready. What you need is "anarchist calisthenics." Every day or so break some trivial law that makes no sense, even if it's only jaywalking. Use your own head to judge whether a law is just or reasonable. That way, you'll keep trim; and when the big day comes, you'll be ready.

For Scott, these small transgressions build up our ethical muscles and prepare us for more important moral exercise. But I also think that some rules are coarse and ineffective ways of achieving a result, like "All dogs must be on leashes" or "Pedestrians can never jaywalk." And I further think that if we're trying to be good people, given how exhausting life on earth can be, taking a little respite from our Moral Exhaustion is okay (and maybe even necessary) just so we don't lose our minds. I say we allow ourselves these moments of rule-breaking, on two conditions:

First: that the rules we violate are not obviously harmful to other people. Let's say you love animals. You give money to the ASPCA, and you once pulled your car over to help a turtle that had wandered out into the road. (That's right. That was you, in that example from earlier. That's how much you love animals.) You're also a huge proponent of adopting pets from shelters instead of buying them from breeders. Then one day a friend tells you she bought a little yellow Lab puppy named Walnut from a breeder, but is now moving and can't keep it. Yes, adopting Walnut would technically violate your own rule to support adoptions from shelters, but there's a compelling counterargument, which is *look at Walnut's ears they're so floppy!* Let yourself off the hook. Take Walnut home. Jaywalking doesn't negate your entire project of being a good person on earth, and taking Walnut home doesn't undo the years of work you've put into the cause of promoting shelters. However, if the rule you want to violate is, say, "Don't flee the scene of an accident," or "Don't start a war in the Middle East under false pretenses," there is no "good deed" bank account with a high enough balance to excuse your behavior.

Second: we need to acknowledge that what we're doing is not ideal. The minimal harm we generate from this small bad action could be compounded if we pretend we're not doing it, because that might alter the way we think of ourselves, and eventually even change what kind of people we are.

There's a concept in public policy called the Overton window, named after its inventor, Joseph Overton-Window.[8] An Overton window describes the range of "acceptability" a political idea has at any given time. Some ideas—say, same-sex marriage—begin as extremely unlikely, or

---

8 Just kidding, it's Joseph Overton.

even unthinkable. Over time, various factors emerge in the culture—
more acceptance of LGBTQ+ people generally, more gay characters on
popular TV shows—and the window shifts a little, making same-sex
marriage more politically possible. As cultural norms continue to evolve
(younger politicians take office, proponents engage in effective activism,
people realize that we all have at least one LGBTQ+ person in our social
circle), the Overton window shifts with them, until finally the range of
possibility described by the window includes same-sex marriage actually
being recognized as the law of the land. Something once unthinkable
becomes possible, and then eventually it becomes reality.

Regarding our little transgressions, we see the potential problem,
right? Overton windows can represent any kind of range, including what
we consider acceptable behavior for ourselves. So, we know jaywalking
is wrong, but we do it anyway . . . and then we've become "people who
occasionally jaywalk." No big deal. But once that's true, it's a short journey to becoming "people who *always* jaywalk." Then one day we can't
find a garbage can, and we think, "I mean, tossing a gum wrapper on
the ground isn't *that much* worse than jaywalking," so we do that . . . and
soon we're littering all the time, and since littering is now acceptable we
start parking illegally, which shifts our window to allow for stiffing con-
tractors out of payment, and once we do that it's a hop, skip, and a jump
to cheating on our taxes, and then embezzling money, and cheating on
our spouses, and smuggling endangered rhinos out of India, and selling
black market weapons to international terrorists.

Now. Is this *likely?* Of course not. That's a deliberately absurd "what
if," like one of those cops in a 1980s PSA warning kids that if they smoke
a single cigarette they're on a fast track to heroin addiction. But there's
a serious point here: the shifting of an Overton window often happens
gradually, and we readjust to its new range very quickly,[9] so there is risk in

---

9 When I was writing on *The Office*, the showrunner (and my mentor), Greg Daniels,
would warn us against jokes that made Michael Scott too cartoonishly stupid. He would
cite *The Simpsons*, which he'd written for, saying that in the early days of the show the

allowing ourselves to do *anything* we know is bad just because we want to. In fact, even with good intentions and level heads, if we give in to our lesser instincts too often there's a far more likely outcome than "we become black market weapons dealers." It's simply that we become *selfish*. We start to believe that our own "right" to do whatever we want, whenever we want to do it, is more important than anything else, and thus our sense of morality concerns only our *own* happiness or pain. We become . . . Ayn Rand.

Bad Writer, Worse Philosopher

Rand (1905–1982) was a novelist and philosopher who offered her readers the deal of a lifetime. Developing a nineteenth-century idea called "rational egoism" or "rational selfishness," she suggested that the true path to moral and societal progress involves people caring only about their own happiness. She called her theory "objectivism," and it's basically the exact opposite of utilitarianism—instead of trying to maximize pleasure and minimize pain for *everyone*, we do it *only for ourselves*. Or as she wrote in the afterword to *Atlas Shrugged*:

> My philosophy, in essence, is the concept of man as a heroic being, with his own happiness as the moral purpose of his life,

---

staff would write a "stupid guy" joke for Homer that stretched the amount of stupid he was, hesitate, then decide to put it in an episode. Later they'd pitch another joke that made him even stupider, and they'd think . . . , "Well, I mean, he *did* say that other stupid thing last week, and this isn't *that* much stupider." In a matter of a couple of seasons, Homer went from a kind of doofy dad to a guy so dumb he once got his arms stuck in two separate vending machines at the same time. Now, that show is a cartoon (which makes it more palatable to have characters who are . . . cartoonish), and Homer's rock-headedness is one of its greatest contributions to comedy, but Greg's point was that even something as unimportant as the Overton window for TV characters' personality traits needs to be watched very closely, or things can spiral out of control.

with productive achievement as his noblest activity, and reason as his only absolute.

This is an amazing philosophy. And not in a good way. If our own happiness is the moral purpose of our lives, that means we're obligated to maximize it at the expense of everything else, including, and especially, *other people's* happiness. In Ayn Rand's world, there could be a thousand Steves trapped behind that ESPN generator, and I could be *the only one* watching the World Cup on TV, and I'd *still* decide to let them all fry because *I* am happy and *they* are merely potential hindrances to my happiness. It's bananas. Here's my favorite quote of hers, wherein she takes a brave stance against "being nice":

> Do not confuse altruism with kindness, good will or respect for the rights of others. . . . The irreducible primary of altruism, the basic absolute, is *self-sacrifice*—which means self-immolation, self-abnegation, self-denial, self-destruction—which means the *self* as a standard of evil, the *selfless* as a standard of the good. Do not hide behind such superficialities as whether you should or should not give a dime to a beggar. That is not the issue. The issue is whether you *do* or do *not* have the right to exist *without* giving him that dime. The issue is whether you must keep buying your life, dime by dime, from any beggar who might choose to approach you. . . . Any man of self-esteem will answer: *No.* Altruism says: *Yes.*

Or, to put it another way: "Fuck all y'all."

It's frankly dispiriting that a woman who advocated radical selfishness and utter disdain for everyone but oneself wasn't booed off the world stage, but even today Rand has plenty of adherents, especially among those who call themselves libertarians. (There are more than a few Randites in the U.S. Congress—former Speaker of the House Paul Ryan says he asked all of his staffers to read her books, a request which, based on their length and unreadability, may have violated the Geneva

Conventions.) I suppose at some level, this shouldn't be surprising. She is basically telling her readers that the only thing they need to do to be morally pure is greedily protect their own interests. A diet book that claimed you could lose weight by eating pecan pie and drinking Mountain Dew Code Red would definitely sell a few copies. The appeal of her theories to those interested in achieving and maintaining power is certainly more likely to explain her enduring place than is her actual talent—Rand's novels are endless monstrosities, written in turgid prose that doubles as an effective pre-op anesthetic. As one noted academic put it, "There are only two problems with Ayn Rand: she can't think and she can't write."[10]

The most cursory glance at any of our previously discussed moral theories sends objectivism careening toward the flaming garbage can of history. It's the flat opposite of utilitarianism, so . . . it fails there. I can't imagine Immanuel Kant struggling through 1,172 pages of *Atlas Shrugged*[11] and declaring infinite selfishness a solid universal maxim. T. M. Scanlon seems like a pretty calm and thoughtful person, but it's not hard to imagine him reading Ayn Rand and putting his fist through a wall. And an Aristotelian in search of a golden mean would bristle at a theory that tells the very concept of a golden mean to go jump in a lake. Nonetheless, we live in a world where "Be as selfish as you can!" is somehow a mainstream moral theory. It's out there, floating around, telling us we can do whatever we want, ignore the value of others' lives, treat everyone else as a means to our own end, decide *we owe nothing to anyone*.[12] Our little moral transgressions, harmless though they might be, shift our Overton windows ever so slightly toward a world where Ayn Rand's goofy "rational selfishness" becomes slightly more plausible. The

---

10 It was Todd.

11 I read the first 220 or so, to try to understand her theories better, and then gave up. I'd rather read Kant's treatise on wind.

12 I'm almost obligated to point out that at the end of her life, Rand, the self-appointed queen of individualism and unfettered capitalism, applied for and began to collect both Medicare and social security benefits.

solution, however, is simple: we commit to those regular "check-ins"—to simply note, when we morally jaywalk, *that we're doing it*. Make the "good deed" bank account withdrawal, but pin the receipt up on our cubicle wall as a reminder.

The Free-Riding Ninja: A Case Study

Thinking about the long-term effects of moral calculations we make in small, relatively unimportant moments calls to mind another of philosophy's most famous thought experiments: the Free Rider Problem. Imagine a trolley car[13] absolutely jam-packed with people. Parents and strollers, cyclists with their bicycles, old couples with a million grocery bags—just a sweaty, soupy reservoir of BO and rush-hour misery. Each one of these commuters has paid the required fee to ride the trolley, and miraculously, today, the number of paying passengers is the exact limit of the trolley's capacity. (It's amazing how things like that seem to happen, in philosophical thought experiments.) As the trolley starts to move, a woman named Deb comes running up and jumps onto the outside of the trolley, hanging on to a pole and snagging a free ride. She didn't pay her fare, but she's also not taking up any space that could be used by someone who did. Is she doing anything wrong?

Instinctively, we think: Of course she is. The Kantian whip-crackers immediately point and jump up and down and angrily shout at us in German,[14] since Deb is clearly violating the categorical imperative—she could certainly not will that her action become a universal law. If everyone did what she did (wait until the trolleys are packed and then grab

---

13 Ostensibly, a different trolley car than the one with failed brakes that killed all those construction workers.

14 Todd suggests that they wouldn't shout, but rather "mutter," because "they're not angry; they're disappointed." Whether it's funnier to imagine a German deontologist *shouting* or *muttering* I will leave as an exercise for the reader. (This is the kind of "exercise for the reader" I can get behind.)

a free ride without paying) the entire commuter system would break down, because no one would pay, because they'd all be aiming to snag a free ride. Pretty clearly "wrong," when you approach it from Kant's perspective. But then again, most things are wrong when you approach them from Kant's perspective. People being wrong was Kant's kink.

But . . . no one on the trolley was really inconvenienced—they all got to their destinations in the same amount of time they would've if Deb had *not* hitched her free ride. Which means that from a utilitarian point of view, this kind of worked out—Deb's sneaky maneuver increased the amount of total happiness in the world (more people got to their destinations), without any additional pain. Of course, the smoldering looks of fury directed at Deb from the paying passengers force us to recalculate here—their combined anger might overwhelm the pleasure of Deb snagging a free trip. So: Let's now imagine that Deb is actually *hidden from their view*. Maybe she scrambled up the side of the trolley car lightning-fast and is lying flat on the roof, unseen by anyone. (Deb is a ninja, it turns out. Just go with it.)

The question now becomes: If no one sees Deb the Ninja commit this small act of rule-breaking, so they were neither inconvenienced by it nor made to feel any anger about having to live in a world where ninjas get free rides while everyone else has to pay, *now* what do we think of this action? Good? Bad? We could keep modifying the original act and chewing on the implications forever; like the Trolley Problem, the Free Rider Problem has millions of versions, and maybe even more real-life applications—once you know it, you see it everywhere. The ethics of not taking a vaccine and thus relying on those who *did* for personal safety . . . cheating on your taxes but still using public resources . . . using too much water on your lawn in a drought-ridden city . . . not voting but still complaining about government—these are all Free Rider varietals. But in the name of preventing Overton window shifts and descents into Ayn Rand fever dreams of our worst and most selfish instincts, let's approach this inside out instead of outside in: let's ask what *Deb* thinks about what she did. No one else even knows she did it, thanks to her parkour abilities and ninja stealth, so the only one doing any ruminating on Deb's free ride is Deb herself. Is *she* fine with it? Thinking about Deb's own guilt, or lack thereof, might help us better pinpoint how we feel about making withdrawals from our moral bank accounts.

Deb's feelings about her own action probably depend on a lot of Deb-specific things. Maybe there's context we don't know about. Maybe Deb the Free-Riding Ninja just fought off a group of thugs who were robbing an old man, and then she had to get downtown to meet her sick dad and bring him soup, and her ninja outfit has no pockets for trolley fare, and she thought to herself, "I just did a super-good thing, and I'm not hurting anyone here, so I'm just gonna grab a free ride." In that case, she's probably acknowledging that this isn't an *ideal* way to behave, but then letting herself off the hook. Under similar circumstances in the future, she'll pay for her ride like everyone else. The Overton window describing her own moral range probably won't move very much, if at all.

Or maybe Deb is a bad ninja, not a good one. She walks around all day using her ninja reflexes to steal lollipops from children, and when she saw an opportunity to score a free ride she (literally) leaped at it. In that case, Deb might be on a more slippery slope. Her Overton window might have just shifted; before, her worst actions were petty candy-related crimes, but now she's a person who doesn't pay for subway rides and feels no remorse. Deb's absence of guilt may put her on a metaphorical ride to Selfishtown.

Again, part of the project of this book is to help us accept failure—because, again, failure is the inevitable result of caring about morality and trying to be good people. I really don't mean to argue for perfect living, or moral sainthood, or anything close to that, because (a) it's impossible, and (b) I don't even think it's a good goal. Instead, I'm arguing that when we do fail, in matters great or small, we just take a second to acknowledge our failure to ourselves, and try to remember that feeling the next time we have a decision to make. That's why it's instructive to focus on something as small as jaywalking or hitching a free ride on a trolley. Deb's actions may have been more justifiable than we thought, or less. They may be noticed by other people or go completely unseen. But whatever the case, we can only hope that the little voice in Deb's head chirps loudly enough to keep her from making this a habit, or at least to warn her that she's been doing stuff like this a lot recently and ought to knock it off.

Small Sacrifice, Huge Reward

It's not always easy to know the difference between harmlessly breaking rules and sending ourselves down a slippery Overton window–shifting path. Plenty of great TV shows and movies involve people making tiny bad decisions and then spending the rest of their lives making more and more of them to try to make up for the first one, eventually becoming irredeemable monsters. It's unlikely any of us will, say, decide to start cooking crystal meth like Walter White in *Breaking Bad* and one day find ourselves running a New Mexican drug empire. But if guilt is how we police ourselves, we need to allow ourselves to feel that guilt, and we need to listen to our guilty consciences when they give us pause. That's one of the biggest hindrances to making use of our individual guidance systems—too many of us just don't pin those slightly damning receipts up on our cubicle walls so they can remind us of these little bad things we've done. Again, I can't help but think about the Covid-19 "mask problem." The people who've refused to join the team here—the ones who decided that they simply didn't have to (or want to) follow this new rule—often get *extremely indignant* when store owners or workers ask them not to be "free riders" and go maskless while everyone else covers up. "How dare you," they say. "This is America! I can do what I want, because of liberty! The Constitution guarantees us Freedom of Face, and also Don't Tread on Me and George Washington and Bald Eagles!"[15] Thanks in part to this attitude (and in larger part to the craven media types and politicians who fostered it), we all watched helplessly as the

---

15 This is barely a parody. Their arguments were rarely more coherent than this Stars and Stripes–colored word salad.

virus ripped through the country in wave after wave. Even worse were the states where *authorities* decided not to require mask-wearing—either for similar ideological reasons, or because they feared the wrath of those who held that ideology, or both, or both plus ignorance and stupidity.

The widespread lack of guilt among mask resisters feels like a gut punch, to me. Because again, it's such a minuscule ask—wearing a mask falls roughly at the "don't jaywalk" level of individual sacrifice. Imagine we were in that Hot Day Jaywalking scenario from earlier—it's 103 degrees and the crosswalk is a block away, so we intend to just hustle across the street. Now imagine that someone said: "Hey, I know it's annoying, but if we all agree to head on down and use the crosswalk instead of jaywalking, we can save a hundred thousand people from dying in auto accidents." Imagine how easily we'd make that call! Okay, it's a little hot and a bit inconvenient . . . but 100,000 people? It'd be one of the simplest calculations we'd ever made. And yet here I sit, writing this book, watching the case count for the nation skyrocket because too many people think their own Ayn Randian right to unfettered selfishness outweighs the sum total of literally everyone else's happiness and safety.

It's one of the reasons Scanlon's *What We Owe to Each Other* struck such a chord with me—the title itself orients us, points us in a certain direction. He notably did not call his book *Do We Owe Things to Each Other?* He begins his journey with the point of view that we do, certainly, owe things to each other, and the goal is to find out what those things are. In a fractured national moment of stress and pain, of inequality and injustice, of ethical strain and Moral Exhaustion, we should go easy on ourselves at moments when we fail in our quest to become better people. But we cannot forget this simple truth: *we owe things to each other*. They may be small things, or simple things, but they're *there*, they're important, and we can't ignore them.

One final P.S.: After I completed the first draft of this book and sent it to my editor to look over, something started nagging at me. How hard would it be, *really*, to find a bank that made me feel better about where

I keep my money? I had written that all bank CEOs were monsters . . . but I had focused on maybe the five biggest banks, and realized I'd kind of phoned in the actual research. So I poked around, and found a few banks that (in my opinion) were better institutions than the one I'd been using. They don't invest in fossil fuels, they actively support charitable causes, they have codes of ethical conduct for their employees, and so on. "Well, crap," I thought. "Now I gotta switch."

So I did. And after all my complaining and griping about how hard it would be, and how annoying it would be, you know what? *It was exactly as annoying as I thought.* Maybe more. Paperwork, and confusing phone calls, and incorrect routing numbers, and new ATM cards, and the whole deal. It took months to get things up and running. I'm certainly glad I did it, but it's important not to sugarcoat how irritated I was at multiple points in the process. It served as a good reminder of two different things. One: the work of making better choices is frequently annoying. We just have to accept that. And two: *it can be done*—if we want to do it, and can summon the time and energy to make it happen.

We've talked about failure, and learning to accept it in our ethical lives, but we can now be a bit more precise when we define which kinds of failure are good and which are bad. The good kind comes from *trying* to do something good, and either miscalculating or just flatly making the wrong decision. That's the kind of failure that's 100 percent guaranteed, and 100 percent forgivable—plus, the attempt at virtue that led to it lets us learn from what we did, and gives us a better chance at success in the future. The kind I was gesturing at when I didn't want to change banks came partly from apathy, or maybe "moral laziness." I didn't do something I knew would be a little better than the thing I was doing, because, well, it was hard and annoying. We've just spent an entire chapter declaring that perfection is impossible, and we're entirely within our rights to let ourselves off the moral hook once in a while when we jaywalk (literally or figuratively). That self-forgiveness is necessary, I think, just to get through the day. But if I'm being honest with myself, I gave up a little early with the checking account thing. (I am lucky enough to even have a checking account, and the time and energy to think about the pros and cons of where that checking account is located, and the resources to make a change—as we'll see a little later, people in my position have an obligation to fight a little harder to get things right.) I don't think I'd be a "bad" person if I hadn't changed my bank. But I do feel like a slightly better one because I switched, and the initial thing that almost stopped me was more laziness than anything else.

We've completed two-thirds of our journey, everyone! That's the good news. The bad news is, we're about to get real thorny. We're gonna wade into some deeply confusing and painful applications of moral philosophy, stretching and straining and chewing on really tough questions that plague us in our daily lives, that cause us anxiety and anguish and often lead to loud arguments with our closest friends and family.

But in a *fun* way!

PART THREE

In Which Things Get Really Tough,
but We Power Through and Complete
Our Journeys, Becoming Perfectly
Virtuous and Flourishing and
Deontologically Pure Happiness-
Generating Super-People, and Also
There's a Chapter with Some Cursing
in It, but It's for a Good Reason

Oh, You Bought a New iPhone? That's Cool. Did You Know That Millions of People Are Starving in South Asia?!

In October 2018, my beloved Boston Red Sox won the World Series, beating the L.A. Dodgers in five games. I was at the title-clinching game in Los Angeles with my close friends Nate and Dave and my son, William. I didn't think sports had much more to offer me in the category of emotional gratification, but that moment—the instant they secured the championship—was so pure and wonderful and magical that I felt like I was floating. Dave spontaneously lifted William up in the air. We hugged and cried and laughed and celebrated. Here's a picture of William right after we ran down to the field level:

Look at that face. That's a big ol' face full of joy, right there.

In December, I decided to get William a Christmas present to commemorate the occasion and found for sale a bat autographed by four of the Red Sox's best players. It was pretty expensive for a ten-year-old's Christmas present: $800. Oof. That's almost as much as a new bumper for a 2005 Saab.[1] But then I scrolled back through my pictures and *look at that face full of joy*. I decided: What the hell. This was a moment we will remember forever. So I bought it. And then for a moment, I felt *terrible*. And it's all philosophy's fault.

Well, one philosopher's in particular.

The thousands of decisions we make every day come not just with Moral Exhaustion—the hot new philosophical term everyone's talking about—but with a forced accounting of our moral opportunity cost. "Opportunity cost" is an economics term describing what we give up when we spend our resources—the opportunity cost of a company putting more money into research and development is that it can't hire as many workers; the opportunity cost of spending more on advertising is that it has less money to buy supplies. Moral opportunity cost, then, would be the good we miss out on doing when we choose to do something else. Which brings us to iconoclastic Australian utilitarian, and source of that 2018 buzzkill, Peter Singer.

In December 2006, Singer (born 1946) wrote an article for the *New York Times Magazine* called "What Should a Billionaire Give—and What Should You?" At the time, Bill Gates had pledged nearly $30 billion to his charitable foundation, making him (by the numbers) one of the greatest philanthropists of all time. Singer applauds Gates for his work to eradicate diseases like malaria that ravage poor enclaves of sub-Saharan Africa. But then he says this:

> Gates may have given away nearly $30 billion, but that still leaves him sitting at the top of the Forbes list of the richest Americans,

---

1 Sorry. Couldn't help it.

with $53 billion. His 66,000-square-foot high-tech lakeside es-
tate near Seattle is reportedly worth more than $100 million. . . .
Among his possessions is the Leicester Codex, the only handwrit-
ten book by Leonardo da Vinci still in private hands, for which he
paid $30.8 million in 1994. Has Bill Gates done enough? More
pointedly, you might ask: if he really believes that all lives have
equal value, what is he doing living in such an expensive house
and owning a Leonardo Codex? Are there no more lives that could
be saved by living more modestly and adding the money thus
saved to the amount he has already given?

Singer wants us to think about Gates differently: not as a man who gave
$30 billion to charity, but rather as a man who *still has $53 billion, none
of which* he's giving to charity. What would we think of a man who has
$53 billion[2] and gives none of it away? We'd start with "What an ass," and
probably not move much beyond that. But is that fair to Gates? Given,
you know, the $30 billion he *did* give to charity?[3]

In chapter 5 we discussed the upper limits of virtue, and discovered
the need for some kind of ceiling on what any ethical system can expect
of us. But even as we (reasonably) shrink away from the idea of becoming a "happiness pump," Singer doesn't want to let us off the hook. He
wants us to think, *all the time*, about whether there might be more we
can do (than whatever it is we're doing) to help other people. So now we

2 These numbers were accurate as of the writing of Singer's article. Gates's net worth
at the moment I'm writing this has—somewhat absurdly, given the fact that he retired
years ago and has given so much away—ballooned to $127.9 billion. (The financial im-
pact to him personally in the aftermath of his divorce has yet to be publicized.)
3 Four years later, in 2010, Gates and Warren Buffett announced "the Giving Pledge,"
in which they promised to give at least 50 percent of their wealth to charity and worked
to get other billionaires to sign up as well. Buffett has actually pledged that 99 percent
of his wealth will be donated.

need to ask a new question: When, if ever, are we allowed to ignore the moral opportunity cost of some mundane, everyday decision?

Every Pair of Loafers Is a Human Life: The Peter Singer Story

The people at the top of the human food chain are basically aliens—they live lives we can't possibly imagine. (And I say that as an extremely well-paid TV comedy writer.) Telecom billionaire John Malone owns more than 2.2 million acres of land in the United States. That means he owns property greater than the size of Delaware plus all of New York City plus Houston. Larry Ellison, who founded Oracle Corporation, got bored a few years ago and bought an entire Hawaiian Island. The people at the far end of the "crazy rich" bell curve don't inhabit the same planet as you and I, so on the rare occasion when they emerge from whatever James Bond supervillain volcano they live in and interact with the real world, their actions draw intense scrutiny. When wildfires ripped through Australia in 2019, Amazon CEO Jeff Bezos, the world's richest man, announced that his company would pledge $1 million AUD ($690,000 USD) in aid. For this he was roundly, and appropriately, dunked on—people pointed out that Bezos had made that much money every five minutes *for the entire year*. Then, predictably, people began to review what else Bezos had recently spent his money on. For example, he'd plunked down $42 million to build a clock in a hollowed-out mountain in Texas that was designed to last for ten thousand years. So, $42 million for weirdo futuristic alien super clock . . . $690,000 to save a continent? Barely a month later, Bezos announced he would donate *$10 billion* over the next decade to fight climate change, and it's hard not to see a connection between his public pillorying and his sudden interest in large-scale altruism. (See? Shame can be good!)

It's natural and correct for us to demand that the people who can do the most actually *do* the most. But what's "the most"? How much are they on the hook for in any given situation, and when should we feel like they've met their obligations? Singer's critique of Bill Gates's charitable giving shook me up, so I went looking for other stuff he'd written, and man oh man—if you're ever interested in feeling morally inadequate, read a bunch of Peter Singer books. His 100 percent pure, uncut utilitarianism can lead to very weird places—like shrugging off $30 billion in charitable gifts—but he carries one simple idea throughout everything he writes: there is no difference in the inherent value of a life *over here*— wherever "here" is, for us—than there is in a life *over there*. To prove his point, he offers a compelling thought experiment, which I'll simplify and paraphrase.

Imagine we're walking by a shallow pond, and we see a drowning child. Most people agree that we have a moral responsibility to act—we should rush into the knee-high water and, you know, grab the kid so he doesn't, you know, drown. But what if we saw the drowning child, and we thought to ourselves, "You know, I *should* save that child, but I just bought these new Italian loafers, and I really don't want to ruin them. So . . . good luck, kid!" And then we just walked on by, perhaps whistling a happy little ditty about how soft and leathery our loafers are. We would, of course, be considered horrible, awful people—worse even than a guy with $53 billion who gives none of it to charity, probably, because what was required of us was so basic and our reason for not doing it was so callous. Choosing to save our loafers instead of a human being means we're either sadists, or sociopaths, or Ayn Rand acolytes, or all three. People would tweet about us and drag us for our awfulness, and they'd be right to do it.

But again, most people aren't monsters. Most of us would instantly calculate that a human life is worth more than a pair of Italian loafers, and we would wade into the pond and try to save the kid. But here's Singer's point: We know for a fact that there are children drowning in ponds, literal and metaphorical, all over the world, *right now*. We see advertisements asking for thirty cents a day to help a starving child in Yemen, or get mail from an organization telling us that a dollar a week can save a human life in Syria, and more often than not we ignore them.

In fact, we're *annoyed* by them. Yet a dollar a week is a lot less than we would've spent on those Italian loafers. Why do we value a life *over there* less than we value a life *over here*? Why does the pond have to be literally in front of our faces in order for us to act?

When Singer conducts this thought experiment in his classes, students often cite reasonable concerns with the transaction—we'd be giving money to an organization we *think* is saving lives, but some of it probably gets siphoned off into bureaucracy, and the actual impact of the money is sort of vague. Singer then points out that the cost to us is so small—pennies, really—so even if the money is only, say, 25 percent as impactful as promised, isn't that a deal worth making? Yeah, I know—hard to quibble with, right? And finally, Singer asks us to take the logical next step: collect all the money we were *going* to spend on Italian loafers, or new jeans, or a new iPhone we don't really need, and send it to someone else, somewhere in the world, to help that person live a better life (or possibly: live at all). He asks us to make a full and complete utilitarian sacrifice—give up the small amount of pleasure we get from a new lamp or whatever, and dramatically decrease the amount of pain being felt by someone facing challenges we can hardly imagine.

Singer knows he's onto something here. A lot of us buy tons of things we don't need, and the simple act of pointing out how much more we could do with our money spotlights our own excessive consumerism. In fact, when we start looking at all of the dumb crap we've accumulated in our houses—all the unnecessary throw pillows and extra sweaters we never wear and $800 autographed baseball bats—we realize that Singer is offering us the deal of a lifetime: We can be heroes! Every single one of us can be Oskar Schindler. Granted, Schindler saved lives by risking his own while under the oppressive eye of a fascist regime, and we're just sitting around watching *Jurassic Park* on TNT and eating honey-roasted peanuts . . . but *we can literally save people's lives*, just like he did. All we have to do is *not* buy that lamp, and instead send the thirty bucks to a mosquito net charity in Africa, and then wait for Steven Spielberg to make an Oscar-winning movie about our sacrifice and bravery.

But then we remember the cautionary tale of the happiness pump, and wonder where this ends for us—sitting in an empty house, down to our last can of honey-roasted peanuts? Suddenly we're back in that gray area, wondering at what point we're allowed to just buy dumb stuff we want and not feel a utilitarian guilt because we aren't using the money for something more important. It's impossible to know!

Except no, it isn't, says Singer, channeling his inner Bentham: you can calculate it.

Singer believes that there is a certain amount of money we need for a basic life—food, shelter, a modicum of entertainment or leisure, and so on. That amount varies depending on our circumstances—how many kids we have, where we live, etc.—but it's calculable. We can figure out how much we actually need, build in a little pad for savings and medical emergencies and the like, and *any amount of money we make beyond that* we should give to someone less fortunate. "The formula is simple," he wrote in another *New York Times Magazine* article from 1999, "whatever money you're spending on luxuries, not necessities, should be given away." Singer is the consequentialist answer to Immanuel Kant. The dude is *hard-core.* His view of moral necessity is so intense, I sort of picture him looking like Tom Hardy in *Mad Max: Fury Road.* A postpunk, grizzled, lone-wolf utilitarian warrior, wandering through the desert, guided by an uncompromising sense of justice. In reality, he looks like this—

—which is a lot less intimidating.

Now we better understand his complaint about Gates. Donating $30 billion is wonderful, but if he still has $53 billion, he ought to give almost all of that away too. What does Bill Gates not have that he needs? Nothing. What do famine-stricken children living in Africa not have that they need? Beds, houses, food, clean water, malaria medicine, vitamins, education, soap, and vaccines. And what does Bill Gates *have* that he *doesn't* need? Around $52.999 billion dollars. For Singer this is a no-brainer. The amount we have above this calculable "necessities" total might be $1, or it might be $53 billion, but the action is the same: we don't need it, so we should send it to someone who does.

Again, we should point out the very reasonable objections to his command. First: For most people, paying for necessities, adding a bit for entertainment, and saving a little extra for a rainy day doesn't *feel* very safe. Every one of us will at some point confront a catastrophic "black swan"–type event—a car crash, an illness, a business deal gone wrong, a friend or relative in extreme need. We also (if we can) want to save for eventual retirement, or to help our future kids and maybe grandkids with their lives. If we give all our money away and then suddenly need some for a dire personal situation, we probably won't be comforted by the knowledge that our money was used to deworm a river in Malawi, improving the health of thousands of children.

Though *some* of us would, apparently. There are anecdotes in Singer's books *The Life You Can Save* and *The Most Good You Can Do* that involve people giving one of their kidneys away—not to a specific person, mind you, just to "whoever needs it"—as part of a movement called "effective altruism." (Singer's acolytes are as hard-core as he is.) Part of the calculation these folks do, when donating their kidneys, involves the fact that the chances of dying from only having one kidney are roughly 1 in 4,000—basically the same odds as being killed by a car while riding a bicycle. That means, to them, that by *not* giving their extra kidney away, they are valuing their own lives as 4,000 times more important than the lives of anonymous strangers. Despite that mathematical logic, most of us can't help but hesitate at the thought of just . . . giving away a kidney. Most of us have family or close friends for whom we're a theoretical donor—what if our child needed a kidney in a few years, but we couldn't help her because we'd yanked one out to satisfy the dictates of an Australian ethicist we've never met? Or what if our one remaining kidney failed and we were put in the position of asking one of our family members to give *us* a kidney? That's no fun either. The fact that the odds of these things happening are small is irrelevant. The very thought of them gives us chills.[4]

Another complaint about Singer's worldview is that he's *super* not into supporting what we might call "cultural" charities. When kids are literally dying, he says, it's hard to justify ignoring their pain and sending your annual charitable gift to a local art museum or symphony orchestra. Again, hard to argue with the logic of that statement, but also: Orchestras are nice! For some people, they are incredibly meaningful and vital to their human experience. It seems almost cruel to chastise those people for giving money to the orchestra, using the preventable death of children as a club to bash them with. Singer's point is important and well-taken—some charities are objectively better than others, and the effective altruism movement deserves a ton of credit for researching and highlighting those worthy of our money.[5] But this line of attack can feel like a cousin of my Saab bumper move: you shouldn't care about *this*, because *that* is so much worse. *Oh, you want to give the art museum a hundred bucks? That's cool. You could literally save twenty human lives with that money, but no, go ahead, staring at a Brancusi sculpture is also important I guess.*

Singer's arguments can be frustrating in their inflexibility. Again, their basic logic is inescapable, and we find ourselves repeatedly butting up against that logic even as we *feel* that it's unfair. That's why, when I

---

4 Singer acknowledges these sorts of objections, to be fair. "Most of us," he writes, "put our obligations to our family, especially our children, above everything else. Putting the family first feels natural, and in most cases, it seems right."

5 For more, see their annually updated list of most effective charities at givewell.org.

bought that expensive but utterly "unnecessary" autographed bat after the Red Sox won the World Series, I momentarily got bummed out. I felt the specter of Peter Singer glaring at me. *Eight hundred bucks for a bat, huh? Nothing better you could do with that money?* "Leave me alone, Peter Singer!" I replied, hopefully not out loud, though I can't say definitively whether or not it was out loud. "This matters to me! Let me do this!" The specter of Peter Singer was unmoved. *Okay, man. It's your money. But real quick, why don't you head over to Oxfam's website and take a peek at a few stories about people living in abject poverty?*

Remember Bernard Williams and his criticism of utilitarianism? He said that it denies us our integrity—our sense of being a whole and undivided person—and sacrifices our individual core projects in the name of a nonspecific mass human "happiness." Utilitarianism can sometimes deny us the things that make us "us." Williams would find absurd the idea that I did something morally wrong by buying my son a present celebrating a moment that we lovingly shared, and which represents an integral bonding experience. Ultimately, that's where I personally land too—aligned with Williams and Susan Wolf, who warned us against seeking moral sainthood. Our lives are our own, and we shouldn't feel bad about filling them with experiences and even objects that give those lives shape and dimension. Following Singer's logic, I shouldn't have gone to that game at all, really, because World Series tickets are expensive. We maybe shouldn't have bought nachos and a hot dog for my son, we shouldn't have paid for parking . . . in fact, I probably shouldn't pay for the special MLB cable package that lets me watch Red Sox games. It can get very silly, very quickly.

But Singer, dammit, has a point.

We do a lot of dumb stuff that we don't need to do, and when we do that dumb stuff, we very rarely think about the moral opportunity cost—the other, better things we *could* be doing instead. Singer's unrelenting focus on moral opportunity cost is why I love him, buzzkills and all—his uncompromising utilitarianism serves an important function. In 2019 he rereleased his book *The Life You Can Save* and asked me to write an introduction.[6] After discussing all of the annoying things a reader can feel when diving into Singer's work, I[7] wrote:

> More important than what you feel when you read this book is what you will *not* feel: complacency. You will not feel like other people don't matter. You will not blithely scroll past reports of disasters, whether abroad or close to home, without considering—even if just for a moment—the impacted lives of those affected. Instead, you will have, bouncing around in your head, the thought that there may be something simple you can do to help, something that does not disrupt your life or put you or your family's well-being in peril.

That, to me, is the gift Singer gives us: It's *incredibly* easy for people living in even modest comfort to become complacent—to forget that the great majority of people on earth live in some degree of poverty or distress, and have daily problems and dangers that far surpass our own. Air-conditioning, heat, food, clean water, a washing machine, a refrigerator, ample electricity, medicine, safety from war or crime—these are things many of us take for granted, and most people can't count on. Singer is like a complacency alert system.[8] He's here to tap us on the shoulder—*tap tap tap!*—to remind us how fortunate we are, and to ask if we might consider doing a bit more to help a few more people.

---

6 I had featured the book in an episode of *The Good Place*. I'm not just philosopher-name-dropping again for no reason. I mean, if I did that, my good friend Tim Scanlon would be *furious* with me.

7 Oh man, it's an entirely new kind of name-dropping: *self*-name-dropping! This is a huge breakthrough in name-dropping technology.

8 Singer, it should be noted, has been criticized for some of his views on disability and the allocation of capital to those with severe health problems (which also come from his stringent utilitarianism, and which readers can probably tease out for themselves). But as we've already learned, it's not always a great idea to follow utilitarian views all the way to their logical ends—whether we're talking about charity, or personal use of resources, or anything else.

Singer has plenty of detractors in the academic world. His shoulder-tapping doesn't make us feel good—and frankly, it's not supposed to. No one wants to feel like we're constantly screwing up, so when an intimidating Australian road warrior with a sawed-off shotgun (still the way I think of him, can't help it) points out that we can nearly *always* do more good if we make different choices—who questions our decision-making *every single time* we go to a movie or buy jeans—well, it kind of sucks. It's even more painful and annoying to be told that the literal cost of those jeans is *ten human lives*. However, we also want to be people who *care* and *try*, and Singer's shoulder-tapping can help with that. The crux of what we're talking about here is, again, engagement—the simple act of asking ourselves: *What am I doing? Is there something better I could be doing?* Confronting our behavior may be painful and annoying, but it's also a remedy for apathy, which is the enemy of improvement. We can hardly hope to hit an Aristotelian mean of civil engagement if we feel no consequences when we underperform.

The Covid-19 crisis led to inspiring stories, like landlords forgiving rent payments and citizens banding together to deliver food to the elderly and infirm. It also led to *awful* stories, about other landlords evicting people without mercy, and companies forcing their employees to work with inadequate protection.[9] There were fundraisers for frontline healthcare workers, and miserable projections of how this would affect the poor and disadvantaged, and through it all many people wondered the same thing: What are *my* responsibilities? How much should *I* do to help? I believe the answer (in this situation, and others like it) starts with Scanlon and then drifts over to Singer. When a public health crisis affects everyone on earth at the same moment, the minimum requirements for all of us—the rules no reasonable person would reject, the basic things we owe to each

---

9 Or, in what I think of as the worst corporate story from this whole awful mess—according to claims in a lawsuit—supervisors in a Tyson Foods factory in Iowa *actually placing wagers* on how many of their employees would contract the virus.

other—are easy to determine and non-negotiable: we need to limit our travel to the best of our ability, maintain social distancing, wear masks, and so on. After that—and this is where Singer comes back into the picture—our responsibilities scale up depending on our socioeconomic situations. As one example, if we have people who work for us in some capacity—dog walkers, babysitters, and so on—and we can afford to pay them (whether a whole or partial salary) even if they aren't *actively* working for us during a shutdown, we should. In a crisis, people lucky enough to have money to spare ought to give it to people who need it.

At the top of the food chain we find people like Jeff Bezos and billionaire media impresario David Geffen, who given their wealth (I'd argue) have the *greatest* responsibility to help other people. Which, when Covid-19 hit, they often did not. Early in the crisis, Amazon started a GoFundMe campaign to raise money for its workers,[10] which went over about as well as it had when Bezos tossed $690,000 at Australia to help fight wildfires. A basic calculation shows that Bezos could personally pay all of his 250,000 minimum-wage employees their full yearly salaries and still have about *$175 billion* left over. When you are the world's richest man, and you employ hundreds of thousands of people who are in harm's way, your responsibilities extend far beyond "pay your dog walker." Geffen, not to be outdone, at one point posted an Instagram photo of his $590 million yacht sailing peacefully in the Grenadines, along with an unironic caption about the importance of social distancing. If you're wondering how that went over, he quickly set his account to private and as of this writing hasn't really been heard from since.

I'm not quite as harsh regarding Geffen as Peter Singer would be. I wouldn't say he's morally required to sell his yacht and donate the

---

10 There was some confusion over whether Amazon was actually soliciting donations from the public—they funded the campaign with $25 million, and a spokesperson later denied they wanted the public to contribute. But one wonders: Then why start a GoFundMe campaign at all?

money. But I would say that as a man worth billions, he has a responsibility to do far more than the average person during a pandemic that has disrupted the lives of everyone on earth. I'd also recommend he spend some of that money on a social media consultant, so that when he tries to post a picture of his $590 million yacht the same week a record number of Americans lose their jobs, there'd be someone to grab his phone and toss it into the ocean.

Modern Life's Most Exasperating Mistake: The Well-Intentioned Screw-Up

Singer's moral shoulder-tapping—*tap tap tap!*—does a very good job of reminding us, when we spend our time and money, that there may be ways we can spend it better. But sometimes, we hit another snag. The problem isn't always that we spent money without thinking about whether we could use it to do more good in the world. Sometimes we *actually tried* to do some good—we listened to Singer, dammit!—and just like with our well-intentioned goodness seeker from the introduction, the world smacked us in the face anyway.

In 2004 I moved to Los Angeles and had to get a car for the first time in my life. I settled on a midsize sedan that was kind of expensive, but it looked cool and got good safety ratings. After about three months I hated it—not because it wasn't fun to drive, which it was, and not because driving around L.A. is miserable no matter what car you're driving, which it is. I just hated how much gas it used. As a person who talked a lot about the negative environmental impact of internal combustion engines, I felt (appropriately) like a hypocrite for driving a car that got like seventeen miles to a gallon.

So as soon as the lease was up, I got a Toyota Prius, which at the time was among the most fuel-efficient cars available, averaging between thirty-eight and fifty miles per gallon. Much better! I felt like less of a hypocrite. Until a friend of mine told me that the way the

Prius's hybrid batteries were manufactured was actually, in toto, just as harmful to the environment than a regular gas-powered car, for reasons that now escape me. (Something something chemicals in the batteries something something groundwater leakage something something.) While researching whether that was true, I read an article about how fully-electric cars were now emerging onto the market and vowed to make one of them my next purchase . . . until I then read a *very* strident article about how that would actually be *worse*, because the electricity on the California grid still mostly came from coal-burning power plants,[11] so unless you had a solar grid powering your car, you were actually doing *more* harm by driving a fully electric vehicle, you dummy, and then I had a panic attack and lay on the floor and put a cold compress on my head.

So, we're back to Moral Exhaustion.[12] But this is a new, more virulent strain of Moral Exhaustion[13]—one where we're somehow punished even when we do something that's better than whatever we were doing before. And worse yet, we're often confronted by people who criticize us for screwing up. *How could you support this person for Congress— don't you know that he voted for the Iraq War? How could you buy these paper towels—the parent company pollutes rivers! How could you see that movie, eat this food, travel to that country, play this brand of bagpipes?*[14] It seems like every time we think we've made a good decision, even if we've researched the issue and feel we've gone with the best option, someone writes an article explaining why we're actually Part of the Problem. Plus, annoyingly, some of our friends and family members and helpful online acquaintances absolutely *delight* in pointing out where we've gone

---

11 Again, this was back in the mid-aughts. California now gets a third of its energy from renewable sources, and has vowed to create 100 percent clean energy by 2045.

12 It's gonna catch on. I can feel it.

13 See?! It's popping up everywhere!

14 This would only apply to a world in which certain bagpipe manufacturers are somehow creating more social ill than other bagpipe manufacturers.

wrong. *Oh, you like peanut butter and jelly sandwiches? That's nice. Guess you don't care about the ELEVEN MILLION CHILDREN who SUFFER from PEANUT ALLERGIES and could LITERALLY DIE because of your SELFISH LUNCH CHOICES. #howdareyou #peanutjustice4all #Choosy MomsChooseLIFE.*

This ethical dilemma feels unique to our age: When information is so readily available, how do we escape the guilt (or shame) that comes from learning about our unintentionally bad decisions? No one in 340 BC understood the detrimental effects of personal choices on wildlife ecosystems. But now we know *everything*, and if we don't, there are plenty of people who do (or at least pretend to) and thoroughly enjoy explaining to us how we're blowing it. It's a second-level ethical dilemma: How do we respond to the unintended ethical dilemmas that sometimes result from our attempts to solve ethical dilemmas? This is a real twisty pretzel of a situation, and seems like a job for Aristotle and his "What kind of person should I be?" approach. So, Aristotle, how much should we care about the possibility that we'll act with as much virtue as we can muster and still get punched in the gut?

A virtue ethicist might say, well, if we worry *too much* about the unforeseen ills of something we did, it might drive us into a sort of paralysis, where all we do is consider and reconsider the potential effects of our actions, so concerned with theoretically bad outcomes from even the simplest decisions that we just nervously pace and twitch when trying to determine which brand of canned peaches to buy. But a *deficiency* of caring about unintended consequences might send us careening back toward apathy—not caring *at all* about the fact that things can go unexpectedly wrong when we do stuff threatens to turn us into people who don't give a crap about anything we do. There is some golden mean we should find, wherein we think things through as much as we can but forgive ourselves when our well-intentioned actions have some deleterious effect.

I wanted to avoid the hypocrisy of driving a car that got bad gas mileage while calling for other people to curb their fossil fuel use. That incongruity made me feel crummy and embarrassed, because hypocrisy stinks. It's one of the most infuriating traits we can display. (Our old friend Judith Shklar wrote a whole chapter on hypocrisy, which she, you might imagine, doesn't care for.) But there's also a difference between my original hypocrisy (driving a car I knew was bad for the environment) and my *accidental* hypocrisy (driving a car that was better for the environment than the gas-guzzler, but *accidentally* harmful in a different way). If Aristotle helped get us through the initial wave of confusion and guilt, some kind of Kantian-like approach—factoring in my good intentions— may take us the rest of the way.

Just as in the previous chapter, when we hoped that Deb the Free-Riding Ninja would acknowledge her own shortcomings so as not to nudge her Overton window toward worse behavior, we need to be our own judges. Let's say we give fifty bucks to the Save the American Pelicans Fund, which protects threatened wetlands where pelicans live, and then our friend Nancy finds out and yells at us: "You fool!" she screams. "Save the American Pelicans Fund is a terrible charity! You should've given to the American Fund to Save the Pelicans—everyone knows *that's* the only good pelican charity!" First of all, Nancy, chill out, you're spitting on us. And second, it was an honest mistake—we *intended* to help the pelicans, and we acted in good faith. Our instinct might be to just throw up our hands—how could we have known this was such a terrible blunder? We don't have a month of free time to devote to researching a million similar-sounding pelican charities, Nancy![15] But if we let the annoyance of making a mistake (or being shamed by it) affect us too much, we might decide it's pointless to ever try to help anybody, ever, because who needs the headache? Better to focus on the fact that the *idea* was good—give money to a charity—even if the *result* was less than ideal. The Kantian worldview seems *really* attractive now; by buying a Prius, or donating to charity, we're actively trying to follow a Kantian maxim, to do something good out of a sense of duty to follow a maxim: help

---

15 I know she means well, but honestly, Nancy is the *worst*. I'm done with her.

other people when we can, make the world better, do our part to solve a systemic problem. If we later get sideswiped by a rotten outcome, even Kant—that sniffing, unpleasant moral snob—would acknowledge that we didn't do anything "wrong." We tried, we failed, we'll try to be better next time. And also maybe we'll cut back on the time we spend with Nancy, who's a little much.

Try again. Fail again. Fail better.[16] It's the best we can do, and often, even if we've bought into that philosophy, it doesn't feel that great to live this way. The more carefully we examine our decisions, the more tempting it seems to ignore all the moral dilemmas we'll inevitably discover. They're so complicated and annoying that we might conclude it's easier—and no worse in ethical terms—to simply keep doing what we were already doing.

. . . I mean, is that an option? Maybe?

---

16 This Samuel Beckett quote, which I also used in the intro, was maybe not intended to be as . . . inspiring as we have suggested. The work it's taken from, *Worstward Ho*, is bleak, dreary, despairing, and grueling to read. Because it was written by Samuel Beckett. But I always get an odd sense of optimism from his hilariously grim prose, so I'm choosing to see a bit of hope in these six words, placed in this order.

CHAPTER TEN

This Sandwich Is Morally Problematic.
But It's Also Delicious.
Can I Still Eat It?

In the summer of 2012, Dan T. Cathy, the CEO of fast food chain Chick-fil-A, joined *The Ken Coleman Show* (a syndicated radio program) and spoke out against gay marriage. Because what that debate needed, apparently, was the "chicken sandwich franchise owner" point of view. Here's what he said:

> I think we are inviting God's judgment on our nation when we shake our fist at Him and say, "We know better than you as to what constitutes a marriage." I pray God's mercy on our generation that has such a prideful, arrogant attitude to think that we have the audacity to define what marriage is about.

If you don't remember what happened after that, you can probably guess. LGBTQ+ groups called for boycotts. Anti gay–marriage politicians and advocates posted pictures of themselves proudly eating Chick-fil-A sandwiches. Everybody started yelling.

At the time, I was working on the show *Parks and Recreation*, and the writers' room was up in arms.[1] I had never eaten at Chick-fil-A and casu-

---

1 Most (but not all) comedy writers' rooms tend to be politically progressive.

ally posited that I never would now, because I didn't want to support an organization that didn't believe in the basic human (and Constitutional) freedom to marry whoever one wants to marry. You can imagine how shocked I was when a few of the writers said they would continue to go to Chick-fil-A without hesitation. When I asked them why, they gave several reasons:

- Not going wouldn't make a difference, really, because one person's chicken order is a drop in the corporate profit bucket.
- Their chicken sandwiches are *so good.*
- Not patronizing the store would only hurt the employees who worked there, some of whom might be laid off if business sank, so really we'd only be hurting *them.*
- Seriously, though, their chicken sandwiches are amazing.
- Every other fast food restaurant CEO is probably just as bad on political and social issues, so where do you draw the line?
- The pickles they put on their sandwiches? Incredible.

This stunned me. Here were several good friends of mine, whom I knew to hold LGBTQ+ rights as something of a core value, punting on a pretty simple act of resistance . . . for the sake of a chicken sandwich?

We debated this for hours, and got nowhere. I found it endlessly frustrating that those on the opposite side of the debate conceded the points I made and *still* shrugged and said they wouldn't change their fast food habits. They also whatabouted me like crazy—bringing up artists or stores I patronized in order to point out that I wasn't so perfect either, points *I* then had to concede and which made me think: "Well, maybe they're right. Maybe it isn't that big a deal to buy a sandwich from Chick-fil-A, even now. Maybe I'm overreacting?"

This debate exemplified one of the thorniest moral issues of our time: Can we separate the things we like from the people who make them? And should we?

A Fun Little Moral Surprise: Everything We Love Is Terrible!

We all have at least a dozen problematic personal affinities. We root for the Kansas City Chiefs, Atlanta Braves, Florida State Seminoles, or some other sports team that callously dresses its mascot in an offensive Native American costume. We cheer for athletes who have committed domestic abuse, express repugnant political views, take banned performance-enhancing substances, or cheat in some other way. We watch and love entertainment made by Woody Allen, Roman Polanski, or Brett Ratner, produced by Les Moonves, Scott Rudin, or Harvey Weinstein, starring Sean Penn, James Woods, Mel Gibson, or Charlie Sheen. We listen to music by Michael Jackson, Eric Clapton, R. Kelly, or Placido Domingo. These are people accused of a range of behaviors, some admitted and others denied, but if we don't know of at least one person or thing whose actions make it problematic for us to be their active fan, it's only because we're hermits who haven't looked at the internet in twenty years.[2] Here's our old friend Moral Exhaustion,[3] with another new fun twist. It's hard enough to figure out what we're supposed to *do* all the time—now we have to be responsible for what we *like*?

We've been saddled with this problem for a long time, but only

---

2 It continues to shock me how many famous or successful people from history are deeply problematic. As I've been editing this book, Bill Gates, he of the record-setting philanthropy, has been accused of workplace harassment (although his private office denied this in the *Los Angeles Times*), *and* apparently spent much more time with Jeffrey Epstein than had been previously reported. Literally today my wife and I listened to a podcast about Gertrude Stein, early supporter of Picasso and Hemingway, godmother of the Parisian art scene in the early twentieth century, novelist and poet and feminist and gay icon . . . and found out she cozied up to the Vichy government during the Nazi occupation of France—going so far as to translate some of Marshal Pétain's anti-Semitic speeches into English. I mean, for cripes' sake—Gertrude Stein?!

3 Wow, there's that term again. A lot of people seem to be using it. Someone should maybe write an article about how it's penetrating the culture.

recently did we really start to care about it. An increase in cultural conversation around topics of social justice, more social media shaming, and an emerging awareness that maybe it's not okay to assault women or use other cultures as Halloween costumes have meant that people's bad actions are much more likely to be exposed, and thus *we* are much more likely to be called to account for watching, listening to, and rooting for them. But here's the problem: It's not just that so many of the people we love, who have made great art or sung great music or hit key home runs in the World Series, are morally problematic. It's that they're *the people we love*. They're the people whose art and accomplishments helped us form our identities, bond with our parents and friends, define our childhoods. We *love* them. Some of us can't even swear off a chicken sandwich after a provincial goober burps up some homophobia on a radio show—so what happens when we hear that our all-time favorite singer or actor or sports hero has done something awful? We are emotionally interwoven with the parts of the culture that shaped our identity, so just detaching ourselves from them is *painful*. It's not like removing a splinter—it's more like amputating a limb. Or, to extend the previous metaphor: it's not just that the chicken sandwiches taste really good—it's that the chef is our best friend.

There are two subcategories to this dilemma. The first we might think of as "Bad Things We Love That Can Change." And we'll use as our example the miserable, awful story of the football team formerly known as the Washington R*dskins. (Note: I will be quoting articles that used the actual slur and will leave it intact for clarity, so proceed with caution.)

Scenario 1: The Leopard Can, but Won't, Change His Spots

Daniel Snyder bought the franchise in 1999, and as of this writing they've since compiled a record of 149-202-1. They have mostly stunk, due in large part to the fact that Snyder is—and I don't use this term lightly—a doofus. He has done so many doofy things since buying the team that in 2010 a journalist named Dave McKenna wrote a piece for the *Washington City Paper* called "The Cranky Redskins Fan's Guide to Dan Snyder" in which he listed something boneheaded, offensive, or thoughtless Snyder had done for every letter of the alphabet. The list was detailed and compelling, but instead of examining his behavior, Snyder sued the *City Paper* for defamation and demanded $2 million in damages. Which is a classic doofus move.[4]

The controversy over the team's plainly racist nickname[5]—a point of contention since long before Snyder took over—was thus overseen by a very big doofus for more than two decades, and it went about as well as you might imagine. In 2013, after yet another extremely reasonable call from Native groups to recognize the nickname as offensive, Snyder said this:

> We will never change the name of the team. As a lifelong Redskins fan, and [*sic*] I think that the Redskins fans understand the great tradition and what it's all about and what it means, so we feel pretty fortunate to be just working on next season. We'll never change the name. It's that simple. NEVER—you can use caps.[6]

---

4 He also kept right on doing boneheaded and/or offensive and/or thoughtless things. Were that article written today, McKenna would likely have five entries for every letter of the alphabet.

5 Snyder has often claimed that the name is *not* racist but rather some kind of "celebration" of Native culture. This, to quote Jeremy Bentham, is nonsense upon stilts. A history of the term in the *Washington Post* cites this entry: "1863: The Winona (Minn.) Daily Republican features an announcement that uses the term 'redskin' as a pejorative: 'The State reward for dead Indians has been increased to $200 for every red-skin sent to Purgatory. This sum is more than the dead bodies of all the Indians east of the Red River are worth.'"

6 Snyder also, in 2013, wrote a letter to his fans in which he cited a bunch of surveys and anecdotal comments that to him proved that Actually the Nickname Is Fine. "After 81 years," he wrote, "the team name 'Redskins' continues to hold the memories and meaning of where we came from, who we are, and who we want to be in years to come." In other words, as we're about to discuss: *This is the way it's always been done.*

Several aspects of this statement are offensive to me. Some of them involve his terrible grammar and syntax, but the more important ones relate to his apologia, which amounts to: It's tradition! It's the way it's always been done, so we can't change it. "This is the way it's always been done" is the last defense of the true ignoramus. The amount of time something has been done is not, by itself, a good reason to keep doing it. By relying solely on precedent and failing to critically examine the problems that precedent might create for us, we're basically just flipping the middle finger to the idea of progress, or finding ways to be better people.[7] We're actively *not* trying to be better, and worse, we're seeing the not-trying as a *virtue*. This benefits no one.

Snyder *could* change his views, of course; he just didn't wanna. Now, if he weren't powerful and influential, that wouldn't really matter, because he'd just be a crotchety dork in his living room barking at his TV. But since he *is* powerful and influential, he became a bottleneck for those who found the nickname problematic; his stance created anguish for any Washington fans in favor of a name change, who then had to figure out what *they* were supposed to do about the tension between their fandom and their belief system. They *love* this particular chicken sandwich, and yet it also clashes with their understanding of a just and virtuous world, and Snyder is the only guy who can make things better. When he defiantly announced he would never change—because This Is the Way It's Always Been Done—his problem became *their* problem.

I found a great explanation for why people take this stance from the writer Jordan K. Ngubane, author of *An African Explains Apartheid* (1963). Ngubane wrote the book in South Africa at a time when criticisms of the Apartheid regime weren't exactly received well by those in power; in the preface, he thanks his friends and colleagues who helped

---

7 This, remember, is partly why William James developed his pragmatism—to give people tools to build a bridge between previously held beliefs and newer, better, more fact-based beliefs that arise, from which they might benefit.

him with the book, but does not name them for fear they would be punished. (The date is listed as August 18, 1961, less than a year before Nelson Mandela was captured and spent nearly three decades in prison.) Here's what Ngubane writes about the reasons an Afrikaner nationalist might perpetuate Apartheid, even in the face of its inherent moral rot:

> He sees it as a way of life, a world outlook by which to create for himself the social order after his design. . . . History to him is a continually unfolding experience whose real validity lies not so much in its being a guide to the future as in being a justification. . . . When pressed to modify it, he is bewildered. In his view, all this is tantamount to saying he should renounce the world he has created for himself.

Saying "this world is problematic" amounts to saying "I, who have helped build this world, am problematic." For people deeply invested in *the way things are*, any change would mean confronting decisions they've made that created or sustained the troubling reality. And it doesn't have to be something as huge and society-wide as Apartheid. Recently, many people in the LGBTQ+ community have made requests regarding which pronouns people use when addressing them. This might be because some people are born with a physiological gender that doesn't match the gender with which they identify, or it might just be an aversion to gendered pronouns themselves. The results were predictable: Some people adapted quickly, granting this minimally intrusive request. Other people . . . didn't do that. They dug in their heels and refused to budge. They have been doing things a certain way for a long time, they "understand" that version of their world, and any alteration of that world causes stubbornness or outright panic.

But what does such a stance mean for the rest of us? When people raise an ethical issue and a person in a position of power proudly declares, in all caps, that upon zero reflection he's decided not to look into the matter because he's definitely right, the anguished are left with few options. We don't have to be Washington football fans to understand the problem here, because again, chances are we all love something that would be easier to love if it would just . . . change, a little. Get with the times. Adapt. It might be an older actor whose interviews involve a cringey, retrogressive attitude toward his female costars, or a university that still has a statue of a slave-owning Confederate general in its courtyard, or your aunt Connie, who's really sweet and sends you a birthday card every year but also has some troubling thoughts about Mexicans that she loudly shares with you every Thanksgiving. When we realize the leopards that cause our moral anguish won't change their spots, we then have to make our own decision: Do we keep supporting them, or do we cut our emotional and financial ties? To answer that, we can apply our schools of ethical thought to Snyder's actions—to see if he has a leg to stand on—and also to our *own* actions, to see if our support of his team is morally defensible. (For simplicity's sake, we'll use Washington's football team to stand in for all of these "problematic things we love, that have the ability to change.")

We begin by using our Quick-Start Guide: the contractualist argument. Could we reasonably reject a principle that allows racist characterizations of persecuted people to be used as team mascots? Of course. We'd pretty easily reject that. In fact, if Snyder suggested that rule during one of our contractualist rule-pitching sessions, he'd be roundly laughed at—especially since his defense amounts to: "I've been a fan of this team since I was young, and now I own them, so I can do what I want." The question *what do we owe to each other?* does not include an exemption clause for either "length of time you have cared about something" or "being rich and powerful." Snyder is actually doing something akin to our old friend from chapter 4, Wayne the Lamborghini Driver—he's suggesting a rule that, owing to his wealth and status, *essentially applies only to him* (and people like him). And by the way, we've also argued that the richer and more powerful you are, the *more* you owe other people, because when we're sitting around coming up with rules that define what we owe to each other, the powerful can more easily bear the weight of sacrifice. A contractualist rejects Snyder's rule, which probably suggests we ought to stop supporting the team.

Deontology won't be any more lenient with him. Snyder's arguing that he could will into existence a world where once anyone gets enough money or achieves enough influence, he can stop considering the feelings or needs of those less fortunate. That's the world the pigs create in *Animal Farm*, and I don't think George Orwell wrote *Animal Farm* as like a "how to" guide for running a society. Plus, co-opting Native American imagery and using it as your mascot is a pretty straightforward case of "using other people as a means to an end." Kant would reject Snyder's actions, and since we're supporting a franchise that's blatantly violating both[8] formulations of the categorical imperative left and right, Kant probably wants us to find another way to spend our Sundays.

Applying virtue ethics: we're essentially asking how compassionate we should be when it comes to issues that cause people anguish or pain. Being *excessively* compassionate might lead to lack of integrity, or backbone, or something—nearly everything in the culture is *some* kind of iffy, so we'd constantly be dropping whatever we were doing and searching for something else that comes with no moral entanglements at all (an impossible pipe dream, here in 2022). On the other hand, a *deficiency* of compassion leads to . . . what Daniel Snyder is: shut down, defiant, impenetrable, resistant to new ideas, calcified, and utterly uninterested in the emotional health of other people. Somewhere between those extremes is a golden mean of compassion. Given

---

8 (*exhausted sigh*) In order not to run afoul of those mean, learned professors from the Q&A in the beginning of this book, I should point out that there are actually *three* formulations of the categorical imperative; we just didn't talk about the third one back in the Kant section. And with an even more exhausted sigh I will also add that Kant wrote about something he called the "Kingdom of Ends" which some scholars count as a fourth formulation, but which others don't consider a distinct idea. This is a good explainer for how difficult Kant's writing can be—experts can't even totally agree on how many damn categorical imperative formulations there are.

that the name of his team creates such extreme and unnecessary anguish, and could be changed so easily, I believe Snyder is deficient in consideration for others. His seesaw is out of whack here. And given how easily he alone could change the name, it's probably wrong to support the team.

Utilitarianism is a little trickier. When Snyder declines to entertain a name change, he *might* have a consequentialist leg to stand on. It is, I suppose, *possible* that if he changed the name, the total pain felt by Washington fans who *don't* want it to change would be greater than that felt by Indigenous people if he chose to retain it. But are these two pains comparable? Remember, it's not strictly *the number of people who feel pain* in each of the two different outcomes—it's the *total amount of pain felt*, and the *intensity* of that pain, and its *duration*, and like four other things from that jaunty little poem. For the utilitarian, it's better to have a hundred people get paper cuts than one person take a baseball bat to the knee. So even if the *number* of people who feel pain (Native Americans and their allies, in this case) were smaller than the *number* of people who feel pleasure, there might be significantly more *total* pain if Snyder keeps the name the same. Not to mention that when we use Bentham's good ol' hedon/dolor calculator to figure out how deep, lasting, or intense the pain felt by pro-status-quo R*dskins fans would be if Snyder did change it, we ought to remember that what they'd be going through is common and banal. Sports teams change their nicknames, uniforms, and logos all the time, and fans quickly adapt. The R*dskins themselves used to be called the (still offensive, but less so) Boston Braves. The St. John's R*dmen (a pretty direct analog, here) changed their name to the Red Storm in 1994—when's the last time you heard someone grumbling about that? Sometimes, when teams *don't* change their nicknames or logos—surely citing "This is what we've always been called and we're not gonna change" as the reason—the results are absurd. The Minneapolis Lakers moved from a place with a lot of lakes to a place with basically none, and now the name "Los Angeles Lakers" just makes no sense. The New Orleans Jazz was an appropriate nickname—the Utah Jazz is most certainly not. (Utah is a lovely state with many things to offer. Jazz is not one of those things.[9]) Given how commonplace name changes are, even a consequentialist argument for Snyder's decision falls apart pretty quickly.

But what about the utilitarian argument regarding *us*, and our fandom? How much "bad" does us continuing to root for the team really create? Some of that depends on what "supporting the team" really means. Do we spend money on tickets and merchandise? Do we publicly tweet or post videos, spreading the racist logo online? Do we wear a hat or jersey out in public where others will see it? It's likely that if our fandom is relatively private, we're not creating that much consequentialist "harm."[10] But it also leads us back to one of those "integrity" questions regarding utilitarian acts. We may create only a tiny amount of "bad" by sitting at home and watching our favorite team play. But we're

---

9 It's actually hard to even conceive of a less appropriate nickname: The Arizona Polar Bears? The Kansas Mountaineers? The Las Vegas Dignity?

10 To be fair to the utilitarians, they did make another argument against the oppression of the weak by the strong. Mill wrote this, in his original text of *Utilitarianism*: "The interest involved is that of security, to every one's feelings the most vital of all interests. All other earthly benefits . . . can, if necessary, be cheerfully forgone, or replaced by something else; but security no human being can possibly do without; on it we depend for all our immunity from evil. . . . Nothing but the gratification of the instant could be of any worth to us, if we could be deprived of anything the next instant by whoever was momentarily stronger than ourselves." He had to come up with *something*, because utilitarianism's basic tenets seem to defend majoritarian tyranny: If 51 percent of us oppressed the other 49 percent, well, that's (in theory) 51 percent happiness and 49 percent sadness. A utilitarian thumbs-up. So Mill concluded that a basic safety from oppression supersedes all other considerations, because *all* people would fear someday being in a situation where *they* were oppressed, and without basic liberty all else crumbles. It's not that the argument has no merit, but we might point out that (a) it doesn't seem to be the case, with a lot of oppressors—they don't seem to fear being oppressed themselves someday, like *at all*, and (b) if your ethical theory needs to explain why it actually *doesn't* give the green light to oppression as it appears to, there might be something big-picture wrong with your ethical theory.

the ones who have to live with our choices. We are, as Bernard Williams put it, "specially responsible for what [we do], rather than for what other people do." Relying solely on a utilitarian calculation that justifies quietly rooting for the team might not be reason enough to justify the choice. We should also just do a gut check here, and ask ourselves if *we* are okay with it.

And look: we might be.

We might mull over all of our options—practical imperatives and doctrines of means and utilitarian accounting and personal gut checks—and when we consider the totality of what matters to us, we may just get to a point where we cannot imagine life without Washington football fandom. It's an ingredient that was stirred into our personal chowder at an early age, and it's impossible to separate that flavor from the rest of the dish. The "integrity" issue cuts both ways—our own senses of who we are as complete people, of what matters to us and which specific building blocks we're comprised of, might mean that when something threatens the structural integrity of one of those building blocks, all of the moral reasoning in the world can't get us to pry it free. What the hell do we do then?

Press pause, for a moment, while we look at the second of the two subcategories mentioned earlier: "Things We Root For That *Can't* Change."

Scenario 2: The Leopard *Can't* Change His Spots, or Maybe He Just Never Got Around to Changing His Spots and Now He's Dead

What if the thing we love or root for isn't the Washington Football Team, who literally at any moment could change their mascot to something less racist? What if we're talking about Michael Jackson's music, Roman Polanski's movies, or Thomas Jefferson's writing—where the thing causing us moral anguish is an unchangeable fact of history? Hell, what if we're writing a book that relies a whole lot on the wisdom of Aristotle, a true genius who also believed the only people capable of virtue were "free males" and put a lot of time and effort into explaining why slavery was totally fine?

When I was about ten years old I had to stay home sick from school, and my mom rented me the movie *Sleeper* by Woody Allen. All I remember is laughing and coughing and laughing and coughing. I watched it twice in a row. My dad then told me that Allen had three books of comedy pieces and short stories, and in maybe four days I read all of *Side Effects*, *Getting Even*, and *Without Feathers*. I can definitely say that my career as a comedy writer was launched by those books. Woody Allen's sense of humor isn't just a thing I like—it's part of my core identity. So you can imagine what happened in my brain when Allen (a) married his extremely young quasi-stepdaughter, and later (b) was accused of sexually abusing a child.

Frankly, I probably should've seen something like event (a) coming. A shocking number of Allen's movies and other writings include a troubling theme: old men attracted to very young women—or more accurately and, as Todd points out, "less credibly," very young women inexplicably attracted to much older men. In *Manhattan* (1979), Allen plays a forty-two-year-old man, Isaac, who has an affair with a seventeen-year-old girl named Tracy, played by Mariel Hemingway. In real life, Allen was forty-four and Hemingway was sixteen. In the movie, Tracy is in high school . . . and in real life, so was Hemingway. Because, again, she was sixteen human years old. At one point Tracy and Isaac kiss in Central Park. It was the first time Hemingway had ever kissed another person. Then two years after filming, according to Hemingway's memoirs, Allen flew to Idaho to convince her to run off to Paris with him, but left when it was clear she wasn't attracted to him, and didn't want to share a room.

There's a word for this behavior, and it's: "gross."

Allen certainly didn't invent men being gross about younger women. He may have perfected it, though, both in films and in real life. In *Annie Hall*, Tony Roberts's character, Rob, bails Allen's character, Alvy Singer (whom Rob calls "Max"), out of jail. Here's how that dialogue goes:

ROB: Imagine my surprise when I got your call, Max.

ALVY: Yeah. I had the feeling that I got you at a bad moment. You know, I heard high-pitched squealing.

ROB: Twins, Max. Sixteen-year-olds. Can you imagine the mathematical possibilities?

So . . . statutory rape, in which two sixteen-year-old girls are also possibly committing incest. Hilarious. I bring all this up less to draw further attention to Allen's ickiness than to spotlight my own questionable behavior—I knew all of this about him for years. Decades. I have several of his movies essentially memorized—I just typed that back-and-forth from *Annie Hall* by heart, because I've seen it a hundred times. And yet I never really asked myself whether it was . . . *okay* that he wrote men and women like this. Then in 1997, a sixty-two-year-old Allen married twenty-seven-year-old Soon-Yi Previn, who'd been adopted as a child by his former partner Mia Farrow. They began dating when Allen was fifty-six and Previn was twenty. Although they hadn't had a lot of interaction before starting the romance—Farrow and Allen were not traditionally "together" for most of Soon-Yi's childhood—a key moment in their relationship apparently occurred when Allen helped her with an injury she suffered in soccer practice when she was in eleventh grade.

There's a word for this behavior and it's: (*pained, guttural groan while clutching stomach*).

But when news of the relationship broke, I didn't emit a pained, guttural groan. I did what a lot of people do when confronted with information that challenges their core identities:[11] I explained it away. Soon-Yi

---

11 Recall the footnote in chapter 7 related to the backfire effect, which often causes people who are confronted with information that challenges their core identities to dig in their heels and double down on their original belief. See especially the work of Brendan Nyhan and Jason Reifler, explained in the podcast *You Are Not So Smart*. Like most of these thorny, complex issues, however, there is also some evidence that the effect is not quite as strong as their work suggested.

wasn't really *his* adopted daughter, she was *Mia Farrow's* adopted daughter. And those movies are just fiction. And it's not like he invented the idea of young women and older men! And on and on. Allen's writing was melted cheese on my personal identity pizza—if I scraped it off, my understanding of comedy wouldn't be the same, and thus neither would I. It only got worse when, years later, Allen was accused of sexual abuse by his daughter Dylan. The details are sordid and some are disputed, but at the very least, a judge overseeing a custody hearing proclaimed in his decision that Allen's general behavior toward Dylan (not specifically related to the charge of sexual abuse) was "grossly inappropriate and that measures must be taken to protect her." Unlike with the Washington R*dskins or Chick-fil-A, there's no fixing this. Snyder can change the name. Chick-fil-A can change their anti-LGBTQ+ stance. Cities can take down statues of racist police chiefs or Confederate generals. But I creatively worship a guy whose actions are (a) dicey at best and abhorrent at worst, and (b) a matter of history. When the person or thing we love or admire contains unalterable flaws, and they either don't own up to them or are dead and cannot—like with Thomas Jefferson's slave-owning, or JFK's philandering and sexual assaults—the only possible change is ours, and the change is painful.

Again, our schools of thought will likely tell us we should, indeed, swear these things off. Consequentialism, for example, falls apart in exactly the same way it did in the "Things That *Can* Change" version: It first seems to allow for the possibility that it's okay to watch Woody Allen movies when we consider how few people are actively "hurt" by our popping in a DVD we already own. No one would even know we had watched it, and *we* would be happy. But that's exactly the way the consequentialist argument *feels* wrong sometimes—this is one of those moments where it denies us our individual integrity. The things that make us "us" are the things at risk, here—both the love of the thing and the anguish that loving the thing causes—and utilitarian accounting ignores those questions of internal conflict. We may *feel* icky about watching the movie, which is completely separate from the "good or bad" caused to other people. (The calculation would obviously change a great deal if we were, say, in a position to finance one of Allen's films.)

The purity of Kant seems tempting: a categorical imperative to turn away from any "fruit of a poisonous tree" (art by an artist who has committed an unforgivable sin) appears to take care of the whole situation. But it's also a slippery slope, as Kantian purity often is. What counts as "unforgivable"? What about an actor who didn't commit a crime but merely supports a presidential candidate we abhor? Is that enough to force us to follow the imperative? And then there are the really confusing cases. For example, Mel Gibson's anti-Semitism and misogynistic comments to a Malibu police officer in 2006 aren't as bad as sexual assault, but they sure ain't great . . . *but*, he also later quit drinking and apologized for what he said . . . *buuuuuut* in 2010 the actress Winona Ryder related a charming anecdote from 1995 wherein Gibson apparently found out her friend was gay and asked "Am I gonna get AIDS?" from talking to him, and then when he found out Ryder was Jewish, he called her an "oven dodger." What do we make of his case? (Ryder said that he subsequently apologized and Gibson has said the allegations are untrue.) Should we give Gibson the same cold shoulder we'd give Allen, if we're being hard-core Kantians?

Again, this feels like a "What kind of person should I be?" question, more than a "What should I do?" question. There are just too many versions of "bad behavior" to lump all these possible scenarios together and find one umbrella rule we can follow. So let's try virtue ethics. If we don't care *enough* about the moral shortcomings of the people who make our movies and TV shows and music, we're callous and insensitive. We teach them a bad lesson—that they can say or do whatever they want, and we will continue to give them our money and attention. But if we care *too much*, and refuse to spend our money on anything made by anyone with a skeleton in their closet . . . well, given the human penchant for skeleton-having, we might never follow sports, listen to music, or watch anything on a screen ever again. Is there some amount of caring that is good and lets us feel like we are being thoughtful, considerate citizens and consumers who factor in morality when we make entertainment decisions, but also gives us a little bit of a break so we can love the things we love? Hopefully?

The "Extra Chicken Nugget" Defense

Here's an analogy that may help us find an answer. I became a vegetarian about ten years ago.[12] Being a vegetarian is frequently and actively difficult for me, because meat tastes good! Staring at the words "buttermilk fried chicken" or "pork ribs" on a menu and then ordering a goat cheese salad is a *tremendous* bummer. I made the decision for two reasons: my health (it's an easy way to lower cholesterol, and mine has always been bad), and morality (animals aren't treated well, by and large, and also they're nice and cute and eating them seems wrong, and also the meat industry is doing unforgivably awful things to the environment). With respect to the "morality" half of the argument, a large part of the point of becoming a vegetarian is to reduce the amount of meat purchased by stores and restaurants, which reduces demand, which leads to reduced meat production. But what if someone else—say, your ten-year-old daughter, Ivy, who loves chicken nuggets—has already ordered chicken nuggets, and then didn't finish them? My eating the rest of those nuggets does not send a positive feedback message to the restaurant—no extra chicken has been ordered, which means no additional chicken would ever be tallied up as being necessary in the future. And the nuggets look really good, by the way, in this theoretical example. They look awesome, and they're just sitting there on her plate, and oooh look there's ranch dressing, and we're just gonna throw them away?! That's nuts. *Someone* ought to enjoy them. I mean, what's the harm?[13]

---

12 If you're keeping tabs on my personal meat-eating history, it was soon after the Chick-fil-A incident, so at the time of that debate, eating at Chick-fil-A was still an option for me.
13 Shocking note from Todd, here, who is also a vegetarian: "True confession: I have been there, because my oldest son, a weightlifter, eats hamburgers. Not only have I finished the last couple of bites when he doesn't eat them, but when he wraps it back up in the bag and puts it on the top of the garbage I have occasionally gone into the bag, pulled out those last couple of bites, and eaten them. Not proud of this. Just sayin'." Philosophers: they're just like us!

I think it's clear that eating Ivy's leftover chicken nuggets is not *as bad* as ordering my own. It's not *great*, because I'm still eating meat, but it's *better* than ordering new meat. There are levels here, is what I'm saying. Is it possible that there are levels in terms of our entertainment consumption too? For example, the "watching an old movie on DVD" situation I mentioned earlier. No new money is going to Woody Allen if I watch *Annie Hall* on a DVD I have owned for twenty years. I'm not buying a ticket to a new film and thus putting new money into his pocket. I still have to reckon internally with my decision to watch art made by a man whose actions I find reprehensible, but if that movie meant so much to me as a kid, and contributed directly to my life and career as a writer, maybe that's okay, somehow?

The most important part of becoming better people, I'll say yet again, is that we *care* about whether what we do is good or bad, and therefore *try* to do the right thing. If we love a problematic person or thing too much to part with it altogether, I think that means we have to keep two ideas in our head at the same time:

1. I love this thing.
2. The person who made it is troubling.

Forgetting about (1) means we lose a piece of ourselves. Forgetting about (2) means we are denying that this thing causes us (and others) anguish, and thus we're failing to show concern for the victims of awful behavior. We can think both of these things at the same time. And if we do—if we really confront the wrongs of the artists as we consume their work, instead of making excuses or living in denial—we can to some degree forgive ourselves for keeping them in our lives. In certain cases, we will find it impossible to continue to enjoy the thing we love—the artist will do something we simply cannot abide, and it will prove so ugly and damning that we just cannot spend our time or money to support them, even in private. But in other cases, when something is so inexorably woven into our core identities that life without it feels unthinkable, maintaining those two ideas simultaneously can help us avoid the pain of severing all ties while still striving for self-improvement.

But what does this mean *practically speaking*, for us? How do we actually confront this problem day to day, person by person? Is it *always* enough simply to keep two conflicting ideas in our heads at the same time? How do we know when someone has crossed over from "troubling" to "indefensible"?

This part of the question doesn't have an answer, I think. Sometimes in philosophy, people throw around the word "heuristic." A heuristic is a tool that allows us to input a problem and get a solution—a rule of thumb that gives us a guideline for our behavior. (Scanlon's "rules no one would reasonably reject" is a heuristic—though a slightly abstract one—because in theory we can take any situation, run it through that machine, and determine the proper way forward.) There is no heuristic to answer the questions "Can we separate the art from the artist?" or "How do we deal with loved ones whose beliefs cause us pain?" or "Can I cheer for a team whose owner gets sexual pleasure from strangling baby giraffes?"[14] We can and should apply any of our moral theories to all of these situations, but at some point we'll just have to act. To *choose*. We will decide we have to banish *this* thing or person from our lives, but maybe not *that* one, based on nothing more than our reasoning and our guts. People who want to avoid this thorny issue like to say, "Where do you draw the line?!" as if merely pointing out its blurriness absolves us from trying to bring it into focus. But as the comedian John Oliver likes to say: *somewhere*. We draw it *somewhere*. You and I may draw it in different places, but we need to draw it, each of us, for ourselves.

Now, the instant we draw these lines, we *guarantee* that we'll eventually find ourselves in a contradiction. We will continue to love and

---

14 To the best of my knowledge, Daniel Snyder does not strangle baby giraffes in order to achieve sexual excitement. But also, if I found out Daniel Snyder strangled baby giraffes in order to achieve sexual excitement, I would nod and say, "Yeah, makes sense."

support one person and not another, even when the two of them seem roughly equivalent in their behaviors. Our friends will jump up and down and point and gleefully ask how we can possibly watch *this* movie but not *that* one, or how we can cheer for *this* baseball player but condemn *that* one, and so on. Those contradictions are not excuses to throw our hands up and abandon the entire project of outlining our integrity, our sense of being a "whole and undivided person." They're reasons to dig back in, mull everything over, and if necessary erase the line we drew and redraw it somewhere else. Contradictions within our own system of integrity are simply opportunities to *try*, again, to make decisions true to our own beliefs, our understanding of ethics, and our sense of who we are. These moments—when we are caught in a situation that has no clear answer, no heuristic to employ that will spit out a theoretical but practically impossible "correct" decision—are when we see the true value in failure. We're deciding to do something that *will*, someday, backfire. The more we chew on it and work it through, the more meaning we can derive from that backfire when it happens.

And the capper, of course, is the even thornier question: When do we not only curb our behavior, but actually *speak out* against those people and things and behaviors we've deemed incompatible with our sense of integrity? These issues aren't like the fender bender that I haphazardly turned into an unfair public shaming. If Aristotle is right—if there is some amount of anger that should be directed at the right people for the right reasons, or some amount of shame that people should feel for their bad actions—these are the situations he's talking about. Remember your pleasant and birthday-remembering Aunt Connie, who's generally lovely but also has some troubling thoughts about Mexicans? Standing up to Aunt Connie sounds *hard*. Just the thought of an actual confrontation with a family member makes our stomachs ache and our voices tremble. So we frequently take the easy way out, and . . . do nothing.

I've been guilty of this, a million times. Plenty of people in my life have said or done things I find abhorrent, and I've remained silent because I didn't want to cause a scene, start a difficult conversation, or risk an argument. (I'm pretty conflict-averse, a fact I'm often not proud of.) As Overton windows shift along the continuum stretching from tradition to revolution, we find ourselves in a constant state of conflict with those older than us, who cling to ideas that have long since been revealed as offensive or outdated, and those younger than us, whose criticisms of the status quo can sometimes seem overly strident. Confronting either attitude can seem both difficult and—given how rarely people seem to change their minds about stuff—pointless. But if I can't quite find "an answer" to these problems, I can at least tell you what *isn't* the answer: doing nothing.

It doesn't help anyone to dig in our heels and ignore pleas from people who accuse us of a lack of caring or sensitivity. It also doesn't help anyone to remain silent when our friends or loved ones or casual acquaintances say something racist, sexist, or offensive. Action is called for here, in the name of openness and improvement, both for us and for other people. Now, when Aunt Connie casually drops a racist talking point about Mexicans in the middle of Thanksgiving dinner, it seems horribly Pollyannaish to suggest: "Talk about it! Have a dialogue!" What does that even look like? What good would it do? How would she react? Will you ruin Thanksgiving? Will Aunt Connie ever speak to you again? We've already seen how shaming people can backfire, making them dig in their heels and double down on their beliefs—why would we think this would be any different?

But we've also heard, from Aristotle, that "the person who is deficient in shame or never feels shame at all is said to have no sense of disgrace." If we love Aunt Connie, and care about her, wouldn't we want *her* to feel a little shame if she's saying something shameful? Wouldn't we want to help *her* flourish? And don't we want to work at finding the golden mean of mildness—expressing the *right amount of anger* in the *right situations?* Virtue ethicists know means are hard to find, and they know exactly what they're asking of us—to do the grueling work of seeking them. If it were easy, we'd all be flourishing already. So maybe we don't stand up in the middle of Thanksgiving dinner and declare our aunt to be an irredeemable racist. But maybe we *do* pull her aside later, and try to explain why her views are wrong or hurtful. Maybe we try to get to the bottom of her views, find their root cause, and work to change her mind. Maybe we explain that while she may think she's just expressing an opinion or making a joke, her words risk damaging our relationship with her, and that remaining silent as she says these things threatens our own sense of integrity. No matter what we do, we keep two conflicting thoughts in our minds at the same time:

I love this person.

This person is causing me anguish.

We treat those thoughts with equal weight. And we hope the person in question will do the same.

Unsurprisingly, Snyder Loses Again

There's a postscript to this discussion: the R*dskins finally changed their name.

In the summer of 2020, as the entire country wrestled with police brutality and the Black Lives Matter movement put racial injustice front and center, Snyder finally decided to join the rest of us here in the twenty-first century and agreed the nickname was no longer appropriate. Of all the ways we can become better people, "dragged kicking and screaming" isn't ideal, but it's better than nothing. (Feels worth mentioning that not long after the decision to change the name, a *Washington Post* piece exposed a disturbing pattern of sexual harassment committed by executives in the team's front office that turned into a full-blown PR nightmare. I'm sure that's just a coincidence, though.) I prefer to focus not on the winding path of doofusness that brought us here, but on the relief and happiness of the Indigenous people and their allies who earned the win in this hard-fought battle. It hammers home what we've been saying about *trying*. Snyder shouted, only a few years ago, that he would NEVER change the name of his team. But a bunch of people kept trying. They kept lobbying, and lightly shaming him, and making their case. And little by little, the Overton window shifted. Other teams changed their names. Social justice crept forward. And finally, the window's range included something that was once unthinkable.

This was a hard one. These are all hard ones. It can wear us out, thinking about these problems, especially when we come armed with 2,400 years of philosophical theory and *still* can't find a definitive solution. In moments like this, a tempting voice calls out to us—*Stop caring! Life is so much easier when you don't try so hard to be good, especially given that it sometimes feels impossible. I mean, we're just little flecks of dust on a tiny rock in outer space—does anything we do even matter?*

So . . . does it?

CHAPTER ELEVEN

Making Ethical Decisions Is Hard. Can We Just . . . Not Make Them?

You've probably heard the term "existentialism," and chances are that when you heard it, it was being used incorrectly. Any literature that's bleak, or deals with death, or is vaguely European, runs the risk of being labeled "existentialist," and it's usually not. "Existential" is one of those fancy words people like to use when the word they really mean is much simpler:

WHAT PEOPLE WHO WANT TO SOUND FANCY SAY	WHAT THEY MEAN
Kafkaesque	Eerie
Surrealist	Weird-looking
Ironic	Annoying
Existential	Dark/sad/bleak/despairing
Freudian	Penis-related
Postmodern	Recent
Orwellian	I got banned from Twitter for being racist

I suppose we can't really blame people for using the word incorrectly, because existentialist writing—most closely associated with a philosophical and literary movement in mid-twentieth-century France—is famously difficult to understand. But buried in its texts, under a thousand layers of Gauloises smoke and Gallic angst, is a new angle on ethical decision-making that sidesteps most of what we've discussed so far and urges us to be good people in a dramatic (and, yes, kind of bleak) way.

Jean-Paul Sartre, Famous Optimist

Existentialism, in a hilariously reductive nutshell, believes the following: Human existence is absurd. There is no "higher power" or deity or meaning to be found beyond the fact of that existence, and this condition fills us with dread and anxiety. The movement's overall goal (though the details vary from writer to writer) was to make sense of what we can do in the face of that absurdity, dread, and anxiety. Even at its height, existentialism was largely misunderstood and criticized. On October 29, 1945, French existentialist Jean-Paul Sartre attempted to set the record straight, giving a speech entitled "Existentialism Is a Humanism" in Paris. The title itself was meant to surprise people—a *humanism*?! This dude is claiming that his philosophy is "optimistic" and pro-people?! We're talking about Jean-Paul Sartre—one of the most famously grim people in history. He named his cat "Nothing." He wrote books called *Nausea* and *Being and Nothingness*. Imagine writing a book called *Being and Nothingness* and then asking, "Why does everyone think I'm depressing?"

Sartre was trying to dispel misunderstandings about existentialism—essentially, he wanted people to stop using the term wrong.[1] He apparently spoke without notes of any kind, which is astounding, and he comes across like a lawyer making a closing argument on behalf of his

---

[1] "Indeed, the word is being so loosely applied to so many things that it has come to mean nothing at all."

client; he's (literally) defensive, but for good reason—his existentialist writings had made everyone mad at him. As Arlette Elkaïm-Sartre (his adopted daughter, and sometime translator) writes in the preface to the 1996 French edition:

> Christians chastised Sartre not only for his atheism but for being a materialist, while Communists reproached him for not being one. . . . In many people's minds, Sartre was becoming the anti-humanist par excellence: he demoralized the French at a time when France, lying in ruins, most needed hope.

In a very short time—really between 1943 and 1945—Sartre had managed to piss off Communists, atheists, and artists, even while being an atheistic novelist who wrote for underground Communist journals. That's hard to do. This existentialism is powerful stuff.

The religious objection to existentialism doesn't take much explanation: Sartre completely denies the presence of any omnipotent God that watches over us or judges our actions. To Sartre, we're born out of nothingness—poof!—and then it's entirely up to us what we are and do, and then we die—poof!—and that's it. Nothing "guides" us, we're not following any playbook from religion or spirituality or *anything*. All we have, and all we ultimately are, is the choices we make while we're alive. The belief that we exist before there's any meaning attached to our lives is a condition Sartre calls "subjectivity," and explains by saying: "Existence precedes essence." The most important conclusion it leads him to is this: if there's no giant structure that fills the world with any kind of meaning before or after we exist, then: "Man is responsible for what he is."

> Man first exists: he materializes in the world, encounters himself, and only afterwards defines himself. If man as existentialists conceive of him cannot be defined, it is because to begin with he is nothing. He will not be anything until later, and then he will be what he makes of himself.

For anyone brought up in one of the Abrahamic traditions—Judaism, Christianity, or Islam—life without God is like a baseball game with no umps. No one is keeping score or enforcing rules, so anything goes. As Dostoyevsky famously wrote: "If God does not exist, everything is permissible."[2] If you remove God from the equation—and thus any kind of grand design for humanity—then we're all just a bunch of dodos wandering around the planet, accountable to nothing but ourselves. And that's exactly what Sartre believed—in fact, it's the very guts of his entire philosophy. Existentialism is a little like when your parents yelled at you when you were fifteen because you did something stupid, saying "You're a grown-up! You're responsible for your actions!" except in this case it's a French philosopher yelling at you, and his conclusions deny the existence of God.

For Sartre, life with no God to create systemic order for humanity may indeed be disturbing, but it's also *freeing*. Without commandments we have to follow, or "meaning" to be found in religion, or national identity, or your parents being dentists and demanding you become a dentist too, or anything else, we're truly *free*—in like a big-picture, eagle-eye-view-of-everything way—to choose what we are. "Signs" or "omens" exist only because we choose to see them, and we should never make a decision based on one; or if we do, we should recognize that the sign isn't making the decision—*we* are simply choosing to interpret the sign in a way that points to *our* decision. Religious instruction, education, family traditions, a Magic 8 Ball—they're all equally bad crutches to rely on when we face a choice. Every person, whether Peruvian or Mongolian, a pauper or third in line for the Danish throne, is perfectly and completely free to make whatever choices she wants.

---

2 He actually didn't write this at all. The actual quote is much longer and more intricate, but that pithy version is the one you see all the time. It's another "Play it again, Sam" kind of a deal. More than a century later, Kurt Vonnegut would update and rephrase this sentiment in a way I find much more fun: "I'm telling you, we are here on Earth to fart around, and don't let anybody ever tell you any different."

But—and this is kind of tricky—when we make our choices, we're actually making them for all people.[3] Yeah. Wrap your head around that for a second. When we choose to do things, says Sartre, we're creating an image of a person as they *should* be, which can then be viewed and followed by everyone else. Here Sartre weirdly converges with Kant, because he wants us to ask ourselves, "What would happen if everyone did what I am doing?" He wants us to determine our own morality but also model that morality for everyone else. This might seem like a contradiction: There's no God, no "meaning" to the universe, no guidebook to follow, everyone can make whatever choices he wants . . . but also those choices should be a model for everyone else? Then, we might ask, wouldn't thinking of yourself as a model for others be in conflict with the idea that everyone makes choices for herself, not following any external guide or rulebook? But don't worry, there's a good reason that this seems like a contradiction: it's a contradiction. It's honestly a little unclear how Sartre maintains all of these ideas simultaneously, or even why he would want to. He did sympathize with the Communists in postwar Europe, so maybe his political beliefs seeped in a bit here as he tried to find a way that humans were connected to each other? All I know is, people have been writing about this contradiction for seventy years, so the odds I untangle it in this paragraph are . . . slim.

Now, if you're thinking, "You just told me there is no God and no 'meaning' to our existence, and that all we have are our choices, and now you're telling me to make choices that model behavior for all of humanity? I kind of have a stomachache here, man," well, that's exactly the point. In fact, Sartre acknowledges that this particular human condition fills us with anguish—"the kind experienced by all who have borne responsibilities." He knows how hard it is to be a human being on earth under the circumstances he describes, and refuses to let us off the hook. Life is anguish. Welcome to existentialism!

---

3 Sartre, of course, used "men" and not "people."

And yet, for all the anguish it entails, Sartre believed, about existentialism, that "no doctrine is more optimistic."

The way Sartre puts it, in his trademark "everything I say is kind of terrifying, even when I'm trying to reassure you" style, is this: "Man is condemned to be free." We have no crutches, or "reasons" to do whatever we choose to do, except that we have chosen to do them. (And I know what you're thinking—what if I just don't choose anything? No go. "If I decide not to choose, that still constitutes a choice," he says.[4]) The "optimistic" thing about this condition, for him, is that "man's destiny lies within himself." If we embrace the idea that all we are is our choices, we are *forced* to freely make any choice we want, whenever we want. We have no other option—there's no other way out of this anguish-filled mess. All of which makes existentialists *super* fun at parties. True story—our own Todd May went through a hard-core existentialism phase in college, and responded to everyone who asked him a question by saying, "I am *choosing* to—" whatever his answer was. So, someone would say, "There's a party tonight at my dorm, you wanna go?" and Todd would reply, "I am *choosing* to not go to your party." Todd has been married for many years and has three grown children, and when I heard that story I wondered how any of that was remotely possible.

In his speech from 1945, Sartre gives the example of a former student, a young man who lived with his mother. The man's father had been a Nazi collaborator, which shamed the mother, and the man's older brother had already been killed in the war. He had to decide whether to go off and join the freedom fighters in England, trying to avenge the death of his brother, or stay and care for his mother, who had already lost so much. The guy knew he might be killed long before he arrived

---

4 Or, in the words of Canadian rock power trio Rush in their song "Freewill," "If you choose not to decide / You still have made a choice." Bet you didn't think when you bought this book on philosophy and got to the chapter on existentialism you were gonna get a Rush lyric thrown at you, huh? Well, too bad. It happened.

in England, but he also knew that staying home meant not fighting for the cause he believed in or avenging his brother's death. It was a real World War II–flavored pickle. Sartre's point is that nothing can "help" the young man make his choice. There's no oracle he can consult, no Kantian rule or moral theory or anything else that addresses this fraught decision. There is only his decision, and his decision is just his decision, whatever it is, so he should make it, and own it, instead of relying on the Bible or reading J. S. Mill or consulting a psychic at a carnival.

So here we are, two hundred pages deep in this book, having learned all about deontology and utilitarianism and contractualism and virtue ethics and a bunch of other stuff, and along comes a morose French-man to tell us that there's no God and people define themselves through action and we have to just make decisions with no guidance except "the essential anguish of our own existence" or something. He's telling us that Kant and Bentham and Scanlon and Aristotle are about as helpful to our moral lives as a coin flip. Should we listen to him, and junk all these other theories?

Albert Camus, the Non-Existentialist Existentialist

Before we even entertain that notion, we should talk about the other great French existentialist, Albert Camus (1913–1960). Sartre and Camus were contemporary French philosophers who both won the Nobel Prize in Literature, but they also had some key differences. For one thing, Camus accepted his Nobel Prize, while Sartre turned his down, which is super punk rock and *extremely* French.[5] Camus's existentialist mus-ings are also even more stripped down and intense than Sartre's. As I mentioned earlier, Sartre did some (kind of contradictory) work to make

---

5 Camus had already died by the time Sartre won and turned down the prize, but I bet if he'd been alive he would've been annoyed that he didn't have the idea to do that first.

his philosophy compatible with Communist political movements in postwar France; Camus didn't care about that. Sartre thought we should perform actions that could serve as models for others; Camus didn't care about that either. His existentialism is like a balsamic reduction of Sartre's—sharper, more intense, more potent. In fact, Camus actually claimed repeatedly that he *wasn't* an existentialist, but come on, dude, yes you were. I mean, look at you:

You're telling me *that guy* isn't an existentialist?[6]

Camus broke down his version of existentialism (which, again, he denied it was, blah blah blah) this way: Humans desire meaning from the universe, but the universe is cold and indifferent and denies us that meaning; in fact, nothing "means" anything, really, or at least nothing is more "meaningful" than anything else. So we're just little specks of nothingness on a big dumb rock floating in space, desperately searching for something we'll never find, and thus, the human condition is fundamentally absurd.

I said that the world is absurd, but . . . what is absurd is the con-

---

6 Also, not that this matters, but what a looker, am I right? It's funny to think of philosophers as sexy, but you gotta give it up—Camus was a stone-cold hottie.

frontation of this irrational[7] and the wild longing for clarity whose call echoes in the human heart. The absurd depends as much on man as on the world. For the moment it is all that links them together. It binds them one to the other as only hatred can weld two creatures together. This is all I can discern clearly in this measureless universe where my adventure takes place.

. . . Great. So, then, what do we do? How do we deal with this fundamental absurdity? Camus says we have three choices.

1. We can kill ourselves.

Seems . . . less than ideal. To be clear, Camus doesn't say we *should* commit suicide. He just says it's technically a way out of the absurdity of longing for meaning in a meaningless universe, because it eliminates half of the equation (the person who desires meaning).

2. We can embrace some kind of structure—religion, family, work, anything—and find meaning in it.

Better than suicide, right? For Camus, actually, no. Or: barely. He refers to this process of imbuing something with meaning as "philosophical suicide." It's an attempt to get rid of the *other* half of the absurd equation—the cold, indifferent, meaningless universe—by manufacturing meaning we can then cling to. But to create "meaning" out of any societal structure is to deny the inescapable fact that we're just little specks of nothingness on a big dumb rock floating in space, searching for meaning in a cold and indifferent universe that will never provide it, and for him that's ultimately harmful: "The doctrines that explain everything to me"—that is, the structures that theoretically offer him meaning—"also debilitate me at the same time." So what's option number three?

---

7 In translation, Camus uses "irrational" as a noun, referring to the unknowable meaning of things in the universe.

3. We can acknowledge the fundamental absurdity of the human condition, and just kind of exist within it!

I added the exclamation point to try to hide how bleak a sentence that is. But for Camus, that's the only real answer.

> I don't know whether this world has a meaning that transcends it. But I know that I do not know that meaning and that it is impossible for me just now to know it. . . . These two certainties—my appetite for the absolute and for unity and the impossibility of reducing this world to a rational and reasonable principle—I also know that I cannot reconcile them.

The only way to cope with our desire for meaning inside an empty, pointless universe is to *recognize* how absurd it is that we exist in an empty, pointless universe and still desire meaning. He wants us to stand in the middle of the hurricane of absurdity, neither denying it nor allowing it to defeat us.

In *The Myth of Sisyphus*, Camus discusses the famous fable wherein Sisyphus is condemned to roll a heavy rock up a hill, after which the rock rolls back down the hill, whereupon he has to descend and roll it back up the hill, forever. He's been assigned this eternal fate because he pissed off the gods in a bunch of different ways, so they gave him an absurd repetitive task that stretches out infinitely. But Camus saw it differently: So Sisyphus has to complete this same ridiculous task over and over forever—so what? "The workman of today," he points out, "works every day in his life at the same tasks, and this fate is no less absurd." And in the case of Sisyphus, "His fate belongs to him. His rock is his thing." Camus says that Sisyphus's existence was made *deliberately* and *inexorably* absurd, which means it's all Sisyphus can think about, and thus he *understands* how absurd it is, and therefore it frees him from the distracting illusion of meaning: there is only this singular task, this one struggle. Camus concludes, in a sentence that has been rocking the worlds of college freshmen for seventy years: "One must imagine Sisyphus happy."

So, here we have a couple of new theoretical approaches to ethics, which have to do with the idea of absolute, radical freedom. Can they help us, somehow, in our quest to become better people?

"We Had No Choice!"

Sartre's critics offered a decent comeback, which recalls the question I imagined some of you may have had at the beginning of this book: *Who the hell are you to judge me?* If there is no higher power, how can it be that any individual has any authority to say others should do what he does? Sartre's response was to say that we make our choices individually but "in the presence of others," so if we determine someone is relying on religion or some other structure as a "reason" for making a choice, she screwed up—he calls such a reliance on external factors or structures "an error" and suggests we should announce it as such. It's not exactly an entire "ethical" system, but Sartre is certainly concerned with what we do and why we do it. Similarly, if our friend asks us what we think of her ugly shirt and we look to Camus for advice, and he smiles insouciantly and says, *You should simply stand naked within the incongruous farce of existence,* well, that's maybe not super helpful. But that doesn't mean it has nothing to offer us in our quest to be good.

The complete freedom that existentialists shove down our throats—the insistence that we can't defend our choices using any external structure—keeps us from using those structures as a crutch. Let's imagine we're in one of those really weird ethical tangles where there's no easy answer. Our friend Sue is furious with our other friend Gina because Gina has been spreading rumors about Sue cheating on her boyfriend. When Sue vents to us, we tell her we are on her side, because Gina tends to do stuff like this. (I mean, you know Gina—she's a mess.) Then later, coincidentally, Gina calls and asks if we want to use her lake house for the weekend because she has to go take care of her ailing mother. We know that doing this will annoy Sue—"How could you accept her offer when she's being so awful to me?!" she'll likely say (I mean, you know Sue, she has a bit of a martyr complex). But on the other hand . . . we have nothing to do with this beef, really, and it sounds relaxing to sit by a lake all day, and also Gina is paying us back for that time last year that we picked her up from the airport, and saying no would require us to either (a) tell her that we're saying no because of her beef with Sue or else (b) lie to her, and we read in a book somewhere that Kant told us we're never supposed to lie, and (c) Gina actually told us we'd be doing her a *favor* by looking after her house and she's already stressed about her ailing mother. And so on. These complex decisions arise all the time—they contain fifty different considerations and ethical vectors and loyalty tests, and sometimes, even if we're determined to be good little utilitarians or virtue seekers or deontological maxim–obeyers, it can be impossible to make sense of all of it.

And when that happens, we're tempted to look for something solid to hang on to, a *reason* that justifies what we're going to do as though that were really the only possible choice. Reasons make us feel better because they reframe our choices as inevitable, thus absolving us of responsibility. "We *had no choice* but to accept Gina's offer, because not doing so would be rude." Or "We *had no choice* but to reject it, because of our friendship with Sue." The existentialists are there to remind us: it's *always* our choice. For all its confusing French[8] linguistic gymnastics, there's a simplicity to Sartre's existentialism: we choose to act, and the choices are ours and ours alone. And there's a comfort, sometimes, in Camus's existentialism: just being human often feels ridiculous, and true happiness may come from accepting that ridiculousness as inescap-

---

8 Not all existentialists were French. Søren Kierkegaard was Danish, and people often call some of the great nineteenth-century Russian novelists (like Dostoyevsky) existentialists. But again: Come on. It's *so* French.

able. Both men also encourage us not to dwell on our mistakes. Okay, we blew it. Next time: don't. If Aristotle tells us to keep trying different things in order to find the bullseye of virtue, existentialists say: keep making choices, because choices are all we have in our absurd, meaningless universe.

However: despite Sartre thinking his existentialism is "humanistic," or how liberating Camus's existentialism might be for the mythical Sisyphus, it can be pretty unforgiving for real people. Let's now imagine a low-income woman in rural Alaska who wrenches her knee. A doctor prescribes her absurdly powerful opioids because he's corrupt and has a side deal with a pharmaceutical company to sell as much OxyContin as he can. She becomes addicted to the opioids, can't afford her habit, and eventually steals money from a gas station to pay the corrupt doctor. Is she a thief? Sartre would say yes—she made that choice, it's her choice and hers alone, etc. But exhortations like *we are responsible for our decisions* are not exactly helpful when a diabolical pharma company has invented a powerful drug and lied about its addictive qualities, and a corrupt doctor has gotten you addicted to that drug.[9] Saying that all we are is our choices ignores the fact that sometimes choices *are made for us*. People don't choose to be put in many situations that they're in— they're just *in* them, and those situations often force them to make other choices that in a more forgiving (or at least neutral) world they wouldn't make. We'll deal with this in greater detail in the next chapter, but it's relevant here: the choices we make may be our own, but the life into which we're born, and many of the events that befall us after that, are things we often have little or no control over.[10]

---

9 Todd notes that Sartre would also say that addiction is a choice. Mike notes that Sartre needs to cool it a little.

10 Note from Todd, to ward off protests from the pro-Sartre crowd: Sartre sorta, kinda recognizes this point obliquely in his concept of despair, which says, "We must limit ourselves to reckoning only with those things that depend on our will, or on the set of probabilities that enable action. Whenever we desire something, there are always ele-

We've now heard a large number of theories, spanning dozens of centuries, all of which have given us reasons to care about whether what we're doing is good and playbooks for how we might try to be better. But there's one essential aspect of the human condition that none of them really deals with: *context*. Few of these philosophies grapple with the plain fact that moral choices are a lot harder for some of us than they are for others, depending on our circumstances. How can it be that the same exact rules apply to me, Prince William, that poor woman whose doctor got her addicted to OxyContin, a South Korean dental hygienist, Cardi B, a sugarcane farmer in Guyana, and you? As we've talked about what "we" should do in any given situation, we've ignored that within "we" are a whole bunch of different "me"s, and each "me" describes a unique life with unique challenges and privileges, which might make the work of being good harder or easier for *that* "me" than the "me" who lives right next door.

So, enough collective "we" action. Let's get *specific*.

---

ments of probability." But come on, Sartre, it's poverty we're talking about, not blackjack.

I Gave a Twenty-Seven-Cent Tip to My Barista, and Now Everyone's Yelling at Me on Twitter, Just Because I'm a Billionaire! I Can't Even Enjoy the Soft-Shell Crab Rolls That My Sushi Chef Made for My Private Dirigible Trip to the Dutch Antilles! How Is That Fair?!

The effort we put into being ethical matters, certainly, but it also matters to what degree we can even try. To quote the great pre-Socratic Greek philosopher Xenophanes on the subject of daily existence, "This shit ain't easy,"[1] and the playing field isn't exactly level. We do not all have equal amounts of time and energy and money to put toward making good decisions. As our old friend Julia Annas writes:

> There are very many people in the world today who live in terrible conditions of poverty and violence (for example, in the slums of large cities) which make it unreasonable to expect them to reflect on and criticize the lessons they are taught by the role models they have, people who frequently (and understandably) emphasize the importance not of the virtues but of looking out for your-

---

1 There's no evidence Xenophanes ever said this, but a lot of pre-Socratic Greek philosophical writing was lost or destroyed, so, you know, he might have.

self, not getting held back by caring about others, becoming used to violence and cruelty, and worse. . . . Most of these people fail to become virtuous because of the difficulties of their situation, not because they are not capable of it.

We may all be born with those virtue starter kits we talked about back in chapter 1—we all have the *potential* to be virtuous—but Annas points out that it shouldn't be held against people when circumstances deny them the chance to develop that potential into actual virtues. Remember how obsessed the Greeks were with teachers? Well, what happens when we can't learn from Aristotle because we don't have enough money to pay for his fancy elite academy, and the "wisest man" in our neighborhood is some skeevy guy who sells knockoff Affliction shirts out of the back of his van? Many people in this world might want to spend their time thinking about ethics and virtue, but they have to focus instead on more pressing matters, like *not starving*, or *not dying of disease*, or *not being killed by roving gangs of paramilitary troops*. How is that their fault?

Kant's zero-tolerance policy is hardly better in this regard. Formulating and following universal maxims can be an impossible luxury if your life has taken a wrong turn or contains too many daily stressors to think about anything other than survival. And as for utilitarianism, well, what if we're not a trolley *driver* but rather one of the construction workers, slaving away on the tracks in the hot sun for minimum wage, vaguely aware that at any moment we might get flattened because of faulty brakes? How can we be held to the same ethical standard as the passenger, who can ponder the correct moral response to the situation without fear of death? What if we're not Jim, the tourist who happens upon Pete holding a gun on the ten locals, but *one of the locals*, and our daily lives include the super-fun variable that at any moment we might get rounded up and shot as a way for Pete to maintain his demented law-and-order regimen? Can we really be expected to spend the same amount of time and energy thinking about ethics as Jim, who happened upon this nightmare accidentally and after it's over will get to go back to his resort and sip a frozen daiquiri by the pool?

It's a Hard(er for Some People Than for Others)-Knock Life

It seems unfair to demand the same level of ethical effort from an unwittingly opioid-addicted woman as we would from Jeff Bezos, or me, or any average citizen. But when we're considering circumstance as a factor in our ability to navigate life's myriad pitfalls, we don't even need to consider someone living under *rare* or *extraordinary* pressure. The most basic facts of existence can create wildly different living experiences for two people who otherwise may appear roughly similar. The writer John Scalzi crystallized the problem of ignoring context and privilege in a 2012 blog post titled "Straight White Male: The Lowest Difficulty Setting There Is."

Imagine life here in the U.S.—or indeed, pretty much anywhere in the Western world—is a massive role playing game, like World of Warcraft except appallingly mundane, where most quests involve the acquisition of money, cell phones and donuts, although not always at the same time. Let's call it The Real World. You have installed The Real World on your computer and are about to start playing, but first you go to the settings tab to bind your keys, fiddle with your defaults, and choose the difficulty setting for the game. Got it?

Okay: In the role playing game known as The Real World, "Straight White Male" is the lowest difficulty setting there is.

This means that the default behaviors for almost all the non-player characters in the game are easier on you than they would be otherwise. The default barriers for completions of quests are lower. Your leveling-up thresholds come more quickly. You automatically gain entry to some parts of the map that others have to work for. The game is easier to play, automatically, and when you need help, by default it's easier to get.[2]

The fundamental problem with applying the same ethical theories equally to all people is that all people aren't living equal lives. Centuries of history, socioeconomic development, racism, genderism, and coagulations of power and capital mean that two people born in roughly the same place at the same time may face *very* different hurdles in their lives. Again, while we may be equal in our *potential* for virtue, not everyone can apply the same amount of precious resources to the *development* of virtue. And if *caring* and *trying* are the most important aspects of ethical engagement, that means it would be silly to ask all people to care and try the same amount.

There is a certain strain of modern Western sociopolitical thinker that aggressively admires "meritocracy." Every society should be a meritocracy, argue these adherents, and we should not pass laws that favor one group of people over another, for any reason. There should be no affirmative action laws for university admissions, no initiatives to gender-balance workforces. The cream shall simply rise to the top! These people (usually heterosexual, rich, white men, with a bookshelf full of Ayn Rand novels) conveniently forget that for a meritocracy to work—for a society to properly value and celebrate hard work and individual success—the people within the society *need to start from the same point of origin*. Otherwise, the cream isn't rising to the top—the people who were *closest to the top already* are rising to the top, and the whole concept of meritocracy crumbles to dust. What they are actually calling for, these people, is a pseudo-meritocracy that does not distinguish between the accomplishments of a man with a Mayflower last name who

---

2 Scalzi is focused on race and gender, not class, but I feel like you can apply his metaphor to any class structure as well; in other words, a straight white *working-class* male will be playing an easier "version of the game" than a gay East Asian *working-class* woman, etc.

inherited a billion dollars from his dad and those of a Black woman who was born into poverty in a redlined neighborhood in a state that enforces draconian, racist laws. (Some people, as the old saying goes, were born on third base and think they hit a triple.) It's not a meritocracy if some runners start the race ten feet from the finish line and some are denied entry to the race because of systemic biases within the Racing Commission.

We were all born into circumstances over which we had no control, and which conferred on us certain advantages or disadvantages. I was born a healthy white dude in America in 1975, to two married, college-educated parents, who never had a lot of money but lived a decent middle-class life in central Connecticut. I didn't have a say in the matter—that was just my roll of the dice. What did that lucky roll mean for me? It meant I was born with immunity to the following societal ills:

- racism
- sexism
- ableism
- misogyny
- famine
- poverty
- low-quality, underfunded schools
- war (in my home country)
- lack of clean water
- lack of medical care[3]

I escaped all of those booby traps, which can throttle people as they attempt to make their way in the world, *through no effort of my own*, just because of the random, specific embryo that I grew out of. I started

---

3 America's health system leaves a lot to be desired, but I could, like, go to the dentist twice a year and get vaccinated and stuff.

my life with a massive societal advantage, and when we do a general checkup of my ethical report card it makes perfect sense to factor that in. Demanding applause for being a generally ethical person would be like me starting a marathon twenty-five miles in, beating someone who started at the actual starting line,[4] and then bragging about winning. I have gotten to play the video game of life on the easiest possible setting, so if I make a bad choice, I have made a *really* bad choice. Think again of Jean Valjean in *Les Misérables*. He steals a loaf of bread to feed his sister's family and ends up serving nineteen years in prison. But he was poor, his family was starving, and he felt he had no choice. Now consider this: What if I—now an adult television writer with plenty of money and a nice house and no cute little starving French urchins to feed—steal a loaf of bread, just . . . because? Kant would say the two actions—Jean Valjean stealing bread and me stealing bread—are the same, because both violate the same universal maxim. Sartre might agree—we both simply made a choice. But I would say that when Jean Valjean stole a loaf of bread to feed his starving family, he was courageous, valiant, self-sacrificing, and generous, whereas when I did it I was just a rich asshole who stole a loaf of bread for no reason. My crime would be *worse*.

The Luck of the Draw

Now, after the circumstances of our births put us on a course we had no choice in taking, our lives unfold in any of a billion possible ways. People born white, rich, and male in America contract debilitating diseases. People born female, bisexual, and South Asian become wealthy pop stars. Lives ebb and flow; fortunes are made, lost, or ripped away; we're

---

4 *Barely* beating them, probably, because I hate running so much I'm not even sure I could commit to it for one mile.

in the right or wrong place at the right or wrong time and either benefit[5] or suffer; our friends and family demand more or less from us. In short, even if we start our journeys with a certain level of ease or difficulty, we're still somewhat at the mercy of chance. A lot of life—before we're born and after—is just *luck*, good or bad, so we ought to understand how exactly that luck affects us and our ability to be good.

Some years ago, a social scientist named Robert Frank was playing tennis with a friend and had a massive heart attack. His friend dialed 911, and the dispatcher called for an ambulance. Emergency vehicles were usually sent from a location miles away and would've taken thirty to forty minutes to get to the tennis courts, but as it happened, two ambulances had just reported to the scenes of two different car accidents only a minute from where Frank was lying motionless. One of those ambulances was able to peel away, get to Frank immediately, and save his life. Frank later learned he had suffered from "sudden cardiac death"—a pretty goddamn intense-sounding medical condition that is 98 percent fatal, and the few who do survive it often have intense and lasting side effects, which he did not.

When Frank woke up and learned what had happened, he had a lovely reaction: From that moment on, he thought, *everything* that happened in his life was due directly to good luck. Without the random good fortune of the nearby ambulance he would've had no more moments *of any kind*, which means that *everything he experienced afterward* was fruit from that lucky tree. (It's also sort of "meta-lucky" that this event happened to a social scientist who was able to examine it intellectually and find meaning in it.) That realization led him to hypothesize that people generally underestimate the role that luck has played in their lives. "Why do so many of

---

5 Recognize again, however, that some of us are far more likely to benefit by being "in the right place at the right time"—like "a fancy dining club" at "the moment when a titan of industry is looking for a new executive vice president of international development." That's not a "time and place" that most people would have the ability to take advantage of.

us downplay luck in the face of compelling evidence of its importance?" he asks. "The tendency may owe in part to the fact that by emphasizing talent and hard work to the exclusion of other factors, successful people reinforce their claim to the money they've earned." In other words, people who achieve (or inherit) a high level of wealth and success are invested in the idea that they *earned* it.[6] That belief allows us to feel like we have control over this big dumb scary world—that if we're smart and work hard we will be appropriately rewarded and everything will be fine. Conceding that a lot of this is dumb luck—including, most significantly, embryo-related stuff that happened before we were even conscious beings—is to concede that there were other factors at play beyond our own incredibleness, and that we're maybe not as amazing as our lot in life would indicate.

Frank wants us to understand that a person's journey to success actually begins long before it might appear to. Take Michael Jordan, who's generally regarded as the greatest basketball player who ever lived.[7] No one worked harder, at anything, than Jordan worked at basketball. His determination was unparalleled, his commitment to his craft was off the charts, his intensity and competitive drive are legendary. Thinking of Jordan as a guy who didn't *earn* everything he got—all the championships, the MVPs, the accolades—seems ludicrous. *And yet.* Jordan is six foot six. He didn't achieve that height because he, like, worked really hard at being tall. He was also born in America, to parents who supported and encouraged his passion. Those two facts make him *lucky*. If you take Jordan's exact personality, talent profile, and work ethic, and put them in the body of a five-foot-two goat herder in Bangladesh, he does not become Air Jordan, six-time NBA champion. He becomes the most intense and irritating Bangladeshi goat herder in history, who's

---

6 To quote Cal Hockley, Billy Zane's character in *Titanic*: "A real man makes his own luck." That's the kind of aphorism you only espouse if you're rich, lucky, and utterly ignorant of how lucky you are that you're rich.

7 LeBron's better.

constantly yelling at the other goat herders for not being good enough at herding goats. In fact, forget about changing his height and birthplace— if Jordan had been born *exactly the same person*, but seventy-five years earlier, we likely never would have heard of him. Baseball players like Oscar Charleston, Cool Papa Bell, Satchel Paige, Josh Gibson, and Buck O'Neil aren't often listed among the all-time greats, because they were born into an era of segregation and denied the chance to play alongside Joe DiMaggio and Ted Williams. Were they less talented, or less diligent? Obviously not. They were victims of bad luck, born into a racist world that kept them out of the major leagues.

Thinking of it this way, everyone who achieves *anything*, no matter how talented or driven, benefits in some way from chance. Some people—far too few, but some—understand that. Warren Buffett, who as noted earlier has pledged to give 99 percent of his wealth to charity, writes this on his givingpledge.org page:

> My wealth has come from a combination of living in America, some lucky genes, and compound interest. Both my children and I won what I call the ovarian lottery. (For starters, the odds against my 1930 birth taking place in the U.S. were at least 30 to 1. My being male and white also removed huge obstacles that a majority of Americans then faced.)

Again, no one would dispute that Warren Buffett is a genius. But he is a rare genius indeed, in that he happily acknowledges the many strokes of good fortune that facilitated his rise. Walking us through the history of Microsoft, Frank writes:

> Most of us would never have heard of Microsoft if any one of a long sequence of improbable events had not occurred. If Bill Gates had been born in 1945 rather than 1955, if his high school had not had a computer club with one of the first terminals that could offer instant feedback, if IBM had reached an agreement

with Gary Kildall's Digital Research, or if Tim Paterson had been a more experienced negotiator, Gates almost certainly never would have succeeded on such a grand scale.

The people and events he references there are footnotes in the life of Bill Gates—early deals or nondeals, events that almost occurred but didn't—that at the time seemed of minuscule importance but which nudged Gates's life along a slightly different path from the one he was on. They were, for him, *lucky*—utterly unrelated to his talent or hard work or anything else. Just the Ping-Pong balls of the universe bouncing randomly around and landing in an arrangement that benefited him as he launched his remarkable career. No one on earth would say Bill Gates and Michael Jordan don't *deserve* what they have—they're geniuses! But Frank's point is: It's okay to admit that *part* of what they have is due to luck. It doesn't diminish their achievements. It simply acknowledges that we *all* owe part of our success to chance, and celebrates those smart and capable and talented enough to capitalize on the breaks that go their way. And as we move around the world, bumping into people and interacting with them in a million big and small ways, that gives us a crucial perspective on their lives.

The Gods of Luck Demand Tribute!

I like to go to Las Vegas maybe once a year. I play mostly low-stakes blackjack, $10 or $15 a hand, and usually end up losing a couple hundred bucks. On the rare occasion when I end my trip in the black—up $100 or something—I feel nervous and unhappy. Why? Because I consider myself to be among the very luckiest people on earth. So when I lose $150 playing actual games of chance, it makes sense—it's like a sacrifice I'm making to the gods of luck, to thank them for the million-to-one slot machine jackpot that helped get me where I am. (The simple fact that I can afford to lose a couple hundred bucks in a casino without it affecting my life at all means I'm probably in the top 0.1 percent of all people on earth, luck-wise.) I work hard, and I think I'm good at what I do. But consider the following facts of my life:

1. I stayed home sick from school one day and my mom rented me the movie *Sleeper*, which caused me to fall in love with comedy.

2. I got into Harvard—through hard work, certainly—but Harvard had the *Lampoon* magazine, which had been churning out professional comedy writers for decades before I got there and joined the staff, which meant that when I graduated,

3. I had friends working at *Saturday Night Live* who agreed to help me submit a packet of material, which led to me getting hired there, and when I did,

4. I sucked at writing sketches for a full year. This isn't false modesty—I was *bad*. My sketches bombed very hard at the table reads, and by any rational measure I should have been fired. Except that

5. right before I got hired there was a big staff shake-up, because an NBC executive had fired Norm Macdonald for making too many jokes about O.J. Simpson (who was a friend of the executive in question)—this was a true rarity for *SNL*, to have NBC execs weigh in on staff decisions. Plus, three weeks before I got hired Chris Farley had tragically died of a drug overdose and he was being mourned by the show (and the whole country), and those two events had thrown the whole *SNL* ecosystem into turmoil. So, basically,

6. nobody even noticed I was there—no one paid attention to the new guy who sucked, granting me crucial time to figure out how to do the job, which I eventually did. After a couple of years my friend Robert, who'd been producing the Weekend Update segment, left to take a job in Los Angeles,

and I was appointed to replace him, because there weren't that many other people who either wanted it or were that much more qualified than I was, so

7. I began producing Weekend Update, which at the time was hosted by Tina Fey and Jimmy Fallon, who were so good at what they did and had such excellent comedic chemistry that the segment became incredibly popular—arguably as popular as that segment had ever been. After three years, my girlfriend and I decided to move in together, and she lived in Los Angeles, so even though I had a really good job, it made more sense for me to move there (where there are more writing jobs) than it did for her to move to New York. I arrived in L.A. at the exact moment that

8. Greg Daniels had decided to adapt the British show *The Office* for American TV and was looking for writers. Because Greg is so thorough and hardworking, he read something like five hundred sample scripts in order to hire his small writing staff, including *my* sample, which he liked. *The Office* was a highly risky endeavor and NBC had only picked it up for six episodes (a very small commitment, showing little faith in the show's long-term prospects), and I was potentially getting another offer from a show that had a thirteen-episode order—obviously a safer bet, with more than twice the guaranteed salary. But the night before that meeting I had insomnia (very rare for me) and when I met the producers I was miserably tired and boring and low-energy, and they didn't offer me a job, so when Greg *did* offer me a job, I took it, and

9. Greg turned out to be the greatest mentor and teacher in all of show business, walking me and the other very green writers on the staff through the process of creating and executing stories step by step (which most people in his position don't do, because it's such painstaking work). So I

learned how to write half-hour comedy from a true master of the form—everybody needs a teacher!—and then we made six episodes of *The Office* and it debuted on NBC in 2005 and

10. everyone hated it. The ratings were terrible. It had no chance to get picked up for a second season . . . except that the executive in charge of NBC at the time, Kevin Reilly, deeply believed in it, and he decided to essentially risk his entire career on its success (again, not something executives normally do). In the interim, meanwhile, Steve Carell had done a movie called *The 40-Year-Old Virgin*, which had been a wild and unexpected success, so NBC thought, "Well, fine, we have this movie star under contract, might as well give this show another shot." When we came back for season two,

11. the ratings massively increased, in part because

12. our timeslot followed a new show called *My Name Is Earl*, which was very popular right out of the gate, and in those days people would just kind of leave their TVs on and passively watch things that came on after things they *chose* to watch, so more people sampled *The Office*, and came to enjoy it, thanks in large part to some very smart creative decisions Greg made between seasons. So it took off and became an enormous hit, which led to

13. Greg asking me to develop a show with him. Because NBC was desperate to capitalize on its success with another Greg Daniels show, they said he could do whatever he wanted, really, and they'd guarantee that it would get a full-season commitment (common now, an extreme rarity for the time). So he and I developed *Parks and Recreation*, but we had no idea who could play the lead role, until

14. Amy Poehler decided to leave *Saturday Night Live*, where she had just finished a multiyear run as one of the most talented

and beloved cast members in that show's history. We asked her to do it and she said yes, which meant that

15. the first show I ever created (a) had Greg Daniels as my mentor, (b) had Amy Poehler as the star and creative partner, and (c) was guaranteed a full season on the air to find its sea legs. And yet it only *barely* survived, because we didn't really write it very well in the first few episodes and didn't figure out how to create a character that played to Amy's strengths until the end of the first season, but we eventually did and the show improved, and also by the way

16. Chris Pratt was in the cast, mostly because

17. my wife had worked with him on *The O.C.* and told me when we were casting it that he was otherworldly talented, and since he happened to be available we scooped him up, and he turned out to be endlessly funny and wonderful, as did

18. all of the other people in the cast, like Rashida Jones (whom I'd met on the second day of our freshman year in college and became friends with) and Nick Offerman (who'd auditioned for a role in an *Office* episode I'd written but was unavailable, but whose name I wrote on a Post-it note, vowing to cast him in something, someday), and Aubrey Plaza, who

19. had herself *just* arrived in L.A. when we were casting the show and happened to appear in the office of our casting director, Allison Jones, who called me and said, "I just met the weirdest twenty-two-year-old woman I've ever seen, I think she's really special," and an hour later Aubrey met with me and the other producers and we thought she was hilarious and immediately wrote her into the show, and

20. so on and so on and so on, to infinity.

Do you see why I like to make a sacrifice to the gods of luck? My own abilities and work ethic notwithstanding, my actual journey through

Hollywood is a goddamn *Jenga tower* of luck. That list of good fortune I just laid out doesn't include about a thousand other things that broke right for me at various times in my life. They're countless. I think about them all the time. I also think about what my life would be if I'd been born somewhere else, at another moment, in another body, with fewer opportunities—about how in many crucial ways, I have played this video game on the easiest setting. And what I take from that is that I can't just lose a couple hundred bucks in Vegas to pay off my debt to the gods of luck. It means my moral requirements, on a day-to-day basis, are far greater than average. I owe more to most people than they do to me.

That doesn't mean unlucky people get to run wild through the streets, doing whatever they want. We should always remember that there is a baseline of morality—some combination of calculations based on virtue ethics, consequentialism, deontology, and so on—that everyone must adhere to. But it *does* mean that the higher up the scale we go, with re-spect to good fortune and wealth and status and (thus) freedom to move about the world without fear or pain, the higher the ethical standard is to which we should adhere. People are not all the same—but all people are subject to forces beyond their control, and different people benefit or suffer from those forces to different degrees. A just society accounts for the fact that people can't choose the context into which they're born, or the random winds that buffet them once they arrive. All of which makes me think of John Rawls.

The Veil of Ignorance: Let's Level This Playing Field a Little!

Rawls (1921–2002) was a political philosopher and ethicist whose work drew heavily from Kant and Mill, and he was a friend and colleague of T. M. Scanlon. His most famous work is a six-hundred-page beast called *A Theory of Justice* (1971). Sometime in the 1960s, Rawls finished a much shorter first version and showed it to a bunch of colleagues and students who gave him extensive notes and feedback, which apparently he incorporated *all* of, because *woof* is this thing long. But *Justice* does contain one of my favorite ethical ideas, which is easily understood: the veil of ignorance.

When kids want to split something—a piece of cake, or a pile of M&M's, or whatever—parents will often tell one kid she can divide it into parts, but must give the other kid the first choice. The veil of ignorance is essentially this idea, presented more thoroughly. Rawls says that we ought to decide the rules for our society from what he calls the "original position"—meaning ideally, we'd all decide how we would divvy up things like salaries and resources for our society *before* we knew which role we were going to play *in* that society. We'd conceive of these rules from behind a "veil of ignorance" regarding who we're all going to become—it's like deciding what the rules will be for grown-up humans, back when we're all embryos. This, he says, guarantees a decently just world, and further guarantees that we'll all *think* of it as just. "Certain principles of justice," he writes, "are justified because they would be agreed to in an initial situation of equality."

So, let's say we're about to start a society, one that (like all societies) will have limited resources and capital, and today we're going to establish salary ranges for a bunch of jobs: truck drivers, mechanics, baseball players, nurses, and teachers. This society is some kind of cool science fiction society, though, where once we've established all the rules, we walk through a magic portal and emerge on the other side with a set of talents (and therefore, a likely career) that will be randomly assigned to us—so, it's *possible* that we'll become a baseball player, but *more likely* that we'll become a nurse or a teacher (simply because there will be more of them than baseball players). The portal, in other words, is *luck*—it will stamp us with abilities, qualities, and life circumstances that we have no control over, like height, ethnicity, intelligence, hand-eye coordination, bagpipe-playing ability, and a million other things. When designing societal guidelines for how we pay and treat people of different professions, then, we might think the following: (a) We could end up being a baseball player! That would be amazing. Baseball players' talents are rare and desirable, so we should make sure that baseball players' potential salaries are high. But also (b) we're more likely to end up being a mechanic, or nurse, or teacher, so we should ensure that the *minimum* salaries for them aren't so low that they end up miserable, and (c) also we might want to ensure that the laws governing our society provide ample resources for schools and hospitals and the like, because if we're a teacher and our school has no money we'll be bummed out. Since there's only so much money and capital to go around, we won't allow any one profession or sector of society to drain too many of our resources.

We can see how Rawls's work is a close cousin of Scanlon's, right? Instead of proposing rules for our world that no reasonable person could reject, Rawls wants to propose them *before we're out in the world,* walking around and doing stuff—because if we make rules before we know what we'll all become, we'll all surely agree to them. Behind the veil of ignorance, we will all immediately realize that there's no way for any of us to gain an upper hand here—no one can know any more or less about what any one of us will become when we go through the portal. Scanlon (as Pamela Hieronymi pointed out to me) took that idea of symmetry and just shifted it later in the process—his "reasonable people" formulation asks that all of us engage in a similar kind of symmetry *after* we've (metaphorically) walked through the portal and learned what our lives are like. His version is more optimistic—because it suggests we can equate our own lives and needs and desires with everyone else's *after we've already been living them,* meaning that people who have led good and/or lucky lives will recognize that they need to be empathetic toward those who've been less fortunate. But Rawls's version would likely be more effective, if it were possible in some kind of cool science fiction universe, due to the exact reality we've discussed in this chapter: people who are successful are often overly invested in the idea that they and they alone are responsible for their success, and are sometimes ignorant to, or unwilling to allow for, the important role luck has played in their lives.

So: this isn't utilitarianism, where individuals are coagulated and flattened out into one big indistinguishable mass of "happiness" or "pain." In Rawls's world, before we know what job we're going to have or what set of abilities we'll be assigned, we allow for and accept the inevitable differences in talent and "societal value" of the theoretical professions we might be assigned—in other words, after we move through the portal, we retain our integrity as individuals. We acknowledge that some people will be better than others at certain skills that are more highly valued by our society—and thus that some jobs will pay better than others—and we're okay with that. But we also take *luck* into account. The magic portal thingy means that we don't control what we become, so we set a high enough floor for *everyone* that means nobody will end up suffering due only to the caprices of luck. "No one," writes Rawls, "should be advantaged or disadvantaged by natural fortune or social circumstances in the choice of the principles. It also seems widely agreed that it should be impossible to tailor principles to the circumstances of one's own case." In Rawls's scenario we divide up the pile of M&M's, but since the universe decides who gets which portion, we're gonna divide it (somewhat) equally.

Rawls had essentially the same beef with utilitarianism that Bernard Williams did. As Rawls phrased it, utilitarianism "does not take seriously the distinction between persons." He wasn't interested in trying to maximize overall happiness in the world as it stands, but rather wanted to design a society that every member would theoretically sign up for, with the comfort of knowing it would be relatively just. That world could reward the Tom Hankses and Serena Williamses among us by allowing them to be appropriately compensated and celebrated, but never at the expense of teachers or postal workers or nurses or auto mechanics or anyone else. And though Rawls doesn't deal with this aspect much, I like to imagine another benefit: the Hankses and Williamses would always acknowledge the incredible portal-based fortune that allowed them to become what they are, no matter how much natural talent they were born with or hard work they put into developing it.

Remember the Portal!

Let's take Rawls and Frank on a quick jaunt back to the question from chapter 4: Do we have to return our shopping cart to the rack? When we're faced with one of those mundane questions, after we apply contractualist rules or seek a golden mean or follow a Kantian maxim or do all of these things in whatever combination we see fit, we need to remember one final thing: If we can even afford to be asking what we should do here, it probably means we're pretty lucky people. We have a car full of groceries—and thus a functioning car—and the luxury of posing philosophical questions, instead of having to think only about our health or safety or where we're going to find our next meal. If we determine that relative to others we're lucky, which means we *can* afford to do a little extra, then we *should* do a little extra. And I don't mean "Warren Buffett" lucky—just lucky enough that we're able to do something to make other people's lives a bit easier, at little or no real cost to our own. There are billions of people for whom that isn't the case, so we have a duty to pick up the slack. Do a bit more than we're ethically required to do. Pay back the gods of luck. And if we're *not* lucky—if life has dealt us a series of blows that mean our internal batteries are running at 1 percent and we're barely scraping by, well, we fall back on those contractualist rules—we do whatever we can to address the minimum amount we owe to each other.

We're almost at the end of our journey. We've learned what we're doing, why we're doing it, whether we could be doing something better, and why it would be better. We're flourishing like ethical rock stars over here! But we've also screwed up. A lot. We knew that would happen—the inevitable outcome of a life of caring and trying is a never-ending stream of screwups, great and small. So there's one last thing we have to do, and it stinks. We have to apologize.

CHAPTER THIRTEEN

I Screwed Up. Do I Have to Say I'm Sorry?

Anyone with kids will recognize this scene, which plays out in my home once a week:

> KID 1: Dad! He yanked the remote out of my hand and he won't give it back!
>
> KID 2: She wasn't even using it!
>
> PARENT: You can't just yank things out of people's hands. It's not okay to do that.
>
> KID 2: (*tossing it back*) Fine.
>
> PARENT: Say you're sorry.
>
> KID 2: . . .
>
> PARENT: Come on. Say you're sorry. Apologize.
>
> KID 2: . . .
>
> PARENT: We can stand here as long as you want. But you have to say you're sorry.

(*They stand there "as long as Kid 2 wants." Minutes go by. Then hours. Day turns to night. No one eats. Phones ring and go unanswered. Somewhere in the distance, a lone wolf howls. The sands of time slowly fall through the hourglass. Civilizations are made and unmade, forests rise and then burn to ash, a reminder of the only true constant in the universe: change itself. Then . . .*)

KID 2: (*mumbled*) Sorry.

Doing something wrong hurts. It stinks. It's embarrassing. But *apologizing* can hurt more and stink more and be *more* embarrassing. Feeling private guilt is one thing; apologizing compounds that guilt with the shame of a public admission. But tempting though it is to avoid that shame after we screw up, apologizing is the final ascent on the mountain we have to climb in order to become better people. It's the punctuation mark on the end of an Aristotelian sentence that describes our search for virtue; it's an easily formulated Kantian maxim, a utilitarian happiness increaser, and a contractualist debt we can pay off, all in one. Without an apology, the wound of a moral wrong can't completely heal.

But it stinks!

But we gotta do it.

But it stinks.

Part of the trouble with apologizing is that all we can think about, in the moments leading up to the act itself, is the awkward, halting mortification of admitting fault in front of other people. The *good* parts—the healing and growth and resolution—are harder to see. Apologies are not "ethical" actions, per se, but I feel like they're ethics-adjacent. If caring and trying are the key to ethical improvement and failure is the inevitable result, apologies are like an exit interview for that failure. What did we do? Why did we do it? What did we learn about how it affected other people? The ickiness we feel when we apologize—the flushed-face shame that comes from admitting fault to a person we've wronged—is *good*. It means *we* feel the pain we've caused, and we care that we caused it. (A person incapable of shame, said Aristotle, has no sense of disgrace.) Those feelings are like flu symptoms—it's our bodies working to cure what ails us.

But because apologies are so fraught with that ickiness, people, as a whole, are *terrible* at them. Like anything else, there are good and bad versions of apologies; if we're going to take a deep breath, confront our fear of shame, and actually make one, we ought to do it right. In 1985, Tom Petty did a concert tour for his album *Southern Accents* whose stage design featured a huge Confederate battle flag. Years later, after many people had pointed out to him what that flag represents, he said this in *Rolling Stone*:

> The Confederate flag was the wallpaper of the South when I was a kid growing up in Gainesville, Florida. I always knew it had to do with the Civil War, but the South had adopted it as its logo. I was pretty ignorant of what it actually meant. It was on a flagpole in front of the courthouse and I often saw it in Western movies. I just honestly didn't give it much thought, though I should have. . . . It left me feeling stupid. That's the word I can use. I felt stupid. If I had just been a little more observant about things going on around me, it wouldn't have happened. . . . I still feel bad about it. I've just always regretted it. . . . When [Southerners] wave that flag, they aren't stopping to think how it looks to a Black person. I blame myself for not doing that. . . . It was dumb and it shouldn't have happened.

I love this statement. It's clear and straightforward. He doesn't dig in his heels or make excuses; instead he just explains how it happened, acknowledges that he blew it, names the people he hurt, and expresses regret. This is the correct way to apologize. If you were a person who felt pain because a popular rock star validated a symbol of hate, and then (even years later) you saw this statement, the pain might dissipate.

Now let's swing on over to the other kind of apology. In July of 2020, Representative Ted Yoho accosted his colleague Alexandria Ocasio-Cortez on the steps of the Capitol, and called her (among other things) a "f*cking b*tch." Pressured to apologize, Yoho took to the floor of Congress and said this:

> I rise to apologize for the abrupt manner of the conversation I had with my colleague from New York. It is true that we disagree on policies and visions for America but that does not mean we should be disrespectful.

So far so good! I mean, I don't think you were asked to apologize for the "abrupt manner" of the conversation as much as the actual words you said, but we'll give you the benefit of the doubt.

> Having been married for forty-five years with two daughters, I'm very cognizant of my language. The offensive name-calling words attributed to me by the press were never spoken to my colleagues and if they were construed that way, I apologize for the misunderstanding.

Uh-oh. Anytime someone who claims to be apologizing for something drags his wife and kids into the mix for no reason, alarm bells should go off. I can't be a bad person, because someone loves me and also I'm a parent![1] Also, it's not really an apology if you deny the incident in question happened. If it didn't happen . . . why apologize? And finally, "if they were construed that way"? How exactly *should* Ocasio-Cortez have "construed" the phrase "f*cking b*tch"? Jocular, good-natured ribbing? But keep going, Congressman, I guess, and let's see if we can get this train back on track.

> My wife, Carolyn, and I started together at the age of nineteen with nothing.

Nope. More off-track. Wheels coming loose, dashboard flashing red warning signals, ominous smoke pouring out of engine.

---

1 The most popular recent version of this "I have a family!" defense involves men speaking about other men's sexual assaults or offensive language toward women, and citing the fact that because they have daughters, or wives, or mothers, they find those behaviors offensive. This implies that they *wouldn't*, really, find the behavior offensive if they were single and had no female children. If you ever hear someone say "As the father of a daughter . . ." just walk away. The rest of the sentence is ethical gobbledygook.

We did odd jobs. And we were on food stamps. I know the face of poverty. And for a time it was mine.

Ted? Buddy? Why are we getting into your financial history? You're apologizing to someone, remember?

That is why I know people in this country can still with all its faults rise up and succeed and not be encouraged to break the law.

. . . I'm lost now. What are you even doing here, guy? Which people? Who was encouraged to break a law? What law?! *What are you talking about?*

I will commit to each of you that I will conduct myself from a place of passion and understanding that policy and political disagreement be vigorously debated with the knowledge that we approach the problems facing our nation with the betterment of the country in our mind and the people we serve.

Woof. That's one tortured sentence. That looks like he typed "I will commit" and then just kept hitting the "autopredict text" button. And finally, at the end, a nonsensical toothpick stuck in this gibberish sandwich:

I cannot apologize for my passion or for loving my god, my family, and my country.

So, to sum up: *I'm here to apologize. But I won't apologize. I didn't do the thing you think I did—you construed it wrong. At one point, I was poor. Also I won't apologize for loving God and America. Yoho out.*

This is a very bad apology. He barely acknowledged the person he was apologizing to, he denied the event occurred, he brought up being on food stamps for some reason, and then he self-righteously refused to apologize for his awesome qualities, which no one had asked him to do. This is plainly not an apology. It is—and I swear this is an actual philosophical term—*bullshit*.

This Is the Part Where There's a Lot of Cursing (for a Good Reason)

Harry G. Frankfurt (born 1929) is professor emeritus of philosophy at Princeton University. He has also taught at Yale, been a visiting fellow at All Souls College at Oxford, received grants from the Guggenheim and Mellon Foundations, and written an entire book about bullshit. Specifically, *On Bullshit*, a paper he published in 1986 that was released in (adorably small) book form in 2005. It became something of a phenomenon, landing on the *New York Times* bestseller list for twenty-seven weeks—presumably because, as he notes in its opening sentence: "One of the most salient features of our culture is that there is so much bullshit."

Frankfurt aims to distinguish *bullshit* from *lying*. "Telling a lie," he writes, "is an act with a sharp focus. It is designed to insert a particular falsehood at a specific point in a set or system of beliefs, in order to avoid the consequences of having that point occupied by the truth." In other words, a liar knows the truth and deliberately speaks in opposition to it. A bullshitter, however, is "unconstrained by a concern with truth." The bullshitter couldn't care less what the truth is—he wants only to make himself appear a certain way or achieve some effect on the listener. Frankfurt imagines, for example, a puffed-up, rah-rah American giving a Fourth of July speech and bombastically celebrating the Founders, the Flag, Mom, and Apple Pie. It's immaterial what this guy *actually thinks* about America, says Frankfurt—he may truly love the country, he might hate it, he might be indifferent. That's not the point. The point is that

> the orator intends these statements to convey a certain impression of himself. He is not trying to deceive anyone concerning American history. What he cares about is what people think of *him*.

The bullshitter has only one goal: to make the listener think of him as a certain kind of person, whether it be a patriot, a moral avatar, a sensitive and caring soul, or whatever else advances his personal interests.[2] "The essence of bullshit," said Frankfurt, "is not that it is *false* but that it is *phony*."

Yoho was caught doing something bad—accosting and cursing at a woman he works with, who'd committed the unforgivable crime of not sharing his political stances. When he was caught, the *right* thing to do was to apologize. Instead, he delivered a line of bullshit intended to make other people—his political allies, and not the woman he cursed at—see him a certain way. (This is not a partisan phenomenon. Contemporary Republicans may have raised it to an art form, but the history of political oratory reveals heaping mounds of bullshit from both sides of the aisle.) Another classic disingenuous apology move—which Yoho employed a version of—is to say "I'm sorry if you were offended," which of course is less an apology than an accusation. That's saying both "I did nothing wrong" and "You're so dumb you *thought* I did something wrong and got upset, so I'm sorry you're so dumb." Apologies don't undo whatever bad thing we did, but when they're sincere and honestly delivered, they can help heal a wound. They won't do *anything*, however, if we're defensive, hedging, or disingenuous—if what we offer is not actually a sincere plea for forgiveness.

Our resistance to one-on-one apologies carries over to the larger

---

2 The excellent *Gawker* essay "On Smarm" by writer Tom Scocca (which uses Frankfurt's essay to make its point) locates smarm alongside bullshit this way: "Smarm is a kind of performance—an assumption of the forms of seriousness, of virtue, of constructiveness, without the substance. Smarm is concerned with appropriateness and with tone. Smarm disapproves. Smarm would rather talk about anything other than smarm. Why, smarm asks, can't everyone just be nicer?" Both the smarm-meister and the bullshitter have a goal in mind that ignores the actual issue at hand—the smarm-meister pretends to take offense at the *tone* or *incivility* of his accuser, while the bullshitter just waves his hand and spews words indiscriminately to achieve the effect he's after.

sphere of institutional or governmental ones. Periodically, some will call for American state apologies for the nation's large-scale past horrors, like the internment of Japanese Americans during World War II, slavery, or the Native American genocide. The counterargument amounts to: "That was a long time ago. What's done is done. Get over it." I find this argument . . . lacking. National sins require national apologies, no matter how long ago they were committed. Those apologies can take the form of a simple declaration, or—far better—a declaration *and* actual restitution paid to the descendants of those who suffered. But the first step is the simple admission of wrongdoing.

In 1992, Pope John Paul II apologized, on behalf of his predecessor, for a mistake made by the Catholic Church. The notable thing about this was that the man he apologized to was Galileo Galilei, and the mistake had been made in 1633. Galileo had confirmed the Copernican theory of the universe, which posited that Earth revolved around the sun and not vice versa, and for that he was called a heretic and threatened with imprisonment and death and everything else the church could throw at him. Ultimately, his fame earned him a mere house arrest, conditional on his recanting his findings.[3] Almost 360 years later, Pope John Paul said, in essence: "Our bad." Admittedly, he did hedge a bit by saying that the Catholic Church was merely working with the information they had at the time, but he apologized, and it mattered. He resolved the open cadence of this historical wrong, and when institutions do that, it declares once and for all that they are fallible, and that they owe something to those they've wronged. If instead of apologizing the pope had said, "We never did this, historians are wrong, and also the church has done

---

3 Galileo did indeed recant, because, you know, he didn't want to die, and as the story goes, he then muttered under his breath: *"Eppur, si muove,"* which means "And yet, it moves." ("It" being Earth.) This is super badass, that he muttered this under his breath in front of a potentially murderous pope, and it makes me think that Galileo was a cool dude.

a bunch of good charitable work, and we'll never apologize for our faith in God," well, that wouldn't be an apology. That would be . . . you get it.

People ought to apologize when they screw up. So should politicians, and religious institutions, and countries. Apologizing *matters*. I say this as a person who has failed to apologize for countless mistakes I've made in my life. My age-forty-ish journey into moral philosophy caused me many sleepless nights, mostly due to the realization that I've hurt people and never told them I'm sorry for having done so. If we're lucky enough to live on this planet for more than a couple of years, we're condemned to cause damage to people we love, people we don't even know, and everyone in between. Only recently have I fully understood the inevitability of that, or the fact that when we inevitably do it, we have one move left: Suck it up, and say we're sorry. And do it sooner rather than later. Waiting 359 years to apologize takes away some of the impact.

I have one final question to ask, in a book full of them, but this one is easy to answer. What do we hope will happen when we apologize? When we face our fear of embarrassment, brave the shame and flushed face and shaky voice and admit our wrongdoing? We simply hope that whoever we've wronged will recognize our sincere regret and our desire to be a little better today than we were yesterday. We hope for whatever mix of kindness, empathy, grace, and understanding leads people to say *it's okay* even if they're still mad at us, even if we lied to them when we knew we shouldn't have or told them to wear a zebra-print fedora to an office holiday party to disastrous results. We hope for forgiveness.

So here, near the end of our journey, is where the rubber of ethics meets the rough road of everyday life, with all its messiness and complexity. We have said, over and over, that caring about what we do requires us to accept and endure a lifetime of screwing up. Getting it wrong. Hurting people. Sometimes the bad we do will be minuscule— barely a tenth of one dolor, floating off into the universe, hardly noticed and largely unimportant. Sometimes it'll be far, far worse: a *real* pain, felt in a *real* way by some number of people whose lives have been made markedly worse because of *something we did*. It's right and appropriate to speak up (in the right way, at the right times, in the right amount) when people fall short of virtue and cause some pain or suffering. But if they've done something forgivable, we should remember what we hope for when *we* screw up, and try to summon that same grace and understanding. (What does "forgivable" mean, you might ask? That's a deeply complicated philosophical question that would take a whole other book to answer, and honestly, I'm not sure Todd has the patience to put up with me for another two years.) The point is this: to demand perfection, or to hold people to impossible standards, is to deny the simple and beautiful reality that nobody is perfect.

Okay, Kids: What Have We Learned?

Dear Ivy and William,

Parents and moral philosophers, I've come to learn, are annoying in exactly the same way. Both groups spend their lives thinking about what makes a person good and trying to convince other people to buy into their theories. For the philosophers, those "other people" are everyone on the planet; for parents, mostly, it's their kids. You had the misfortune to be born to a parent who's also into moral philosophy—a real double whammy. Twice the theories, and twice as many attempts at convincing you to listen. But bear with me just for a few pages here as I try to summarize why I care about this stuff, and why you should too.

Right after Ivy was born, I took a walk with your grandmother and marveled at how many new things I had to worry about. "You worry about one set of things when they're babies, and then another set of things when they're toddlers," I remember saying, "and now I can imagine worrying about them as kindergartners, and middle schoolers, and on and on." Nana said nothing. "I guess that's just the deal with parenthood," I continued, working it out for myself. "You worry and worry and worry, until they're finally grown-ups and they have jobs and stuff."

"Oh, it doesn't get any better when they're grown-ups," said Nana. "I worry about you all the time."

So far, she's been proven right. As I write this, William is twelve (!)

and Ivy is ten (?!?) and not a day has gone by that your mom and I haven't worried about you. Sometimes it's because of what you've done, or not done—like when William (taking after his mom) gets waaaay too angry when he loses at Ping-Pong, or when Ivy (taking after her dad) decides the best response to any kind of conflict is to just go completely silent. Other times I worry because the world you're inheriting feels impossible to navigate even for the very luckiest humans alive—a group you two belong to—and if it feels impossible for *you* to navigate, if its problems and threats and moral tangles present a path so treacherous that no parent in the world would wish to see her child try to walk it, what that parent is left with is *worry*.

But if Montesquieu was right, and knowledge makes people gentle, maybe it makes them safer too.

That's the bet I'm making, really. I'm placing a decent-size bet on the idea that understanding morality, and following its compass during decisions great and small, will make you *better*, and therefore *safer*. Not safer from harm, necessarily—though I hope for that too—but from all of the traps that modern life sets, especially for people lucky enough to be born into privilege. I'm talking about selfishness, callousness, cruelty, hypocrisy, snobbery—those qualities people display when they decide we are not actually living all together, here on earth, but instead are living alone, individually, eight billion siloed ego states, competing with each other in a race that (they seem to forget) inevitably ends with everyone in a dead heat.

So far, I think you're good people! You understand right and wrong, and you generally try to do right. You're kind to your friends, and when you're not you feel bad and (sometimes) apologize. Your virtue starter kits arrived intact. You also understand how very lucky we are, and as often as your mom and I grill you on your understanding of this luck, you're not likely to forget about it. But just understanding the *concept* of good fortune isn't enough. The world moves fast, and it wouldn't take much for you to forget the role luck has played in your lives, which can lead to you feeling *entitled* to things and tossing your moral compasses aside in favor of an inflexible response to the questions you face. It might lead you to do only what you want, without asking yourself some simple questions: *What am I doing? Why am I doing it? Is there something I could be doing that's better? Why is it better?*

You wonder what your mom and I worry about? It's that. (And climate change. We also worry about climate change.)

But here's the good news: A lot of very smart people have been thinking about these problems—how to be good, how we should act, what we owe to each other—for a very long time. They have ideas for how we might avoid disappearing into our own little worlds. Though their ideas vary widely, they're all based on the simple concept that who we are and what we do *matters*—that we should *care* whether we're doing something good or not, and thus try to do the best things we can. And if you can get past the fact that the people who formulated these ideas wrote super-confusing books that will give you an instant headache, you can someday arm yourselves with their ideas, use them when you make decisions, and become the kind of people that would let your mom and me stop worrying all the time about whether you're okay. Or, at least, worry less.

I've tried to explain a few of their ideas in this book so you can have something to refer to as you get older, passing through all of the strange and unsettling eras of life—each of which will twist you into knots and garble your brains in ways you didn't expect. One of the great ironies of aging is that every ten years or so, you look back on the person you were ten years before and shudder—at the mistakes you made, at your immaturity and thickheadedness—and then you breathe a sigh of relief that you're so much smarter and more mature now. Then ten years later . . . it happens again. I'm forty-six, and can only guess which of my current actions will embarrass me ten years from now. (Hopefully one of them won't be: "writing this book.")

So I very much hope that this book will benefit you, someday. But right now you're twelve (!) and ten (?!?) and even a casual discussion of the categorical imperative might be kind of a hard sell. (Your mom and I did not take the same approach to your education that J. S. Mill's dad did with his kid, which means you didn't learn Greek and Latin in kindergarten, but also you don't hate us and aren't horribly depressed, which we think is a good trade-off.) So here, at the end, I'm going to tell you in simple terms what I think matters. Think of this as the two-page Quick-Start Guide to this whole project: it won't cover everything, but it'll be a decent starting point.

You are people on earth. You are not alone here, and that means you owe the other people on earth certain things. What you owe them, more or less, is to live by rules they wouldn't reject as unfair (assuming they're decent, reasonable people). If you, Ivy, are about to do something and you're not sure whether it's okay, ask yourself if William would tell you it's a good idea. William, ask yourself if Ivy would say the same thing. Then keep going—ask yourself if one of your friends would reject it as a bad idea—or one of your teachers, or even a kid you don't like that much but who you have to admit is pretty smart. If you feel like those people could reasonably reject your idea for what to do, maybe don't do it. Maybe do something else.

Or you can try this: You can think to yourself, before you do something, "Would it be okay if *everyone* did this? What would the world be like if every single person were allowed to do whatever I'm about to do?" If that world seems twisted, or unfair, or nonsensical, you should probably do something else.

Or: Think about what you're about to do, and imagine the result. Think of how many people will be happy, and how many sad, and how happy or sad they'll be. Think about how *soon* they'll be sad or happy, and *for how long* they'll be sad or happy. Try to total it all up in your mind, and think about whether what you're about to do will result in more total sadness or happiness. This one is tricky, but sometimes it's the best way to find an answer.

And while you're here on earth, think about the parts of people you love—their kindness, generosity, loyalty, courage, determination, mildness. Aim yourselves at the exact right amount of those qualities, as best you can—not too much, not too little. And know that you're often going to get it wrong. You'll try to be mild, let's say, and you won't be mild enough, then you'll overcompensate and become *too* mild, and that'll keep happening, and it'll annoy people, and that will sting. But hopefully, by trying over and over, you'll get closer and closer to getting it right. The trying is important. Keep trying.

Over the course of your lives, you may find yourself drawn more or less toward one or another of these techniques for determining right from wrong, good from bad. That's fine! Use the ones you like, the ones that make sense to you, but keep the others around just in case. There will be moments when you're befuddled—when the system you put in place to guide you seems to fail, when you're caught red-handed defending one thing while condemning another thing, and you'll come to see that contradiction as inconsistent. It'll be embarrassing. You might have to draw and redraw the lines between "good" and "bad" over and over, and that's fine. The important thing is that you keep drawing them.

I'm almost done, I promise. I can feel you getting annoyed. But I need to say just a bit more about other people.

Humans have this problem: we're kind of trapped inside our own brains. Our default setting is to think about ourselves—how to keep *ourselves* happy and safe and protected. Sometimes that's good! We have *integrity*, which means (in this case) "a sense of wholeness, of being undivided." If someone asks you to do something that doesn't seem like it fits with who you are or how you think of yourself, a little voice in your head might start chirping at you, warning you that *this doesn't feel right*. Don't ignore that voice. It's there to help.

But being trapped inside our own brains also means that sometimes we don't think enough about *other people*. If you were growing up in South Africa or Zimbabwe, you might have been taught to *live through* other people—to think of their happiness as your happiness, their pain as your pain. But you are growing up in America, and America, like a lot of other places, teaches people to look out for themselves first. There's even a very famous writer who told people that selfishness was actually *good*—that the more selfish everyone is, the better the world will be. (I know, it's bonkers. She was a very silly person, and an impressively terrible writer.) So, being raised in America, you need to start thinking about other people a little more.

Sometimes that will be *really hard.* It'll take work, concentration, energy, sacrifice. It'll be tricky and complex and confusing. These are the times you'll blow it—you'll make a mistake and cause harm you didn't intend to cause. Take a deep breath, and apologize. Remember: We are wrong, all the time. We are wrong, and we try again, and we're wrong again, and again, and again. *Keep trying.* Choosing to *not* try is still making a choice, and it won't make you (or anyone else) a better person.

Thousands of years ago, in a part of Greece called Delphi, some people built a temple. They were worried about their kids too—all parents in history have been worried about their kids, it's not just Mom and me—so they chiseled a couple of sayings into a column of that temple to tell their kids, and their grandkids, and their great-grandkids, in as few words as possible, how to try to pull off the nearly impossible task of living a good life on earth. Here's what they wrote:

Know thyself.

and

Nothing in excess.

Honestly, as far as "guides to life" go, I don't think anyone's beaten that in the 2,400 years since. *Know thyself*—think about who you are, check in with yourself when you do things to see if you've made good decisions, remember what you value and care about, understand your integrity, and live a life consistent with that integrity. *Nothing in excess*—because too much (or too little) of anything will screw you up. Practice virtues like kindness and generosity and courage, but not *too much* of them. Drink whiskey, when you're old enough, but don't drink *too much* whiskey. (Single malt, by the way. None of that blended junk.) Watch TV, but don't watch *too much* TV. Don't eat *too many* tacos, or exercise *too much*, or curse *too much* (I struggle with that one). Somewhere in the middle of every kind of virtue you can have, and every thing you do, there's a perfect amount of that thing, and your job is to find it. You want a real Quick-Start Guide for how to live a good life? A guide so pithy you can have it tattooed on your arm with plenty of room to spare?

Know thyself.

Nothing in excess.

There's more, of course. You can't *just* use that. But maybe start there.

Being a good person is a job, and a hard one at that. But if you care about it, it may start to seem less like work and more like a puzzle you can solve. And in those rare times when you have to make a decision and you assemble the pieces in exactly the right way, so the image of what to do comes sharply into focus—you will feel alive and fulfilled and elated. You will feel like you're *flourishing*. Which is really what Mom and I hope for you. We want you to be safe, from harm and from the pitfalls of the specific lives you're leading. We want you to be happy—not in the eating-pizza-with-your-friends way, but in a deeper, more lasting way. We want you to be *good*—to act with good intentions, to cause minimal harm to those around you, to abide by rules you'd want everyone to follow and that other people wouldn't reject as unfair. We want you to apologize when you screw up, and we want you to try to do better the next time. Doing all of these things can help you flourish—to be the very best versions of yourselves.

But again, there will be plenty of other times when you do not flourish. When you straight-up blow it. And then you'll try again, and you'll blow it again, over and over, and you'll be frustrated and you'll feel awful. And if you've tried to do something good a thousand times, and you've failed a thousand times, and the people around you are miserable, and you're at the end of your rope, and you're losing faith in yourselves, you know what we want you to do then?

Keep trying. Keep trying. Keep trying.

Love,
Dad

Acknowledgments

Let's be honest: no one reads this part unless you are a person who thinks you might have been thanked, which means you're reading it either to see your name or else to *not* see your name so you can get righteously angry that I forgot to thank you. If that's the case, I'm legitimately sorry. If I *did* thank you, then congrats on seeing your name! It's cool to see your name in a book. If you are neither a person I thanked nor a person I should have thanked but forgot to, and for some reason you're reading this part, I'll try to make it more interesting by stirring cool little facts and anecdotes into these acknowledgments every so often. Like: There are more than one quadrillion ants on earth! A million-billion ants?! That's so many ants!

This book doesn't happen without the wisdom, knowledge, and all-around good spirit of Todd May. He encouraged me, supported the vision of the book unconditionally, and patiently explained the nuances of various versions of existentialism seven hundred times until I finally felt confident enough to write that chapter. Thank you, Todd, for everything. Sorry about all the commas.

Pamela Hieronymi not only kick-started my understanding of moral philosophy, she also volunteered to read the first chunk of this book and give me notes, which I've come to understand is the academic philosopher equivalent of helping someone move into a sixth-floor walk-up. Her notes were invaluable. Thank you, Pamela. If you ever need me to help you move, just say the word. And sorry I occasionally forget and call you "Pam."

Albert Einstein once used a $1,500 check (roughly $30,000 in today's money) for a bookmark, and then couldn't remember where he put the book. And once at a dinner party his wife mistook a bouquet of orchids for a salad and ate them.

Eamon Dolan from Simon & Schuster provided the perfect combination of editorial acumen, congeniality, tough love, and disdain for the phrase "sort of." He steered a first-time author through the choppy waters of self-doubt with a steady, friendly demeanor I appreciated greatly. Thank you, Eamon. Sorry I left in all those "like"s and "gotta"s.

A whole lot of people at S&S (and elsewhere) had to read this thing a million times and make sure it wasn't all messed up, or write me a million e-mails to ensure I wasn't messing it up in some other way: most notably, Laura Cherkas, Tzipora Baitch, and Kayley Hoffman. Thank you, and sorry you had to read this a million times. Kate Kinast expertly fact-checked the whole thing; any remaining mistakes are certainly my fault and not hers.

In December of 1997 I signed with 3Arts management, mostly because of all the agents and managers I'd met, David Miner seemed like the nicest and funniest. Twenty-five years later, every move I make in my career starts with a phone call either to or from him. I'm eternally grateful for all twenty-five of those years. And our partnership is what led me to Richard Abate, who got exactly what this book wanted to be and knew exactly how to present it to publishers. I should also thank Ken Richman, Matt Rice, and Julien Thuan, whose guidance and advice are a big part of the Jenga tower of luck that is my writing career.

A fun riddle for kids: A wealthy man dies and leaves his collection of elephants to his three kids. To his oldest he leaves half of his elephants, to his middle kid he leaves a third of his elephants, and to his youngest he leaves a ninth of his elephants. Problem is: He has seventeen elephants. The kids seek the advice of a wise woman in their town, and she instantly comes up with a solution. What is it? (Answer in the footnote!)[1]

---

1 The wise woman adds one of her elephants to the herd, to make eighteen. Half of them (nine) go to the oldest kid, a third (six) to the middle kid, and a ninth (two) to the

One of the most fun side effects of working on this book was that it brought me into contact with philosophers from all over the country. Dr. Molefi Kete Asante from Temple lent me his expertise on the *ubuntu* section. I'm also grateful to have made the acquaintance of T. M. Scanlon, who was exactly as charming and thoughtful in conversation as I imagined he'd be. Craig Vasey from the North American Sartre Society invited Todd and me to speak at their annual gathering, which was delightful, and I got a cool NASS pin that I wear with pride. I'm also grateful to Peter Singer and Isaac Martinez at Princeton, and Meghan Sullivan at Notre Dame, for the invitations to talk to them and their students about ethics.

Of course, this book would never have been written if it weren't for *The Good Place*. Making that show was a joy from beginning to end. The conversations we had in the writers' room about philosophy, comedy, ethics—and a whole bunch of stuff that was far less important than philosophy, comedy, or ethics—leave me forever indebted to that writing staff: Demi Adejuyigbe, Megan Amram, Chris Encell, Kate Gersten, Cord Jefferson, Dave King, Andrew Law, Kassia Miller, Dylan Morgan, Aisha Muharrar, Matt Murray, Lizzy Pace, Rafat Sanni, Dan Schofield, Josh Siegal, Jennifer Statsky, Tyler Straessle, and Alan Yang. Each of their senses of humor is in the show, which means they're all in this book. I love all of you weirdos, and am a better person for knowing you. Additional thanks to my assistant, Bridget Stinson, and all of the writers' assistants and PAs we had over the years for their tireless work, and to everyone who watched the show and got something out of it, which was the whole point of making it.

Once Samuel Beckett was walking with his friend in London on a beautiful spring day. His friend commented on how lovely the weather

---

youngest. That's seventeen, and then the woman takes her elephant back, and everyone is happy! (This comes from the book *A Children's Almanac of Words at Play* by Willard R. Espy, my favorite book when I was a kid.)

was, and how nice it was to be walking with his old friend, and Beckett agreed. Then his friend said that it was days like this that made you glad to be alive. Beckett replied: "Well, I wouldn't go *that* far."

Over the course of the show we had various "guest lecturers" come and discuss matters of ethics and social justice. In addition to Todd and Pamela, Joshua Greene and DeRay Mckesson were generous with their time and their words. Damon Lindelof wasn't really a "guest lecturer" per se—more of a spiritual advisor—but without his early advice there may have been no show at all.

The Good Place production team, headed by Morgan Sackett and David Hyman, made sure the ideas that came out of the writers' room could be turned into actual entertainment. Most of what I've done in my TV career has really, actually, been done by them. The talented artists and craftspeople who put the show together are too numerous to mention—naming one requires me to name them all—so please just know I am forever indebted to every one of you for your hard work. And then there are the actors and directors who took these thorny ideas and translated them for an audience—most importantly: Ted Danson, Kristen Bell, Manny Jacinto, Jameela Jamil, D'Arcy Carden, William Jackson Harper, Marc Evan Jackson, and Drew Goddard. Boy oh boy, do I love and miss you all.

The word "buffalo" written out eight times in a row creates a complete and grammatically correct sentence.

I again thank J.J. Philbin—a dedication *and* an acknowledgment? Must be nice—because she read this whole thing when I first finished a draft, and we both know exactly how annoying it is when someone asks you to read something they wrote, and in this case it was like two hundred and fifty pages longer than the kind of thing we usually have to read. The first person to read the entire manuscript (outside of my immediate family) was Dan Le Batard, whose thoughtful notes and general praise put wind in my sails.

I have been a gainfully employed writer since 1997, thanks to the generosity and tutelage of countless people who gave me a shot, kept giving me shots when I didn't really deserve them, taught me how to shoot better, or liked the way I shoot enough to extend my shooting contract: Jon Stewart, Steve Higgins, Lorne Michaels, Mike Shoemaker, Tina Fey, Adam McKay, Bela Bajaria, Tracey Pakosta, Pearlena Igbokwe, Steve Burke, and Jeff Shell. Chief among them is Greg Daniels, a peerless writer and the greatest teacher I've ever had. Thank you, all of you, forever.

Some Alaskan moose in the Western Yukon have been observed having "birthday parties" for each other, complete with "presents" (usually smooth rocks or metal objects that they find in nature) and even "birthday cakes" made out of weeds and mud. They even "sing" a song to each other by grunting in unison![2]

Finally, there are just a whole bunch of writers, some of whom I know and some of whom I've never met, whose work has altered my brain chemistry in that way that only great writing can. Thank you all for spending your time writing comedy, fiction, nonfiction, plays, music, TV, movies, journalism, anything. Writing is a weird job, and I salute everyone who makes it her life's work.

Okay, I'll end this acknowledgments section before I just start listing writers I like. Thanks for reading this book. Or maybe just picking it up in a bookstore and flipping to this page to see if I thanked you.

---

2 I made this one up. Moose don't have birthday parties for each other. That's ridiculous.

Notes

Introduction

7   *Try again. Fail again*: Samuel Beckett, *Worstward Ho*, in *Nohow On: Three Novels* (New York: Grove Press, 1998), 7.

A Few Questions Readers Might Have, Before We Get Started

12   *In 1746*: "Samuel Johnson's *A Dictionary of the English Language*," British Library, accessed April 23, 2021, https://www.bl.uk/collection-items/samuel-johnsons-a-dictionary-of-the-english-language-1755.

13   *defined a "pastern" as*: Adam Kirsch, "Samuel Johnson's Peculiar Dictionary," *Slate*, September 17, 2003, https://slate.com/culture/2003/09/samuel-johnson-s-dictionary-revised.html.

Chapter One

19   *"People are too complicated"*: Philip Pullman, *The Amber Spyglass* (New York: Alfred A. Knopf, 2000), 447.

19fn2 *"Love all, trust a few"*: William Shakespeare, *All's Well That Ends Well*, *The Yale Shakespeare*, ed. Wilbur L. Cross and Tucker Brooke (New Haven: Yale University Press, 1993), 1.1.57–58.

19fn3 *"It doesn't matter what's"*: *The Fate of the Furious*, directed by F. Gary Gray, (2017; Universal City, CA: Universal Pictures).

19fn3 *"I'm gonna knock"*: *Fate of the Furious*.

20   *Cicero even described*: Christopher Shields, "Aristotle," *Stanford Encyclopedia of Philosophy*, revised August 25, 2020, https://plato.stanford.edu/entries/aristotle/#AriCorChaPriDiv.

21   *good things we want*: Aristotle, *Nicomachean Ethics*, 2nd ed., trans. Terence Irwin (Indianapolis: Hackett, 1983), 14.

21   *it has no aim other than itself*: Aristotle, 13–14, 15.

22   *involve rational thought and virtues of character*: Aristotle, 23.

23   *"cause [their] possessors to be"*: Aristotle, 42.

24   *"Each of us seems"*: Aristotle, 170.

24   *children and animals*: Aristotle, 170.

26   *"Virtue comes about"*: Aristotle, 32.

26 *We may have been born*: Aristotle, 170

27fn13 *spent his life trying to conquer and enslave*: A. C. Grayling, *The History of Philosophy* (New York: Penguin, 2019), 83–84.

28fn14 *comedy piece he wrote about Socrates*: Woody Allen, *Side Effects* (New York: Ballantine, 1980), 49.

28fn15 *"read twenty-five books"*: Eliza Relman, "Jared Kushner Says He's Read 25 Books About the Israel-Palestine Conflict," *Business Insider*, January 29, 2020, https://www.businessinsider.com/jared-kushner-says-hes-read-25-books-about-israel -palestine-2020-1.

28 *"Nature, habit, and teaching"*: Aristotle, 292.

28fn16 *"We are what we repeatedly do"*: Will Durant, *The Story of Philosophy* (New York: Pocket Books, 2006), 98.

29 *"the mean concerned with anger"*: Aristotle, *Nicomachean Ethics*, 105.

30 *"It is hard to define how"*: Aristotle, 107.

30 *"This much is at least"*: Aristotle, 107.

31 *"I know it when I see it"*: Jacobellis v. Ohio, 378 U.S. 184 (1964), 197.

34 *"The result"*: Julia Annas, *Intelligent Virtue* (Oxford, UK: Oxford University Press, 2013), 28–29.

36 *The Shklars had to flee*: "Judith Shklar, Professor and Noted Theorist, Dies," *Harvard Crimson*, September 18, 1992.

36 *"To put cruelty first"*: Judith Shklar, *Ordinary Vices* (Cambridge, MA: Belknap, 1984), 8.

37 *Cruelty, she says, is often*: Shklar, 29.

37 *"If cruelty horrifies us"*: Shklar, 13.

38 *"'knowledge makes men gentle'"*: Shklar, 27.

Chapter Two

39 *The original question*: Philippa Foot, "The Problem of Abortion and the Doctrine of Double Effect," *Oxford Review*, no. 5 (1967): 5–15, https://philpapers.org /archive/footpo-2.pdf.

40fn1 *was discussed by a woman*: Judith Jarvis Thomson, "The Trolley Problem," *Yale Law Journal* 94, no. 6 (1985): 1395–1415.

41 *just an innocent observer*: Thomson.

41 *standing on a bridge*: Thomson.

42 *doctors in a hospital*: Foot, "The Problem of Abortion."

43 *he argued for*: James E. Crimmins, "Jeremy Bentham," *Stanford Encyclopedia of Philosophy*, revised January 28, 2019, https://plato.stanford.edu/entries/bentham /#LifWri.

43 *should be given to his friend*: Nick J Booth, "Fake News: Demystifying Jeremy Bentham," UCL Culture Blog, accessed June 28, 2021, https://www.ucl.ac.uk/ culture/projects/fake-news.

43 *Smith preserved Bentham's skeleton*: Ibid.

43 *"did not produce acceptable results"*: Ibid.

43 *"went disastrously wrong"*: "Auto-Icon," UCL Blog, accessed June 28, 2021, https://www.ucl.ac.uk/bentham-project/who-was-jeremy-bentham/auto-icon.

43 *in 1850 Smith donated*: "Fake News: Demystifying Jeremy Bentham," UCL Culture Blog, accessed June 28, 2021, https://www.ucl.ac.uk/culture/projects/fake-news.

43 *"The College did not"*: Ibid.

43 *in February 2020 they put it*: "Auto-Icon," UCL Blog, accessed June 28, 2021, https://www.ucl.ac.uk/bentham-project/who-was-jeremy-bentham/auto-icon.

44 *authoring a groundbreaking work*: Christopher Macleod, "John Stuart Mill," *Stanford Encyclopedia of Philosophy*, published August 25, 2016, https://plato.stanford.edu/entries/mill/#Life.

44fn4 *the cover of the edition we used*: John Stuart Mill, *The Subjection of Women* (Buffalo: Prometheus Books, 1986).

44 *your skin essentially explodes*: "Erysipelas," National Organization for Rare Disorders, https://rarediseases.org/rare-diseases/erysipelas/.

46 *He came up with seven scales*: Jeremy Bentham, *An Introduction to the Principles of Morals and Legislation* (Whithorn, SCT: Anodos, 2019), 9–10.

47 *"Intense, long, certain, speedy, fruitful, pure"*: Bentham, *An Introduction to the Principles of Morals and Legislation: A New Edition, Corrected by the Author*, 1823, sec. 20, https://www.econlib.org/library/Bentham/bnthPML.html?chapter_num=5#book-reader.

48fn8 *"Few human creatures"*: John Stuart Mill, *Utilitarianism*, ed. George Sher, 2nd ed. (Indianapolis: Hackett, 2001), 9–10.

48fn9 *reformulation of a thought experiment*: T. M. Scanlon, *What We Owe to Each Other* (Cambridge, MA: Belknap, 1998), 235.

53fn16 *His full name is*: Andrew David Irvine, "Bertrand Russell," *Stanford Encyclopedia of Philosophy*, revised May 27, 2020, https://plato.stanford.edu/entries/russell/.

53 *"There is nothing new"*: Bertrand Russell, *The History of Western Philosophy* (New York: Simon & Schuster, 1972), 777.

53 *"There is an obvious lacuna"*: Russell, 778.

53 *"His optimism was"*: Russell, 778.

53 *"John Stuart Mill, in his"*: Russell, *History of Western Philosophy*, 778.

54 *"Anything whatever may be"*: Russell, 779.

55fn18 *he was born*: Brian Duigman, "Bernard Williams," Encyclopedia Britannica, accessed April 23, 2021, https://www.britannica.com/biography/Bernard-Williams.

56 *Jim is vacationing in a small town*: J. J. C. Smart and Bernard Williams, *Utilitarianism: For & Against* (Cambridge, UK: Cambridge University Press, 1973), 98.

56 *"each of us is specially"*: Smart and Williams, *Utilitarianism*, 99.

Chapter Three

64 *his routines were so predictable*: Bertrand Russell, *The History of Western Philosophy* (New York: Simon & Schuster, 1972), 704.

65 *"After the earthquake"*: Russell, 705.

66 *"A completely isolated"*: Immanuel Kant, *Foundations of the Metaphysics of Morals* (New York: Macmillan, 1990), 26–27.

66 *"Act only according to"*: Kant, *Foundations*, 38.

66 *"Water, fire, air, and dirt"*: Insane Clown Posse, "Miracles," written by Joseph Bruce, Joseph Utsler, and Mike E. Clark (Farmington Hills, MI: Psychopathic Records, 2010).

68 *"There can be no imperative"*: Kant, *Foundations*, 35.

70 *"Some moralists want"*: Friedrich Nietzsche, *Beyond Good and Evil*, trans. Walter Kaufman (New York: Vintage Books, 1989), 99–100.

71 *"Act so that you treat humanity"*: Kant, *Foundations*, 46.

72fn8 *something called "just war theory"*: Seth Lazar, "War," *Stanford Encyclopedia of Philosophy*, published May 3, 2016, https://plato.stanford.edu/entries/war/.

75fn9 *Taurek is flabbergasted*: John M. Taurek, "Should the Numbers Count?" *Philosophy and Public Affairs* 6, no. 4 (Summer 1977): 293–316, http://www.pitt.edu/~mthompso/readings/taurek.pdf.

76fn10 *The irony of this thought experiment*: Immanuel Kant, *Critique of Practical Reason and Other Works on the Theory of Ethics*, 5th rev. ed., trans. Thomas Kingsmill Abbott (London: Kongmans, Green and Co., 1889), 361–362, reproduced at https://oll-resources.s3.us-east-2.amazonaws.com/oll3/store/titles/360/0212_Bk.pdf.

Chapter Four

84 *Scanlon's suggestion*: T. M. Scanlon, *What We Owe to Each Other* (Cambridge, MA: Belknap, 1998), 4.

84 *But in essence he says this*: Pamela Hieronymi, email message to author, October 8, 2020.

85 *"a shared willingness"*: Scanlon, *What We Owe*, 5.

85fn3 *Pamela described*: Hieronymi, email message to author, August 26, 2020.

92 *"A comprehensive ancient African"*: Johann Broodryk, *Africa Is Best* (Waterkloof, SA: Ubuntu School of Philosophy, 2010), 47.

92 *"It may be asked"*: Broodryk, 47.

92 *"these values are practiced"*: Broodryk, 48.

93 *Broodryk notes that*: Broodryk, *Africa Is Best*, 46.

93 *Doc Rivers said that*: Maggie Ryan, "Why Doc Rivers Says Ubuntu Led Him and the 2008 Celtics to an NBA Title," Yahoo Sports, September 22, 2020, https://sports.yahoo.com/playbook-why-doc-rivers-says-072245595.html.

93 *"A person is a person through other people"*: Eze, *Intellectual History*, 94.

93 *hurt or diminished*: Broodryk, 54.

93 *"magnanimity, sharing, kindness"*: Eze, 185.

93 *"In the old days"*: Nelson Mandela, interviewed in "Nelson Mandela über Ubuntu," YouTube video, June 1, 2006, https://www.youtube.com/watch?v=DxoqGJCm-qU.

94fn9 *"cooperative venture for mutual advantage"*: John Rawls, *A Theory of Justice* (Cambridge, MA: Belknap, 1971), 4.

94 *"The individual does not"*: Quoted in Eze, *Intellectual History*, 94–95.

95 *as Hieronymi pointed out to me*: Pamela Hieronymi, email conversation with author, October 8, 2020.

97 *"Tim, this is not a moral theory"*: T. M. Scanlon, conversation with author, September 19, 2019.

Chapter Five

101 *Jack Lucas was thirteen*: Tyler Bamford, "The Incredible Story of Jack Lucas: The Youngest Medal of Honor Recipient in World War II," National WWII Museum, February 17, 2020, https://www.nationalww2museum.org/war/articles/incredible-story-jack-lucas-youngest-medal-honor-recipient-world-war-ii.

101fn1 *In 1961*: Bamford.

106 *"For the moral saint"*: Susan Wolf, "Moral Saints," *Journal of Philosophy* 79, no. 8. (August 1982): 420.

107 *"If the moral saint"*: Wolf, 421.

108 *"A moral saint will"*: Wolf, 422.

108 *"There seems to be"*: Wolf, 423.

108fn3 *She describes two*: Wolf, 420.

110 *"I believe my own worst"*: Edith Hall, *Aristotle's Way* (New York: Penguin, 2018), 10–11.

111 *One thought experiment we might explore*: Judith Jarvis Thomson, "A Defense of Abortion," *Philosophy and Public Affairs* 1, no. 1 (Autumn 1971): 47–66.

112fn5 *Foot was also discussing abortion*: John Hacker-Wright, "Philippa Foot," *Stanford Encyclopedia of Philosophy*, published August 17, 2018, https://plato.stanford.edu/entries/philippa-foot/#ApplEthi.

Chapter Six

117 *who was nominated for*: "The Life Story of Thich Nhat Hanh," Plum Village, accessed April 23, 2021, https://plumvillage.org/about/thich-nhat-hanh/biography/.

118 *"Emperor Wu asked"*: Thich Nhat Hanh, *The Heart of the Buddha's Teaching* (New York: Harmony Books, 1998), 61.

118 *"the energy that brings"*: Hanh, 64.

118fn2 *He describes a person's life*: Hanh, 124.

118fn3 *The Stoics were*: Bertrand Russell, *The History of Western Philosophy* (New York: Simon & Schuster, 1972), 256.

121 *In his twelfth-century*: *Mishneh Torah*, Laws of Charity, 10:7–14.

124 *"a method of settling"*: William James, *Pragmatism and Other Writings* (New York: Penguin, 2000), 24.

124 *The anecdote he uses*: James, 24–25.

124fn7 *sometimes called Albert Einstein's* annus mirabilis: "Albert Einstein's Year of
Miracles: Light Theory," *Morning Edition*, NPR, March 17, 2005, https://www.npr
.org/2005/03/17/4538324/albert-einsteins-year-of-miracles-light-theory.

124fn7 *"a new experience puts them to a strain"*: James, *Pragmatism*, 31.

126 *"What difference would it"*: James, 25.

126 *"look[s] away from first things"*: James, 29.

126 *"corridor in a hotel"*: James, 28.

127 *"a mediator and reconciler"*: James, 39.

128 *"Everyone wants to be"*: Hanh, *Heart of the Buddha's Teaching*, 34–35.

Chapter Seven

136 We'll build a mosque: David W. Brown, "Gingrich Denounces Ground Zero
Mosque," *Atlantic*, July 22, 2010, https://www.theatlantic.com/politics/archive
/2010/07/gingrich-denounces-ground-zero-mosque/60244/.

140 *"The person excessively prone"*: Aristotle, *Nicomachean Ethics* (Indianapolis:
Hackett, 1983), 48–49 (1108a 34–37).

142fn10 *Pamela Hieronymi related*: Pamela Hieronymi, email message to author,
August 26, 2020.

142 *"The result"*: Julia Annas, *Intelligent Virtue* (Oxford, UK: Oxford University Press,
2013), 28–29.

Chapter Eight

151 *"One day you will be called"*: James C. Scott, *Two Cheers for Anarchism: Six Easy
Pieces on Autonomy, Dignity, and Meaningful Work and Play* (Princeton, NJ:
Princeton University Press, 2012), 4–5.

154 *"My philosophy, in essence"*: Ayn Rand, *Atlas Shrugged* (New York: Signet, 1985),
1074.

155 *"Do not confuse altruism"*: Ayn Rand, "Faith and Force: Destroyers of the
Modern World," in *Philosophy: Who Needs It* (New York: New American Library,
1982), 74.

155 *Paul Ryan says he asked*: Richard Gunderman, "What Should We Make of Paul
Ryan's Fondness for Ayn Rand?" *The Conversation*, October 29, 2015, https://the
conversation.com/what-should-we-make-of-paul-ryans-fondness-for-ayn-rand
-49933.

156fn12 *Medicare and social security benefits*: David Emery, "Did Ayn Rand Receive
Social Security Benefits?" Snopes, June 23, 2017, https://www.snopes.com/fact
-check/ayn-rand-social-security/.

158 *the Free Rider Problem has*: Russell Hardin and Garrett Cullity, "The Free Rider
Problem," *Stanford Encyclopedia of Philosophy*, revised October 13, 2020, https://
plato.stanford.edu/entries/free-rider/.

Chapter Nine

168   *"Gates may have given"*: Peter Singer, "What Should a Billionaire Give—and What Should You?" *New York Times Magazine*, December 17, 2006, https://www .nytimes.com/2006/12/17/magazine/17charity.t.html.

169fn2 *Gates's net worth*: "#4 Bill Gates," *Forbes*, accessed May 17, 2021, https://www .forbes.com/profile/bill-gates/?sh=1a365127689f.

169fn3 *Gates and Warren Buffett announced*: "Warren Buffett," Giving Pledge, accessed April 23, 2021, https://givingpledge.org/Pledger.aspx?id=177.

170   *2.2 million acres of land*: Samuel Stebbins, "Who Owns the Most Land in America? Jeff Bezos and John Malone Are Among Them," *USA Today*, November 25, 2019, https://www.usatoday.com/story/money/2019/11/25/these -people-own-the-most-land-in-america/40649951/.

170   *pledge $1 million AUD*: Chloe Taylor, "Jeff Bezos Says Amazon Is Donating $690,000 to Australian Bush Fire Efforts," CNBC, January 13, 2020, https:// www.cnbc.com/2020/01/13/jeff-bezos-criticized-for-amazons-690000-austra lian-fires-donation.html.

170   *every five minutes*: Uke Darby, "Billionaire Jeff Bezos Donates Five Minutes of His Income to Bushfire Relief Efforts," *GQ*, January 13, 2020, https:// www.gq.com.au/entertainment/celebrity/billionaire-jeff-bezos-donates-five -minutes-of-his-income-to-bushfires-recovery/news-story/02b5dd5281b273d d8a25e20fbb6a8156.

170   *to last for ten thousand years*: Chaim Gartenberg, "Construction Begins on Jeff Bezos' $42 million 10,000-Year Clock," *Verge*, February 20, 2018, https://www .theverge.com/tldr/2018/2/20/17031836/jeff-bezos-clock-10000-year-cost.

170   *Bezos announced he would donate* $10 billion: Amy Held, "Jeff Bezos Pledges $10 Billion to Fight Climate Change, Planet's 'Biggest Threat,'" NPR, February 17, 2020, https://www.npr.org/2020/02/17/806720144/jeff-bezos -pledges-10-billion-to-fight-climate-change-planets-biggest-threat.

171   *a compelling thought experiment*: Peter Singer, "The Drowning Child and the Expanding Circle," *New Internationalist*, April 5, 1997, https://newint.org/features /1997/04/05/peter-singer-drowning-child-new-internationalist.

172   *students often cite*: Singer, "Drowning Child."

173   *Singer believes that*: Peter Singer, "The Singer Solution to World Poverty," *New York Times Magazine*, September 5, 1999.

173   *"The formula is simple"*: Singer, "Singer Solution."

175fn4 *"Most of us"*: Peter Singer, *The Life You Can Save* (New York: Random House, 2009), 131.

175   *he's super not into supporting*: Peter Singer, *The Most Good You Can Do* (New Haven, CT: Yale University Press, 2015), 118–127.

177   *"More important than what"*: Michael Schur, foreword to *The Life You Can Save*, 10th anniversary ed. (Bainbridge: The Life You Can Save, 2019), xvi.

177fn8 *has been criticized for*: Harriet McBride Johnson, "Unspeakable Conversa-

tions," *New York Times Magazine*, February 16, 2003, https://www.nytimes
.com/2003/02/16/magazine/unspeakable-conversations.html.

178fn9 *supervisors in a Tyson Foods factory*: Katie Shepherd, "Tyson Foods Managers
Had a 'Winner-Take-All' Bet on How Many Workers Would Get Covid-19, Lawsuit
Alleges," *Washington Post*, November 19, 2020, https://www.washingtonpost.com
/nation/2020/11/19/tyson-foods-waterloo-bets-covid/.

179 *Amazon started a GoFundMe campaign*: Danielle Zollner, "Jeff Bezos, World's Richest
Man, Asks Public to Donate to Amazon Relief Fund," *Independent* (UK), March 24,
2020, https://www.independent.co.uk/news/world/americas/coronavirus-amazon
-jeff-bezos-relief-fund-covid-19-billionaire-net-worth-a9422236.html.

179 *posted an Instagram photo*: Benjamin Stupples and Kevin Varley, "Geffen's Super-
yacht Isolation Draws Outrage While Industry Sinks," *Bloomberg*, March 30, 2020,
https://www.bloomberg.com/news/articles/2020-03-30/geffen-s-superyacht
-isolation-draws-outrage-while-industry-sinks.

181fn11 *California now gets a third*: "New Data Shows Nearly Two-Thirds of California's
Electricity Came from Carbon-Free Sources in 2019," press release,
California Energy Commission, July 16, 2020, https://www.energy.ca.gov
/news/2020-07/new-data-shows-nearly-two-thirds-californias-electricity-came
-carbon-free.

Chapter Ten

185 *"I think we are inviting"*: Garth Johnston, "Christian Chick-fil-A President Prays
for 'Arrogant' Marriage Redefiners," *Gothamist*, July 18, 2012, https://gothamist
.com/food/christian-chick-fil-a-president-prays-for-arrogant-marriage-redefiners.

187fn2 *has been accused of*: Emily Flitter and Matthew Goldstein, "Long Before Divorce,
Bill Gates Had Reputation for Questionable Behavior," *New York Times*, May 16,
2021, https://www.nytimes.com/2021/05/16/business/bill-melinda-gates-di-
vorce-epstein.html.

187fn2 *listened to a podcast*: Holly Fray and Tracy V. Wilson, "Gertrude Stein and Alice
B. Toklas," *Stuff You Missed in History Class*, February 14, 2018.

188 *Dave McKenna wrote a piece*: Dave McKenna, "The Cranky Redskins Fan's Guide
to Daniel Snyder," *Washington City Paper*, November 19, 2010, https://washington
citypaper.com/article/221900/the-cranky-redskins-fans-guide-to-dan-snyder/.

189 *demanded $2 million in damages*: Paul Farhi, "Redskins Owner Dan Snyder Drops
Lawsuit Against Washington City Paper," *Washington Post*, September 10, 2011,
https://www.washingtonpost.com/sports/redskins-owner-dan-snyder-drops
-lawsuit-against-washington-city-paper/2011/09/09/gIQA3hf1IK_story.html.

189fn5 *"1863: The Winona (Minn.) Daily Republican"*: Ian Shapira, "A Brief History of
the Word 'Redskin' and How It Became a Source of Controversy," *Washington
Post*, July 3, 2020, https://www.washingtonpost.com/history/2020/07/03/red
skins-name-change/.

189 *"We will never change"*: Erik Brady, "Daniel Snyder Says Redskins Will Never

Change Name," *USA Today*, May 9, 2013, https://www.usatoday.com/story/sports/nfl/redskins/2013/05/09/washington-redskins-daniel-snyder/2148127/.

189fn6 *"After 81 years"*: Annys Shin and Dan Steinberg, "Daniel Snyder Defends Redskins Name in Emotional Letter to Fans," *Washington Post*, October 9, 2013, https://www.washingtonpost.com/local/snyder-defends-redskins-name-in-emotional-letter-to-fans/2013/10/09/9a161b06-30fa-11e3-8627-c5d7de0a046b_story.html.

190 *in the preface*: Jordan K. Ngubane, *An African Explains Apartheid* (Westport, CT: Greenwood Press, 1976), ix–x.

191 *"He sees it as a way of life"*: Ngubane, 3–4.

194 *Boston Braves*: Jeff Kerr, "Washington Redskins Change Name: Here's a Timeline Detailing the Origins, Controversies and More," CBS Sports, July 13, 2020, https://www.cbssports.com/nfl/news/washington-redskins-name-change-heres-a-timeline-detailing-the-origins-controversies-and-more/.

195fn10 *"The interest involved"*: John Stuart Mill, *Utilitarianism* (Indianapolis: Hackett, 2001), 54.

197 *the first time Hemingway had ever kissed*: Julie Miller, "Mariel Hemingway Says Woody Allen Tried to Seduce Her when She Was a Teenager," *Vanity Fair*, March 25, 2015, https://www.vanityfair.com/hollywood/2015/03/woody-allen-mariel-hemingway-manhattan.

197 *she wasn't attracted to him*: Miller.

198 *"Imagine my surprise"*: *Annie Hall*, directed by Woody Allen (1977; New York: United Artists).

198 *when she was in eleventh grade*: Daphne Merkin, "Introducing Soon-Yi Previn," *Vulture*, September 16, 2018, https://www.vulture.com/2018/09/soon-yi-previn-speaks.html.

198fn11 *in the podcast* You Are Not So Smart: David McRaney, "The Backfire Effect," *You Are Not So Smart* (podcast), June 10, 2011, https://youarenotsosmart.com/2011/06/10/the-backfire-effect/.

198fn11 *not quite as strong as their work suggested*: Brooke Gladstone, "Walking Back the Backfire Effect," *On the Media* (podcast), WNYC, July 20, 2017, https://www.wnycstudios.org/podcasts/otm/segments/walking-back-backfire-effect.

199 *"grossly inappropriate"*: Maureen Orth, "10 Undeniable Facts About the Woody Allen Sexual-Abuse Allegation," *Vanity Fair*, February 7, 2014, https://www.vanityfair.com/news/2014/02/woody-allen-sex-abuse-10-facts.

200 *misogynistic comments to a Malibu police officer*: Maureen O'Connor, "All the Terrible Things Mel Gibson Has Said on the Record," *Gawker*, July 8, 2010, https://gawker.com/5582644/all-the-terrible-things-mel-gibson-has-said-on-the-record.

200 *the actress Winona Ryder*: Ben Child, "Winona Ryder: Mel Gibson Called Me an 'Oven Dodger,'" *Guardian* (US edition), December 17, 2010, https://www.theguardian.com/film/2010/dec/17/winona-ryder-mel-gibson. (See also "Mel

Gibson and Winona Ryder at Odds over Anti-Semitism Claims," BBC, June 24, 2020, https://www.bbc.com/news/entertainment-arts-53162246.)

206 *was no longer appropriate*: Rosa Sanchez, "NFL's Washington Redskins to Change Name Following Years of Backlash," ABC News, July 13, 2020, https://abcnews .go.com/US/washington-redskins-change-years-backlash/story?id=71744369.

206 *executives in the team's front office*: Will Hobson and Liz Clarke, "From Dream Job to Nightmare: More Than a Dozen Women Allege Sexual Harassment and Verbal Abuse by Former Team Employees at Redskins Park," *Washington Post*, July 16, 2020, https://www.washingtonpost.com/sports/2020/07/16/redskins -sexual-harassment-larry-michael-alex-santos/.

Chapter Eleven

210fn1 *"has come to mean nothing at all"*: Jean-Paul Sartre, *Existentialism Is a Humanism*, ed. John Kulka, trans. Carol Macomber (New Haven: Yale University Press, 2007), 20–21.

211 *"Christians chastised"*: Sartre, ix.

211 *"Existence precedes essence"*: Sartre, 22.

211 *"Man is responsible for what he is"*: Sartre, 23.

211 *"Man first exists"*: Sartre, 22.

212 *"If God does not exist"*:

212fn2 *"I'm telling you"*: Kurt Vonnegut, speech at Case Western University, 2004, as posted at "We Are Here On Earth to Fart Around, Kurt Vonnegut (2004)," YouTube, September 12, 2019, https://www.youtube.com/watch?v=nxpITF8fswE.

213 *we're actually making them for all people*: Sartre, *Existentialism Is a Humanism*, 24.

213 *"What would happen if everyone did what I am doing?"*: Sartre, 25.

213 *"the kind experienced"*: Sartre, 27.

214 *"no doctrine is more optimistic"*: Sartre, 40.

214 *"Man is condemned to be free"*: Sartre, 29.

214 *"If I decide"*: Sartre, 44.

214fn4 *"If you choose not to decide"*: Rush, "Freewill," comp. Geddy Lee/Alex Lifeson, lyrics by Neil Peart, track 2 on *Permanent Waves* (Chicago: Mercury Records, 1980).

214 *"man's destiny lies within himself"*: Sartre, 40.

214 *Sartre gives the example*: Sartre, *Existentialism Is a Humanism*, 30.

215 *Camus accepted his Nobel Prize*: Josh Jones, "Jean-Paul Sartre Rejects the Nobel Prize in Literature in 1964," Open Culture, June 17, 2014, https://www.openculture .com/2014/06/jean-paul-sartre-rejects-the-nobel-prize.html.

216 *"I said that the world is absurd"*: Albert Camus, *The Myth of Sisyphus* (New York: Vintage Books, 2018), 21.

217 *We can kill ourselves*: Camus, 27.

217 *eliminates half of the equation*: Camus, 54.

217 *"philosophical suicide"*: Camus, 28.

217 *"The doctrines that explain"*: Camus, 55.

218   *"I don't know whether"*: Camus, *Myth of Sisyphus*, 51.

218   *"The workman of today"*: Camus, 121.

218   *"His fate belongs"*: Camus, 123.

219   *"One must imagine Sisyphus happy"*: Camus, 123.

219   *"in the presence of others"*: Sartre, *Existentialism Is a Humanism*, 47.

219   *"an error"*: Sartre, 47.

221fn10 *"We must limit ourselves"*: Sartre, 34.

Chapter Twelve

223   *"There are very many people"*: Julia Annas, *Intelligent Virtue* (Oxford, UK: Oxford University Press, 2011), 31.

225   *"Imagine life here"*: John Scalzi, "Straight White Male: The Lowest Difficulty Setting There Is," *Whatever*, May 15, 2012, https://whatever.scalzi .com/2012/05/15/straight-white-male-the-lowest-difficulty-setting-there-is/.

229   *Robert Frank was playing tennis*: Robert H. Frank, *Success and Luck: Good Fortune and the Myth of Meritocracy* (Princeton, NJ: Princeton University Press, 2016), 1–2.

229   *"Why do so many"*: Frank, 11.

230fn6 *"A real man makes"*: *Titanic*, directed by James Cameron (1997; Los Angeles: Paramount).

231   *"My wealth has come from"*: "Warren Buffett," Giving Pledge, accessed April 23, 2021, https://givingpledge.org/Pledger.aspx?id=177.

231   *"Most of us would never"*: Frank, *Success and Luck*, 35.

237   *extensive notes and feedback*: Frank Lovett, *Rawls's A Theory of Justice: A Reader's Guide* (New York: Continuum, 2011), 20–21.

238   *what he calls the "original position"*: John Rawls, *A Theory of Justice* (Cambridge, MA: Belknap, 1971), 17.

238   *"Certain principles of justice"*: Rawls, 21.

239   *took that idea of symmetry*: Pamela Hieronymi, email conversation with author, October 11, 2020.

240   *"should be advantaged or disadvantaged"*: Rawls, *Theory of Justice*, 18.

240   *"does not take seriously"*: Rawls, 27.

Chapter Thirteen

245   *"The Confederate flag was"*: Andy Greene, "Tom Petty on Past Confederate Flag Use: 'It Was Downright Stupid,'" *Rolling Stone*, July 14, 2015, https://www .rollingstone.com/feature/tom-petty-on-past-confederate-flag-use-it-was -downright-stupid-177619/.

245   *"I rise to apologize"*: "Representative Yoho Apologizes for 'Abrupt' Conversation with Representative Ocasio-Cortez, Denies Name-Calling," video, CSPAN, July 22, 2020, https://www.c-span.org/video/?c4894103/representative-yoho -apologizes-abrupt-conversation-representative-ocasio-cortez-denies-calling.

246   *"Having been married"*: "Representative Yoho Apologizes."

246 *"My wife, Carolyn"*: "Representative Yoho Apologizes."

247 *"We did odd jobs"*: "Representative Yoho Apologizes."

247 *"That is why"*: "Representative Yoho Apologizes."

247 *"I will commit"*: "Representative Yoho Apologizes."

247 *"I cannot apologize"*: "Representative Yoho Apologizes."

248 *"One of the most salient"*: Harry G. Frankfurt, *On Bullshit* (Princeton, NJ: Princeton University Press, 2005), 1.

248 *"Telling a lie"*: Frankfurt, 51.

248 *"unconstrained by a concern with truth"*: Frankfurt, 38.

248 *"the orator intends"*: Frankfurt, 18.

249fn2 *"Smarm is a kind of performance"*: Tom Scocca, "On Smarm," *Gawker*, December 5, 2013, https://gawker.com/on-smarm-1476594977.

249 *"The essence of bullshit"*: Frankfurt, 47.

250 *In 1992, Pope John Paul II*: Alan Cowell, "After 350 Years, Vatican Says Galileo Was Right: It Moves," *New York Times*, October 31, 1992, https://www.nytimes.com/1992/10/31/world/after-350-years-vatican-says-galileo-was-right-it-moves.html.

Coda

258 *Thousands of years ago*: Sebastian Bertolini, "Know Thyself," Ancient Greek Courses, September 19, 2018, https://ancientgreekcourses.com/anthropology/know-thyself/.

Index